CW01375943

WEEKEND
Thought for Today with Switched-On Stan
Y'KNOW... PEOPLE OFTEN SAY TO ME..."STAN, THE GOVERNMENT HAS BEEN IN POWER FOR A YEAR NOW...HOW COME IT'S STILL SO POPULAR?"
SCRIPT
"IS IT FISCAL PRUDENCE?", THEY ASK, "DRIPPING SINCERITY? WILLIAM HAGUE?" I ANSWER THUS...
NEW LABOUR IS A BIT LIKE CANNABIS.. BOTH INDUCE MILD EUPHORIA, ACCOMPANIED BY A DISTORTED SENSE OF REALITY—
—AND A TENDENCY TO SPOUT RUBBISH IN A MEANINGFUL WAY...
EVERYTHING TAKES ON ADDED SIGNIFICANCE DESPITE THE FACT THAT NOTHING IS HAPPENING!
OF COURSE, THERE ARE DIFFERENCES...
...CANNABIS IS UNCOOL, ILLEGAL AND QUITE HARMLESS...
...WHEREAS NEW LABOUR CAN LEAD ON TO THE HARDER STUFF... ISN'T THAT RIGHT, MR. X?
CLACKETY-CLACK
THAT'S RIGHT, STAN... COUGH. I... I JOINED MY LOCAL LABOUR PARTY... JUST TO BE SOCIABLE LIKE... AND PRETTY SOON I WAS HOOKED... CHAIRING 4 COMMITTEES, 2 WORKING PARTIES AND A FOCUS GROUP.. I WAS OUT EVERY NIGHT OF THE WEEK... I NEVER SAW MY KIDS, MY WIFE LEFT

The Guardian Year '98

Introduction by **Richard Hoggart**
Edited by **John Ezard**

FOURTH ESTATE • *London*

First published in Great Britain in 1998 by
Fourth Estate Limited
6 Salem Road
London W2 4BU

Thanks to Danny John, *Guardian* executive picture editor, for his role in selecting pictures.

Copyright © 1998 by Guardian Newspapers Ltd
Introduction © 1998 by Richard Hoggart

10 9 8 7 6 5 4 3 2 1

The right of John Ezard to be identified as the editor of this work has been asserted by him in accordance with the Copyright, Designs and Patents Act 1988.

A catalogue record for this book is available from the British Library

ISBN 1-85702-874-0

All rights reserved. No part of this publication may be reproduced, transmitted, or stored in a retrieval system, in any form or by any means, without permission in writing from Fourth Estate Limited.

Typeset by Rowland Phototypesetting Ltd,
Bury St Edmunds, Suffolk
Printed in Great Britain by Bath Press

Contents

Biff *Thought for today* — i
Richard Hoggart *Introduction* — xi
John Ezard *Editor's Foreword* — xv

Camels and corrections

Merrily Harpur *Sorry, I've got a headache* — 1
Francis Wheen *Words of wisdom from the Ayatollah* — 2
Derek Brown *The first time around: a browsers' guide to the teething troubles of the new millennium* — 4
Matthew Norman *Diary of a hypochondriac* — 5
Matthew Engel *Farewell, Ambridge* — 7
Leader *Plenty of postmodern comfort and joy* — 9
Ian Mayes *Corrections and clarifications* — 10
Alex Duval Smith *Michelin tires of inflated image* — 10
Tony May *Hire intelligence trips up job experts* — 11
John Hooper *Crosses made in heaven* — 12
Don McPhee *Angel of the North* — 14
Martin Wainwright *Apple tempts shy sisters* — 13
David Pallister *'Bored' guest walks out on Dobson* — 15
David McKie *Hitler and who?* — 16
Ian Mayes *Corrections and clarifications* — 18

A blessed Good Friday – and after

Martin Argles *Union and Ulster flags fly together at Drumcree* — 19
John Mullin *'Please make it work'* — 20
Anthony McIntyre *'We, the IRA, have failed'* — 21
Conor Gearty *Britain's finest attempt to solve the problem* — 23
Leader *A blessed Good Friday* — 25
John Mullin *Agony of an act of faith* — 26
John Mullin *Adams told: it's time to deliver* — 28
Rory Carroll *A dynasty ended at 3 p.m.* — 30
Jonathan Freedland *The bomb hit right where it was placed* — 31
Henry McDonald *Among the victims* — 33

Contents

'A thorn in the side'

Graham Turner *An award ceremony*	35
Owen Bowcott *The Guardian wins accolade for record sixth time*	36
Simon Hoggart *A dragon with a red rose in its mouth?*	36
Leader *Let the donors be revealed now*	38
David Austin *Teflon Tony*	38
Anne Perkins *Cuts outcry humiliates Harman*	39
Steve Bell *Alien resurrection*	40
Simon Hoggart *Floundering in offshore drift*	41
Leader *Has baby, so must travel*	42
Hugo Young *A spin on the truth*	43
Bel Littlejohn *I'll never speak of my marriage to Roger Pook*	45
Michael White *And the groom wore a green anorak*	47
Michael White *Blair & Co. do hate the* Guardian	48
Armando Iannucci *Faustian pact shock horror*	50
Alexander Chancellor *Dome and dumber*	52
David Austin *The end is nigh*	53
Jonathan Glancey *Nice wallpaper, shame about the paint*	54
Martin Argles *A 'suitably fey Narcissus' in Lord Irvine's apartments*	55
Matthew Norman *A year in the life of Derek Draper*	56
David Austin *Campbell – 'I might have been wrong'*	58

Tony, Gordon and the invisible man

Martin Argles *Tony and Gordon on song*	59
Leader *Brown's blockbuster: it's a stunning statement*	60
David Marquand *The magic lingers on*	62
Steve Bell *Education, education, education*	63
Matthew Engel *A very private wedding*	67
Ewen Macaskill and Lucy Ward *The invisible man*	69
Hugo Young *Labour is working, working, working*	71
Madeleine Bunting *What about the family?*	73

A class apart

Michael Stephens *Clive Harold introduces himself to Prince Charles as a former fellow pupil*	77
Alex Bellos *The prince and the* Big Issue *vendor: from classmates to a class apart*	78

Contents

Tim Radford *A unique hoard emerges from history*	79
Martin Wainwright *A teenager who could take no more taunts*	81
Rory Carroll *Two in a small, secret legion*	83
Owen Bowcott *Olde England stages last supper*	85
Owen Bowcott *'Have you heard of CJD?'*	86
News in brief *Mother dies after daughter*	87

Jean's war

Azadur Guzelian *The burnt-out Jolly Brewer*	89
Nick Davies *A last stand for sanity*	90
Nick Davies *Talking to the Hyde Park Estate's angry young men*	99

Eclipse of the sunrise

David Simmonds *Boom Boom '98*	107
Alex Brummer *A defining moment*	108
Andrew Higgins *Betrayal of the salaryman*	109
Nick Cumming-Bruce *Net closes on Suharto*	111
Alex Bellos *'The flames are huge like sails'*	113
Martin Woollacott *Unmasking tyranny*	115
Ian Traynor *Swiss were 'in grip of Nazis'*	118
David Beresford *Mandela's greatness*	119
Leader *The gangrene of Third World debt*	121
David Austin *All we need is love*	121
Maggie O'Kane *The pitiful victims*	123
Robin Cook *Saddam is to blame*	125
Martin Woollacott *Schoolboy vices*	126

Ulysses and the Little Horrors

Museum of Modern Art *James Joyce, F. R. Leavis and the Director of Public Prosecutions*	129
Alan Travis *How they tried to kill off* Ulysses	130
Pat Kane *Wee girl power*	131
Martin Argles *A critic at the opera*	133
Andrew Clements *Little horrors*	134
Adrian Searle *Power to shock*	135
René Magritte *The Key to the Fields*	135
Harold Pinter *It's actually a state of war*	138
Simon Hattenstone *A tale of two Quentins*	139
Quentin Crisp *A tale by one Quentin*	140
Richard Williams *Fear in Provence*	141

Contents

Jonathan Glancey *A world like this?* — 142
Martin Argles *Abseiling from the Millennium Dome* — 143

The way we live now

Martin Rowson *'Watch telly, get pissed'* — 147
Catherine Bennett *Who we are* — 148
Joanna Coles *Southern comfort eating* — 150
Victor Keegan *Funny old ways of creating wealth* — 151
Flora Luck *Diary of an emergency social worker* — 153
Mark Irving *'To tell the truth, we're desperate'* — 155
Roy Greenslade *Icon still pushes up sales* — 157
Roy Greenslade *Diana: now the press gets off its knees* — 158
Leader *The big bad wolf: Murdoch has his price* — 160
Steve Bell *Scratch Rupert* — 160
David McKie *That old-time, dumbed-down para-religion* — 162

Voices from elsewhere

Don McPhee *Gervase Phinn, with children* — 165
Joseph Harker *Notes & Queries* — 166
Erwin James *Diary of a prison inmate* — 167
Linda Grant *Youth isn't so cool* — 168
Alan Randall *Diary of a hospital chief executive* — 170
Elaine Williams *The master storyteller* — 172
Helen Parnham *My hell from bullying* — 174
Linda Grant *Girls on top form* — 175
John Ryle *Casualties of two conflicts* — 178

Final calls

John Hodder *Trevor Huddleston* — 181
Desmond Tutu *Bishop Trevor Huddleston* — 182
Alastair Campbell *Ellie Merritt* — 183
William Kennedy *Frank Sinatra* — 184
David Robinson *Stephen Archibald* — 185
Sean Smith *Security at Linda McCartney's memorial service* — 187
James Ivory *Geoffrey Kendal* — 189
Hugo Young *Enoch Powell* — 191
Veronica Horwell *Martha Gellhorn* — 193
Linda Grant *Kathy Acker* — 197
Martin Argles *At Jeffrey Bernard's cremation* — 198
W. Stephen Gilbert *Sydney Newman* — 199

Contents

Meirion Bowen *Sir Michael Tippett* — 202
Martin Argles *Sir Michael Tippett* — 203

A cracking few days

Tom Jenkins *Michael Owen, the 18-year-old goalscoring virtuoso* — 207
Paul Hayward *First-class honours for Owen* — 208
Mike Selvey *The cutting edge?* — 209
David Lacey *Petrescu shatters England* — 211
Sean Smith *An alleged England soccer hooligan is arrested* — 213
David Lacey *The lions find their roar* — 213
Richard Williams *Batty bites the roulette bullet* — 215
Tom Jenkins *Tony Adams hoists high the FA Carling Premiership trophy* — 217
Frank Keating *Tim's turn but no final twist* — 218
David Hopps *Victorious England break the mould* — 220
Chris Hawkins *Bradley hits the heights on Suny Bay* — 222

Introduction

Richard Hoggart
Introduction

An admission at the start. Fifty years a *Guardian* reader, almost under the shadow of C. P. Scott, I expect to remain a reader till I die – in spite of some wobbles over recent years. Of those more later.

This anthology does much to reinforce confidence. At its best, and it is surprising how often it hits its best, the *Guardian* is a very good newspaper indeed. It honours good writing and the search for unbiased intelligence and imagination. It tackles directly issues which should haunt us all but which most of our 'gatekeepers' in the press prefer to ignore or distort for their own purposes. The leaders reinforce its regular columnists' efforts.

Such as how to manage best the awful sore of Third World Debt; or the problems of the National Health Service below the obvious level – waiting lists – which preoccupies and obsesses less well-nourished commentators. I do not remember the main question – how to deal with the fact that the service now has two tiers, the public and the private – being raised by the department's spokesmen. Similarly one does not hear much from the Department for Education about the way to tackle the great dilemma of comprehensive education, by which those of us who are in principle in favour of 'the comprehensive idea' are troubled; precisely because it involves contradictory good principles. But at its starkest, as it is here, the question is: how do you protect bright pupils from the downward, populist pressure of the large peer-groups. All this is a continent away from the shallow selective treatment of the tabloids.

When they are brought together, some of the *Guardian*'s less evident strengths emerge from the half-shadow. The obituaries, for example. Except in one instance here, they avoid sentimental fawning, and paint in the warts without any smart-alec clay-foot finding. This anthology's 'Voices from Elsewhere' section, in which people we do not often hear from directly – convicted prisoners writing from gaol, school victims of horrible bullying – are so well chosen as to be their own most telling advocates. The *Guardian*'s courage in chasing corruption in high places, especially the political, was most recently and best shown last year. It deserves another salute here. That battle will not be soon if ever completely won.

Being of a literary bent I especially enjoyed the report on Joyce's *Ulysses*. It is, of course, hilarious. From that, the oddest thought of all is that we were so recently and so blindingly daft about our practice of censorship. Some of the former Lord Chamberlain's higher lunacies were revealed this year from the Public Records Office. Those of Sir Archibald Bodkin apropos Joyce must now stand beside them in any students' introduction to the subject (along with the

Introduction

thoughts on sex-and-the-Common Man of prosecuting council Mervyn Griffith-Jones in the 1960 *Lady Chatterley's Lover* trial. (He asked the jury, 'Is it a book you would wish even your wife or your servants to read?') No one could send up our national moral regulators better than they do themselves. It is an uncovenanted gift that the Public Prosecutor in the Joyce case had so apt a name. Not a bare bodkin, but one encased in conventional prejudices and self-righteous total conviction. Dickens couldn't have done better.

Now the niggles, the worries. There are three, two stronger than the third. The third is the tendency in comic writing, of which the best is as good as you will find anywhere in the broadsheets, to be twee; that's a sign of uncertainty and widespread today. There are only a couple of instances in this collection. More important is not only the obsession with 'Youth' but its peculiar forms. I do not intend to apologise for this observation. I echo Lear's quizzical observation: 'I am a very foolish fond old man', which can be read as less an admission of his own tetchiness than as a criticism of his age-rejecting, youth-preening daughters. The case is that 'Youth' in the eyes of most writers seems to be between the ages of 13 and 16; totally absorbed in the latest, successive, pop-culture fads. As an undergraduate, I would have laughed at those of my peers who behaved like that; and hardly thought of them as potential *Guardian* readers. So there's not likely to be much fruitful seed-corn there. Perhaps it would be better to pay more attention to the old whose numbers are increasing rapidly? At least there are several hints in these pages that 'Youth isn't so cool' after all. Perhaps that excessive attention is beginning to be seen as what it is: mistaken both in itself and as good marketing practice.

'To ask the hard question is simple.' That early Auden line often comes to mind. Its answer has to be: 'To accept the hard answer isn't at all simple.' This is recalled when we meet yet again the sentimental, anti-'judgmental', relativism characteristic of the times. That is the tendency to avoid judgments of character in favour of blaming all failings on society; corner-cutting to avoid the suggestion of personal responsibility, the neglect of complex, hard choices in favour of showing that one's heart is in the right place. Most writers on issues with exceptionally difficult moral implications manage to ignore them. One essay here highlights the difficulties. An otherwise admirable and heart-rending essay on the terrible plight of Iraqi hospitals as a result of the sanctions, in itself virtually ignores the difficult but not justifiably evadable case for those sanctions. True to its principles, the *Guardian* then asks the Foreign Secretary to respond, which he does with equal conviction. But two people uttering their convictions side by side or successively are not the same, not so intellectually testing in the right way, as two people actually engaged with one another; or as one journalist recognising in the one piece the inescapable pros and cons of a dreadful set of choices.

Back to the continuing strengths. In spite of the lapse I described just above, this collection exhibits very well, because in some depth, the *Guardian*'s attention

Introduction

to many contemporary social and personal concerns. Such as the apparently ineradicable corruption and incompetence which allows the Asian forest-fires to continue; and the collapse of many Asian economies. It tells us things we don't want really to know or contemplate, such as the stark poverty of so many in Bolivia in contrast with the high life of those who are appointed to do something about it. It reveals, in detail and with controlled but personally-felt passion, the self-righteousness of the Swiss apropos their finagling over Hitler's gold. It powerfully and sympathetically lays out the dilemma for women in balancing the demands of work and family. It deploys well an imaginative mosaic of responses to the Northern Ireland agreement.

It mocks the razmatazz about the Dome. By the time this book appears the actual construction will, I predict, have been acclaimed as a new wonder of the world (or at least one up on the Eiffel Tower). Then the *Guardian* will need to turn its attention to what it is proposed to put inside the Dome as the Best of British – Yesterday, Today and Tomorrow. I expect they'll do that and with the scorn the present proposals deserve. That will not stop the enterprise being a great populist success. The *Guardian* is not as influential as all that. Still, its voice is needed and is listened to in some relevant quarters.

Most valuable of all, in the year represented here, is the reporting of the new Labour government. The paper promised to be and has been critical and for that the government should be grateful, for this is not the endless, one-sided carping of the manifestly Tory press. But yes, it recalls to some extent the old crack about the relations between the press and government – like that between dogs and trees. As a basic principle in a democracy, that is fair enough.

So a newspaper does right to pursue the matter of large donations to Labour and their possible relationship to advertisements for smoking. It is right also to mock at the choice of Canary Wharf as the iconic venue for the lunch to Chirac. We are told that Blair dislikes, even hates, the *Guardian* nowadays. A great mistake; if so, that's his short sightedness and that of his spin-doctors, not the paper's. The government is lucky to have such frank and honest rather than fair-weather friends.

As I am writing this, the *Guardian* interviewed one of the Prime Minister's close advisers. He talked of the importance of 'making a lot of profits', which he declared is 'not an ethical question'. In the background. aeons away as it now seems, I heard the gruff, gentle voice of Tawney* talking of Brotherhood, Charity and Usury; and happily looked again at David Marquand's long analytic piece on The First Year. Illustrating all this there are also, and as always, the most able and sometimes mischievous team of cartoonists. I am sure Mr Blair's entourage do not at all like those.

A newspaper such as this has to have above all a hinterland, a background,

---

* The social and economic historian Professor Richard Tawney (1880–1962), author of *The Acquisitive Society* (1921) and *Religion and the Rise of Capitalism* (1926), a pioneer of the Workers' Educational Association. For some years he wrote leaders for the *Manchester Guardian*.

Introduction

body, bottom, moral texture; rather than merely a daily succession of rhetorical 'ooh-ahs'. It gives space, and within it can be tautly unsparing. It says, implicitly: 'There is more to life than beer, football, sex, and box-office blockbusters; or than fat cats, glossy modishness, designer clothes and designer food, than 'New Values' for the New British People.

Ranging over this great variety of themes and noting again the responsible consistency of approach, one realises that if these writers have a central core it is the assertion of humane social and personal values. Which are now, in too many parts of Britain, in total decline. Since I come from Leeds I recall from this book insistently and depressingly Nick Davies's two long pieces on 'Jean's War', on Hyde Park and Burley – an area any student at the University now in middle-age and beyond remembers as nearby decent urban villages; but is brought to realise that they are today kinds of Hell – and only one example of a pattern right across the country, places most proponents of Cool Britannia choose not to visit or often think about.

Editor's Foreword

This is the forty-sixth *Guardian* anthology. The first came out when we were still the *Manchester Guardian* but had already had a national readership since the early nineteenth century. That book, in 1952, reported the final trip of the last tram in London and the death of the Queen's father, King George VI. The paper then was only some eight to twelve pages thick, in the long aftermath of the Second World War newsprint rationing. Among the biggest changes has been that today's *Guardian*, especially on Saturdays, sometimes runs in its various sections to 382 pages. So this yearbook is culled from tens of thousands more articles, pictures and cartoons than in the beginning.

This year has seen innovations, among them a daily Corrections and Clarification column (see page 10), the first in the British press though a widespread, proud feature of American newspapers. While it sometimes provokes squeals of anguish from those of us who make mistakes, it is popular with readers, admired by *Private Eye* and has already sparked a healthy increase in corrections by other papers. This autumn too 'a concerted leap into cyberspace' began at the *Guardian*'s already thriving website (see page 4) – offering specialist sites devoted to news, work, politics, football, film and fun. The new weekly Space magazine covering trends in design, is on page 155. Next year, there will be more changes to report on and to reflect in this anthology – and even more by the fiftieth edition in 2002.

J.E.

Camels and corrections

Camels and corrections

10 June 1998
Francis Wheen
Words of wisdom from the Ayatollah

The complete works of the late Ayatollah Khomeini are to be placed on the Internet, according to a brief news item last week. And about time too: we all remember his talents as a severe literary critic who issued fatwas against authors who incurred his displeasure, even if he hadn't actually read them; but how many of us have studied his own books? My knowledge of Khomeini's oeuvre comes from two volumes he published in the 1970s while he was exiled in France, which were brought back from Paris by my then colleague David Caute. They suggest that the Imam missed his vocation as an agony uncle for the *Tehran Times*. In fact, using nothing but his own words,* one could still compose a useful advice column:

Dear Ayatollah, I love my wife, but I'm having an affair. Is this a sin?
'A man who ejaculates after coitus with a woman who is not his wife, and who ejaculates again after coitus with his legitimate wife, does not have the right to say his prayers if he is still sweating from the exertion. But if he first has coitus with his legitimate wife and only afterwards coitus with his illegitimate wife, then he can say his prayers. But if it is dark and he is not sure which is his lawful wife and which the other, then it doesn't matter.'

Dear Ayatollah, I'm a broad-minded sort of guy, but my brother-in-law has been giving me the wink lately. And last week I caught him ogling a leg of lamb in Tesco. Is this normal?
'If a man sodomises the son, brother or father of his wife after his marriage, the marriage remains valid. But if he sodomises his neighbour's camel, oxen or sheep, then the beast becomes contaminated and must be killed and burnt.'

Dear Ayatollah, I'm a 45-year-old woman, but I think I may be going through the change. Is this possible?
'Women from the line of the Prophet attain the menopause at the age of 60; all other women at 50. The blood flowing from the vagina of a woman under nine years of age or over 60 ought not to be considered menstrual blood.'

Dear Ayatollah, As a new mother, I wonder if you can settle an argument between me and my midwife: breast or bottle?

---

* *All quotes from* Pour un Gouvernement Islamique, *or from* Principes Politiques, Philosophiques, Sociaux et Religieux de l'Ayatollah Khomeiny.

Camels and corrections

'Children should be breast-fed for two full years. You cannot marry the wet nurse who breast-fed you or your wife when your wife was a baby. Nor can a man marry a woman who was breast-fed by his own mother or grandmother. A wet nurse should always be a Shiite Muslim who believes in the Twelve Imams and looks beautiful.'

Dear Ayatollah, What are these 'impurities' about which we hear so much these days?
'Eleven things are impure: urine, excrement, sperm, bones of the dead, blood, dog meat, pork, non-Muslims, wine, beer and the sweat of a camel which eats excrement.'

Dear Ayatollah, I'm trying to potty-train my two-year-old. Any tips?
'At the moment of doing one's business it is imperative to squat in such a way as to neither face Mecca nor point one's bum at it. The urinary orifice should be washed once, with water, after the act; but those whose urine comes out by some other orifice should wash this other orifice twice. But if you forget, it doesn't matter. Say extra prayers. The faithful should urinate before going to bed, before coitus and after ejaculation. When crouching to urinate, the weight should always be on the left foot.'

Dear Ayatollah, My wife says she'll divorce me if I don't get some Viagra. Is this fair?
'If the husband is crazy, impotent or without testicles, the wife has been wronged. If the wife annuls the marriage because of her husband's inability to accomplish the sexual act via the vagina or the rectum, he ought to pay her damages equal to half her dowry.'

Dear Ayatollah, What will happen to the Spice Girls now that Geri's gone?
'There will be no more radio music, for if young boys and girls in the full flood of puberty, their bodies afire with fertility, shall be denied carnal knowledge of each other, then why permit Western music and blue jeans designed to emphasise crotch and bum and so inflame the lusts of these same young people? If women in your society wore the chador, you would not suffer constant riots and insurrections.'

Dear Ayatollah, If you were managing Iran's World Cup squad, which teams would you regard as the greatest threat?
'My enemies are those who wage war on God, in particular the Americans, the Kurds, the Jews, the Egyptians, the Russians and the Christian infidels.'

Dear Ayatollah, What about England? Has Gazza been punished too harshly? Has Teddy Sheringham suffered enough?
'One must punish crimes by the law of retaliation, cut off the hand of the thief, whip the adulterous woman . . . For the drinking of alcohol, Satan's brew, 100 lashes! For the smoking of tobacco, Satan's weed, 100 lashes!' •

The late Ayatollah Khomeini's fatwa on Salman Rushdie – which provoked this satire – was effectively revoked by Iran on 24 September 1998.

Camels and corrections

20 August 1998

Derek Brown

The first time around: a browsers' guide to the teething troubles of the new millennium

It was not the best of times. And if it was not the worst of times, the people of Britain at least could have been forgiven for thinking it was, ruled by a king who, even by the relaxed criteria of the day, was rotten at the job.

Ethelred II succeeded in 978, when his older half-brother Edward the Martyr was murdered in Corfe Castle. The assassination, almost certainly ordered by Ethelred's ambitious mother, placed upon the throne a boy of 10 who was to learn little and forget nothing.

His popular name, Ethelred the Unready, meaning the Ill-Advised, indicates that he was unlucky in his associates. But one authority, Keith Feiling, is not inclined to make excuses for a reign he describes as '38 years of ignominy'.

It was, to be sure, a tough era for kings. Danes and other Norsemen were in firm control of huge chunks of territory and key towns. It was, in short, a bloody start to the millennium. The more mystically-minded clerics and chroniclers may have been con founded in their dire predictions of murrains, pestilence and the imminence of the Second Coming (a comet sighted around 996 had been thought particularly propitious), but though Armageddon did not materialise, the reality was scarcely less awful.

1,000 years in 500 days
an **online history** of the **millennium**
www.newsunlimited.co.uk

Further afield, there were momentous stirrings of history. It was about this time that Polynesian settlers arrived in New Zealand. After 2,500 years of relentless expansion, they had become the most widespread nation on earth.

What They Said

'This year there was great commotion in England in consequence of an invasion by the Danes, who spread terror and devastation wheresoever they went, plundering and burning and desolating the country. Of the Danes there was slain a much greater number, though they remained in possession of the field of battle' – *The Anglo-Saxon Chronicle*

On the bleak coasts of north-west Europe, the enterprising Frisians were

Camels and corrections

beginning to build the system of sea-defence dykes to protect what was to become the Low Countries of Holland and Belgium. More ominously, the Chinese perfected gunpowder, using charcoal, sulphur and potassium nitrate. England's more prosaic contribution to human progress was the Danegeld: Ethelred's ruthless levying of huge quantities of silver to pay off the marauding Danes. It was, according to some, the embryonic beginning of one of the great curses of our millennium: systematic tax collection.

What They Said

> 'This year was the great famine in England so severe that no man ere remembered such' – *The Anglo-Saxon Chronicle*

Further instalments of this guide can be read on the Guardian's *News Unlimited website at www.newsunlimited.co.uk/millennium* •

---

11 November 1997
Matthew Norman
Diary of a hypochondriac

Tuesday

The annual bout of SAD (Seasonal Adjusted Depression) has passed, leaving behind a wistful awareness that the ageing process continues its relentless march. For example, my head is like an autumnal tree. Each morning the hairs in the bath look more like Pete Sampras's chest, except that, for my head, the spring shall never come.

Wednesday

Over breakfast, I complain about the hair loss to my wife. Without removing her head from the paper, and with no apparent movement of her lips, she replies, 'Oh, for God's sake, why don't you just accept it? After all, it's hardly as though I married you for your looks.' It is little moments such as this, I reflect once again, that keep the magic in a marriage.

Thursday

At work, the conversation turns to Pathé News and its hilariously jingoistic wartime reports. 'Tell me,' says the defence correspondent, narrowing his eyes

Camels and corrections

to scrutinise my features, 'were you alive during the war?' He is not trying to be humorous or wounding. He is simply interested. 'I was born,' I reply, 'at the end of 1963.' 'Ah, I see,' he says, with unaffected sympathy. 'I see.'

Friday

As a newly diagnosed victim of the ageing disease known to geriatricians as Andrew Neil Syndrome by Proxy, I am excited by news of a miracle cure for baldness. It is the first miracle cure of the year. The drug finasteride, marketed as Proscar, was designed for men with enlarged prostates, and clinical trials are being held on both sides of the Atlantic. I must get on one, and my physician, Sarah Jarvis, has to help.

Saturday

Attempts to contact Dr Jarvis at her emergency surgery have failed. Rebecca, who has formed a friendship with the doctor (or is it a strategic alliance?), has her direct line at the Grove Health Centre, but answers my request with an eloquent snort of derision. Silence, that most immovable piece of marital furniture, enfolds us until I mutter, 'By the way, you know you said you didn't marry me for my looks. Well, what was it, exactly, that you did marry me for?' 'Isn't that funny,' says my wife, ramming another half-orange into the juicer, 'I was hoping you might be able to tell me.'

Sunday

I awake feeling shattered after a deeply troubled night. In the dream, I am lying in a hospital bed, singing 'Let's All Go Down the Strand (Have a Banana!)' in an insane falsetto, when a doctor and a nurse come over. His name badge says 'Dr Radovan Karadjic, Psychiatrist' and hers reads 'Jo Brand, Sister, Ronald Reagan Ward'. 'This one's not quite with us, I'm afraid,' says Jo. 'He keeps insisting he's not quite 34.' As the pair dissolve into mirth, in view behind them, hurtling towards the ceiling on a turbo-charged Stanna Stairlift, comes Dame Thora Hird. 'I want to go with her, I want to go with her,' I shout through toothless gums. 'Didn't I tell you, Doctor?' squeals Jo, the tears rolling from her eyes. 'The poor old chap thinks he should be with Thora and the other young 'uns in the Junior Day Group.'

Monday

Coming downstairs after dinner, I catch Rebecca on the phone to Dr Jarvis. She ignores my attempts to catch her eye, and when she starts to say goodbye I can take no more. Jumping up and down in fury, I dementedly tap the top of my head with index finger. 'Oh, hang on, Sarah,' she says (Sarah!), 'I've a feeling Matthew may want to ask about this new drug for baldness. Oh yes . . . Uh huh . . . Mmm, I see.' She puts one hand over the phone and addresses me: 'She says it might have a side effect.' She returns the phone to her head. 'So what you're saying is, it's a straight choice between losing his hair and impotence. Hang on.' As if examining livestock at a cattle auction, she allows her eyes to descend from the top of my head to the area just below the waist. They linger here a moment, before beginning the return journey. 'Sarah, I'm afraid it's a bit too close to call right now,' says my wife. 'Let me have a think and I'll let you know on Friday.' •

7 March 1998

Matthew Engel
Farewell, Ambridge

I had known for a long time that things could not go on the way they were. The change had to come. Finally, my wife found out. I have now left the village. I have no plans to move back.

The crisis point came as we were discussing some very old friends. 'We haven't seen them for AGES,' she said.

'Yes,' I replied, 'and I've never even met Baby Josh.'

'Josh?' she said. 'Who's Josh? Their baby's called Fred.'

Josh is the son of David and Ruth Archer. It was easy to confuse them with the Nickolds family. One lot live in Cambridge, the other in Ambridge, so it's easy to get mixed up, save only for the small detail that – on the world's stern reckoning of these things – the Nickoldses exist, and the Archers don't.

There had been other, minor, incidents. 'You're being ridiculous,' she might say. 'Why don't you face reality?' 'Yes,' I would answer dreamily, 'Brian was saying the same thing to Jennifer only the other day.'

One of yesterday's papers – I think it was the *Guardian*, but it might have been the *Borchester Echo* – discussed soap operas, and how some pathetic souls cannot distinguish between fiction and reality. But it's OK, I'm now cured, finished, outta there, gone. The train has left Hollerton Junction, and I'm on it.

It is true that I have a history of these afflictions. I was probably the only teenager of the 1960s who was traumatised by missing episodes of *Mrs Dale's Diary*, a situation ended only when the BBC decided the programme was such rot that they took it off.

For many years after that I was only a casual *Archers* user, and I do have an excuse for being suckered into addiction. It happened when, on behalf of this newspaper, I began to do a lot of long car journeys. I discovered it was quite easy to tape the Sunday morning omnibus edition, on a time switch if necessary,

Camels and corrections

and play it back during long treks up the M4 or M6. There is a school of thought that this taping is illegal, though it is only the radio equivalent of what every video-owner does with TV programmes. I am hoping that if this confession leads to my arrest and imprisonment, they will send me to a jail where there is compulsory chapel or something on Sunday mornings, so I don't backslide and start listening to *The Archers* again.

I think heroin users get flashes of insight that their habit is pretty ridiculous. In my case, these grew as I became aware of Ms Vanessa Whitburn (one of these so-called 'real' people), the editor of *The Archers* and a woman alleged to rule Ambridge with a ferocity not seen since Mayor Daley's heyday in Chicago.

Even Mayor Daley never had the power accorded to the editor of a long-running soap. It takes little more than an arch of an eyebrow to have someone taken out and shot or, more likely, since Ms Whitburn's exuberance is beginning to outrun her imagination, written off on the Borchester by-pass or mangled under a tractor.

As many of you will be fed up with hearing, this was the fate which last week befell one John Archer, grandson of Peggy and the late Jack, son of Pat and Tony, and second cousin (or thereabouts) to the aforesaid Baby Josh. The effect of a fictional death on the reader or viewer or listener ought to be a sort of delicious tristesse: shock and sadness, mitigated by the realisation that it has not actually happened. This is as true for the death of Cordelia or Desdemona as for the bloke in *Coronation Street* who was mown down by a Blackpool tram.

According to the *Guardian* (or *Echo*) piece, thousands of people wept at the news of John Archer's death. I do not believe it. It was too crass and cack-handed a story-line for that. It was like the death of Little Nell, as described by Oscar Wilde: you would need a heart of stone not to burst out laughing. It was perfectly well-executed; it was just too melodramatic an event: like the post-office raid, the fascist attack on Usha, the instant transformation of Simon Pemberton from cold-hearted landlord to near-homicidal sex maniac, and various other recent instances from the *Archers* annals.

Occasional sensationalism is essential to a soap opera. But it is even more essential not to snap the thin, taut line that keeps the listener's credulity going. I am just not a believer any more.

I shall leave other listeners to monitor the development of John's younger, surviving brother: a youth who, without leaving Borsetshire, has acquired a distinct Mancunian accent.

And they can also hear how the programme pans out from next month, when there will be six weekly episodes instead of five, and the Sunday omnibus stretches from an hour – its length since the days of Squire Lawson-Hope – to 75 minutes. Given the desperation that seems to afflict Ms Whitburn even now, I simply do not believe that *The Archers* can be sustained at that length. The controller of Radio 4 has made a damn-fool mistake.

It was this that made me understand I would have to return to the real world.

You don't seem to be able to buy tapes longer than 60 minutes a side these days. And the man in the electrical shop assured me that those fancy auto-reverse tape players will only work on playback. It thus seems to be impossible to record a radio programme longer than an hour without standing over the cassette machine. I am definitely not that crazy. So it's now certain. I have left Ambridge forever. Mind you, if anyone does know how you record a 75-minute programme on a 60-minute tape, I would like to know. Just in case, you understand.

John Archer would have known. Mike Tucker, he's practical, he might know. I could ask him. Maybe young Roy could ask one of his university mates for me.

No, I'll ring Eddie Grundy . . . •

10 December 1997

Leader

Plenty of postmodern comfort and joy

Shortly before 7 p.m. last Sunday the nation learned its fate. For the next two weeks we are doomed to a peculiar form of aural torture: the constant repetition of a sugary jingle lisped by four mutant psychedelic gonks. 'Say Eh-oh' is almost certain to top the charts right up to Christmas. Move over shepherds, wise men and kings! Here come Tinky Winky, Dipsy, Laa-Laa and Po with their festive cheer of custard, toast and hugs. Teletubbies! Teletubbies! They bring you good tidings of great joy. Shame about the music.

The new wave of Teletubbymania hits a country which is barely recovering from its bout of Barbiemania. For weeks now some of us have not been able to get it out of our heads. 'Come on, Barbie, Let's go party! Ah-Ah-Ah-Ah! Life in plastic, it's fantastic! Ooo-oo-ooooh! Oooo-oo-oooh!' It is, of course, a relief to escape from the hermetic world of Ken and Barbie. But it is little comfort to find oneself instead in an acid-green Orwellian landscape watched over by a sinister windmill and a troop of menacing rabbits.

It would be some comfort if the success of these two songs were solely attributable to the innocent choice of the under-10s. But we know that a large proportion of Teletubby fans are in fact students who chill out in Laa-Laa land before retiring to bed. Dozens of websites deconstruct the meaning of the Teletubbies — their sexuality, their politics, their potency as narcotic metaphor. One Media Studies lecturer has described them as the biggest campus cult of the decade. Their only rivals are, indeed, Ken and Barbie. Or, possibly Alan Partridge. Or even Mrs Merton. Postmodern irony is clearly becoming not only the dominant cultural force in Britain today, but also a formidable commercial force.

Aha! And Eh-oh! •

Camels and corrections

....

20 February 1998
Ian Mayes
Corrections and clarifications

The obituary for Lord Granville, Page 18, 17 February, oversimplified his parliamentary career when it described him as Liberal MP for Eye 1929–51. He was elected in 1929 as a Liberal. In 1931 he became a Liberal National. He resigned the whip in 1942 and became an Independent. He rejoined the Liberals in 1945.

A transcription error caused us to misquote W. H. Auden in the Endpiece column, Page 14, 16 February. Auden wrote, 'Their steep stone gennels . . .' It appeared as 'gunnels'. A gennel is a narrow passage. A gunnel is a small eel-shaped marine fish.

In the Birthdays column, Page 18, 17 February, we were mistaken both in the day and date of birth of the Labour MP Helen Jones. She is not 68. She was born 24 December 1954. Apologies for the error.

Country Diary on Page 16, 17 February, was headed 'Heald Green, Cheshire'. Heald Green is in Stockport, Greater Manchester. The error was caused by nostalgia. •

....

4 December 1997
Alex Duval Smith
Michelin tires of inflated image

One of the last acceptable faces of obesity, the Michelin man has succumbed to the anti-fat fad: the French tyre company decided he needed a leaner image for the United States and Japan. The roly-poly Bibendum character was relaunched yesterday by image consultants who believe his slimmed-down spare tyres exude calm and authority.

'The change of look is in keeping with major sociocultural changes,' said Stephane Lepicard at the Carré Noir design group.

'Before, Michelin had him running behind a tyre, but our aim was to give him the serenity of a leader, standing still and looking the customer in the eye.' Like Barbie, who recently saw her bust shrink, Bibendum's belly was considered old-fashioned and undynamic, he said. 'Focus groups in the Far East and the US wanted him to be more of a leader.'

But it would be out of character for the Michelin man — who seems to have

Camels and corrections

swapped his spectacles for contact lenses as well – to forsake pot-au-feu and red wine for sushi and green tea.

He was born in 1898 after André Michelin was inspired by a beer poster with the slogan '*Nunc est bibendum*' (Now is the time to drink), from the Latin lyric poet Horace.

Feeling that his tyres swallowed up bumps in the road, Michelin asked the illustrator Marius 'O'Galop' Roussillon to use the slogan with a character fitting his product. Michelin now has a fat turnover of more than £6 billion.

Mr Lepicard said, 'We hope that by cutting Bibendum's cholesterol level, he is closer to the innovative reality of the company.' •

12 June 1998
Tony May
Hire intelligence trips up job experts

The value of SHL fell 45 per cent yesterday after the expert in psychometric testing of job applicants admitted it hired the wrong man to run its US management. The group issued its second profit warning in four months.

The fall in SHL shares of 117p to 146p means the group has lost 75 per cent of its market value since February and, at £78.2 million, is worth £52.4 million less than when it was floated on the stock market in October.

The group's plans for a rapid expansion in the US helped ensure the flotation was enthusiastically received. It then spent $1 million hiring sales staff, a manager and support workers. All of them passed the psychometric tests designed to find ideal recruits for specified jobs. A further $750,000 was spent on set-up costs and marketing.

The main board, all of its members psychometrically tested, had estimated that taking its products to the top companies in the US could push up US sales 140 per cent and boost profits.

It admitted yesterday that this had proved over-optimistic – sales were only half of the target. Half-year profits, which it warned in February would be flat,

Camels and corrections

were down 7 per cent to £4.53 million and would not be recouped in the second half.

SHL has appointed a new – psychometrically tested – chief operating officer to head the North American team, cost-cutting is under way and Nevill Bain, recently made chairman to strengthen the board, said, 'The jury is still out on the salesmen.' •

....

8 December 1997

John Hooper
Crosses made in heaven

And now here are the football results: St Peter's Basilica 5, Radio Vaticana 4; Secret Archives 4, Vatican Fire Brigade 1.

This is not a joke.

Virtually unknown beyond the confines of the world's smallest and most secretive state, a Vatican football league has existed for 27 years. Those were some of last week's results.

There are 16 sides. They include teams put together by the Palatine Guards, the Vatican police, the Vatican museums and the Vatican post office. The so-called Vatican Bank, more correctly known as the Institute for the Works of Religion, fields two sides. Appropriately enough for an organisation best known for its mysterious dealings, one of them goes by the name of Team X. By last week, with eight games played, the Secret Archives headed the league on goal average.

Sides are drawn mostly from among the Vatican's lay workers. But there are two priestly players, both of whom take the field for Radio Vaticana – Father Davide Djudjaj, an Albanian from Kosovo, and Father Salim Del Cristo Tobias, recently arrived from Colombia and apparently one of the league's most exciting prospects.

'With a few kilos less and a bit more speed, he'd be up to international standard,' sighed a Vatican printer, Saverio Di Pofi.

Standards have now reached the point at which the league feels confident enough to field a 'national' team. The Sistine Sporting Society made its debut this season in the Rome and Lazio division of the Italian five-a-side league. Mr Di Pofi, who spends his days turning out Papal encyclicals and the like, is its trainer.

And it has made a pretty impressive start too. With no visible divine intervention, it has won three games, lost one and drawn away against what was thought to be the best side in the league.

'Our distinctive strength is our good behaviour,' said Mr Di Pofi's deputy, Roberto Di Stefano. The Vatican's own league has two end-of-season awards: the league trophy and a prize for '*disciplina*'. The good behaviour cup is 'more important for us'. •

Camels and corrections

The Angel of the North goes up at Gateshead

23 December 1997

Martin Wainwright

Apple tempts shy sisters into contemplation of virtual reality

Contemplating over her Apple Mac, Sister Mary of the Carmelites is trying to make up her mind whether to post a Christmas message on the enclosed order's new Internet website.

'It'd be a nice touch, wouldn't it?' she says. 'But my worry is that if I put a special message on, will I ever get round to taking it off when Christmas is over?'

The small IT problem is a minor glitch in the venture by the shy but spiritually powerful sisters into the world of cyber-chatting, e-mails and virtual convents.

The Carmelites' first rule-maker, patriarch Albert of Jerusalem, and their most famous mentor, St Teresa of Avila, left no guidance on a weapon of communication so awesomely powerful.

'But we do know that it can and should be used for good,' says Sister Mary, who has pondered the role of global information in freeing, for example, the people of the former Soviet Union and apartheid South Africa. 'There has been much discussion among Carmels about how to proceed, and we are very pleased

Camels and corrections

to have our website at last – although I'm finding this version a little slow.'

From her convent at Dysart in Fifeshire, and liaising with Britain's 24 other Carmels, Sister Mary checked out her technology with her computer-minded brother in Australia. The convent also sought advice from lay friends in Scotland, who took a list of requirements which astonished local dealers.

'Apparently they said, "Surely one person can't want a computer to do all this,"' says Sister Mary. 'You see, we have our accounts, publications, graphics, the music we use and a host of other things as well as the website. They thought for a long time and then came up with the Apple.' Unlike its biblical counterpart, which set Adam and Eve down the wrong track, the computer and its busy netlink is already proving a help to the sisters, who spend their lives behind convent walls. The website has received rapid-response requests for prayers and is also spreading details of the order's work and way of life.

'We want to let people know we are here,' said Sister Mary of St Michael, a former president of the Association of Carmels of Great Britain, who is also

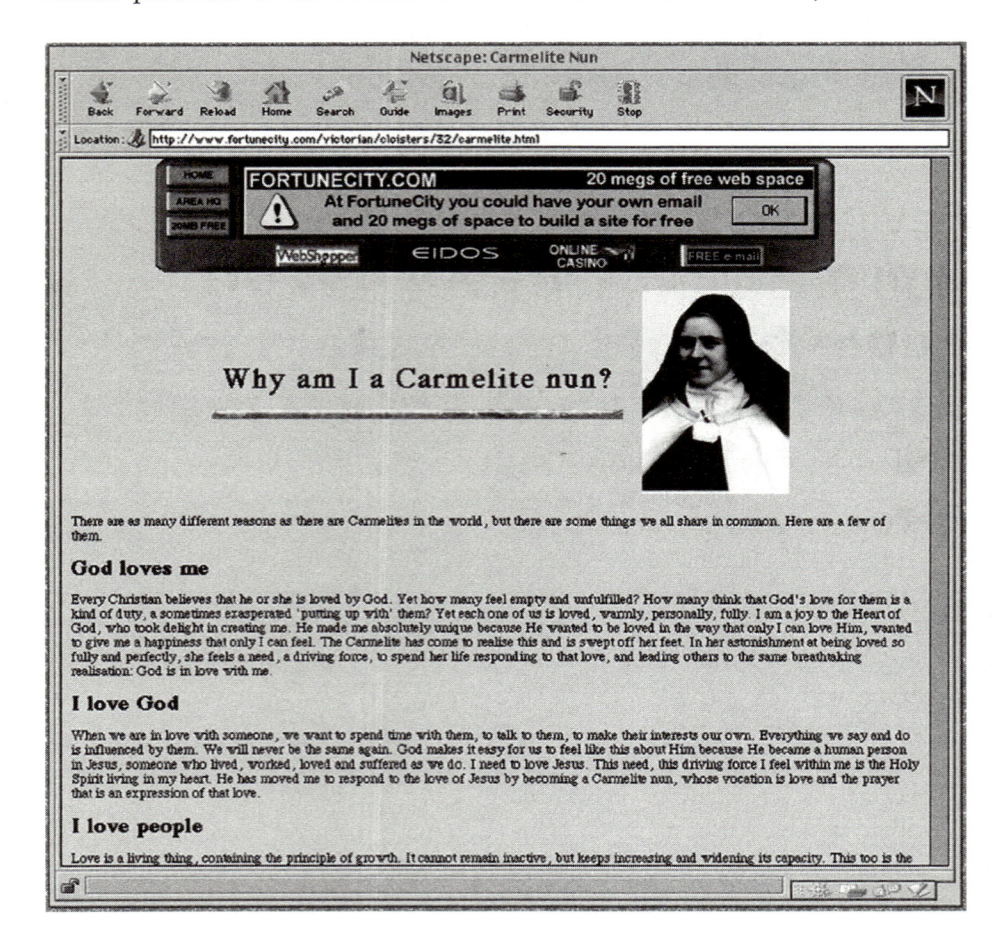

Camels and corrections

wired-up at a convent near Glasgow. 'It isn't for recruiting, because the life of a nun is a vocation not a job, but there are people who seem to have forgotten that we exist. An Internet page puts us clearly on the map and shows that we can embrace new technology.'

The website is relatively simple, but the Carmels are working on links to other Carmelite orders and counterparts in the United States, New Zealand and Europe. Sister Mary in Dysart says, 'We're still feeling our way, and I know there are lots of changes we will probably want to make to the site.'

The order is also considering the implications of inviting the world into the home – albeit virtual home – of religious sisters whose essence since St Teresa's rules of 1562 has been an austere and contemplative, unworldly life.

'We will see how things work out, but many of the sisters – there are some 350 in Britain – are quite at home with computers,' says Sister Mary. 'We're not expecting an avalanche of interest, but the website is already receiving hits. We've only just installed a webcounter and it's just got to 32.'

The Carmels can be reached at www.fortunecity.com/victorian/cloisters/32/index.html •

4 March 1998
David Pallister
'Bored' guest walks out on Dobson

Just after the Parmesan-flecked rocket-leaf starter, with grilled red onions in balsamic vinegar, the Secretary of State for Health stood up to speak. The Queen Elizabeth II conference hall was stuffed with about 700 chemists, local health authority officials and scores of MPs.

It was the annual dinner of the Pharmaceutical Services Negotiating Committee – an event not normally noted for hilarity or churlish behaviour. 'Listening to pharmacists' was Frank Dobson's theme – on the day that the Government announced a rise in prescription charges. But for one guest it was less than riveting. About 15 minutes in, just as Mr Dobson was enthusing about new developments in the drugs industry, he stood up and cried out, 'Frank, I've had enough of this. Frank, you're boring, I'm off.'

A clearly mortified Mr Dobson was heard to mutter, 'I didn't think it was that boring,' before bringing his speech to a hasty close.

Embarrassed pharmacists queued up to apologise as Mr Dobson comforted himself with the lamb main course.

'He was plainly upset,' said one of the guests, Tory MP David Amess.

The chemists couldn't believe the culprit was one of their own. Beverley

Camels and corrections

Parkin, head of public relations at the Royal Pharmaceutical Society, said, 'It was rather boorish and not very good form. Pharmacists would never behave in such an ungracious way.'

The guilty man was Knighton Berry, a director on West Sussex Health Authority, who considers himself a bit of a wit according to the comic letters he occasionally sends to the *Guardian*.

A contrite Mr Berry, who is also an occupational psychologist and human resources consultant, yesterday said he 'deeply regretted' his remarks and would be writing to Mr Dobson to apologise.

Yesterday, the 58-year-old minister shrugged off the slight: 'I'd already given them a few jokes – all very tasteful, like all my jokes. After all, people are entitled to be bored. I had, in fact, pointed out earlier in the speech that I'd actually fallen asleep during one of my own speeches – so perhaps it is not surprising.'

One seasoned Dobson-watcher recalled yesterday that even that joke is one he has used before. •

12 March 1998
David McKie
Hitler and who?

For many years newspapers got along pretty well without much recourse to the word 'arguably'. Now it is everywhere. She is arguably the brightest/dimmest/most erudite/scrofulous of all the new Labour MPs. He is arguably the finest midfielder ever to come out of Bedfordshire. And so on. One can hardly imagine a greater foe of such practices than the philosopher Ludwig Wittgenstein (1889–1951). 'What can be said at all,' he wrote, 'can be said clearly; and whereof one cannot speak, thereof one must remain silent.' It therefore seems foully ironic that Wittgenstein should be the subject of a new book by Kimberley Cornish, *The Jew of Linz*, which, if last week's *Sunday Times* extract is any reliable guide, must represent the elevation of 'arguably' to a whole new art form.

Cornish's thesis is this. Hitler's virulent anti-Semitism, as he records in *Mein Kampf*, was born in his schooldays. But who was the hated schoolmate, 'this boy who turned Hitler into the killer of 6 million Jews'? Although Cornish concedes there is not much to go on in Hitler's book, it is possible to make a fair bet, and the fair bet is Ludwig Wittgenstein – a boy just a few days younger than Hitler who joined him at the Realschule in Linz in 1904. Though there were other Jewish boys at the school, Wittgenstein fits the bill perfectly. 'We face, I think, the astounding possibility that the course of twentieth-century history was radically influenced by a quarrel between two schoolboys.'

Camels and corrections

This is startling enough, but what Cornish calls the denouement is no less spectacular. When Wittgenstein came back to Cambridge in 1929, the celebrated spies Philby, Burgess and Blunt were among his college contemporaries, while Donald Maclean was just down the road. 'Of course,' Cornish concedes, 'the mere fact of their attending Trinity at the same time proves nothing.' But Wittgenstein certainly knew them, through his work, his homosexuality and his membership of the secret society called the Apostles. 'I do not wish to labour the point,' Cornish writes, 'but one has to consider a question that has never been satisfactorily resolved: who was the Soviet recruiter who created the spy ring?' One hypothesis is that this mysterious figure was none other than Wittgenstein. The recruiter must have been a remarkable man; 'that he might have been one of the most brilliant minds of the twentieth-century has not been suspected'.

The extract, of course, represents only a segment of Cornish's book.

Restrictions of space may have denied us equal consideration of another outstanding intellect at Trinity in those days, a man who suffered a huge revulsion from a previous passion for Germany; who like Wittgenstein once venerated Nietszche but later turned to religion; who was touched for a while, we now know, by homosexual love; and whose powers of persuasion far outstripped those of Wittgenstein. I do not wish to labour the point, but one hypothesis is that the master recruiter was Enoch Powell. Was he not, in later years, virulently anti-American? Did he not speak more warmly of Russia than any front-bench Conservative contemporary? He may not fit the bill perfectly, but it is, I think, a fair bet that he fits quite as well as Wittgenstein.

I hope, too, that Cornish has found room in his book to consider my own pet theory that Wittgenstein is to blame for the long decline of Huddersfield Town — once one of the greatest forces in English football, and for 32 years from 1920 a continuous presence in the game's top division. And yet in the season 1951–2 they suddenly lost it. One has to ask: what happened in 1951 to change things so drastically? One hypothesis is that Wittgenstein died. True, there is no actual evidence that Ludwig was a supporter or ever attended a game. But until his sad death at the end of the 1950–51 season there was always that possibility. As they trotted out at Leeds Road in the season which followed, it's a fair bet, I think, that the players were stricken by the knowledge that the famous philosopher could now never take his place on the terraces with his blue and white scarf, his rattle and his mug of hot Bovril, urging them on now and then with some quotation from Schopenhauer, but mostly backing his team with the kind of support which he valued the most: his silence.

If this hypothesis is right, we face the astounding possibility that the course of twentieth-century football was radically influenced by a man who never went anywhere near it. Just as we face the astounding possibility that the *Sunday Times* unloaded on its readers last week one of the biggest loads of steaming old tosh inflicted by any serious newspaper on its defenceless readers in this generation.

Arguably. ●

Camels and corrections

29 April 1998
Ian Mayes
Corrections and clarifications

On page vi of the *Guardian Higher Education* supplement yesterday, we gave the wrong telephone number to be called by undergraduates and postgraduates seeking more information about the Association of Business Schools' Award for business and management students. The number we gave connected callers with the Interactive Chat and Date Service and provided an alternative number for gay callers. The correct number for students to call is 0891 338260. The award is supported by Clerical and Medical, as well as by the *Guardian* and *Observer*.

A Leader headed 'After Israel's soundbites', Page 17, 21 April, referred to letters from Mr Arafat to 'the late Shimon Peres'. Mr Peres is, of course, alive, unlike Mr Rabin, to whom the leader writer meant to refer. Apologies.

In a review on page 10, *G2*, 21 April, of the work of the artist Chris Ofili, we said, 'Along with the wrap-around shades and his 1973 lime-green Ford Capri, and the retro, one-size-fits-all Angela Carter Afro wig, elephant doo-doo is his trademark, a pungent calling card.' We should have said Angela Davis (the African-American civil rights activist) not Angela Carter (the novelist).

In the obituary of Joan Heal, Page 13, 27 April, we referred to the show 'which turned her into a star' as *Grab Me a Gondolier*. Not quite. It should have read '*Grab Me a Gondola*'.

A quotation was slightly mangled in the *Guardian*/Penguin Quiz, Page xii of our supplement for World Book Day, 23 April. His 'Wee, sleeket, cow'rin', tim'rous beastie' became 'sleckit' and 'sae' as in 'need na start away sae hasty' became 'she'. We can't identify the poet here because the competition doesn't close until 14 May. •

Union and Ulster flags fly together at Drumcree

A blessed Good Friday – and after

A blessed Good Friday – and after

11 April 1998
John Mullin
'Please make it work'

They stood at the threshold at dawn; a hard night's haggling left them at the gateway to a new future. There was euphoria, then frustration and later worry as the time dragged on.

The once-in-a-generation chance seemed to be slipping away amid rumours of rekindled rancour. Except that this time, unbelievably, the politicians took that last, most difficult, step.

It was a very special Good Friday in Northern Ireland. Tony Blair, sustained since his arrival on Tuesday on a diet of no sleep, bananas and tea, announced a historic deal while the hailstones fell. Mr Blair, wan but delighted, said he hoped 30 years of violence were at last over. 'When I arrived on Wednesday, I said I felt the hand of history on our shoulders. Today I hope that the burden of history can at long last be lifted from them.'

The deal was done, he said. Now for the tricky bit: making it work.

'I want to say this to the politicians and people of Northern Ireland with all the force I can muster. Even now, this will not work unless, in your will and in your mind, you make it work.'

His was a remarkable coup, and this was his finest day as Prime Minister. In the circumstances, he could be forgiven for forgetting what day of the week he had arrived. It was Tuesday, with the talks apparently close to collapse. Ulster Unionists and Sinn Fein, along with six parties between their polar positions, welcomed a deal brokered after 22 months of negotiations at Stormont. No one had dared believe it possible.

The settlement provides for an assembly in Northern Ireland, raising the possibility of David Trimble and Gerry Adams sitting alongside each other in a power-sharing executive. There will be cross-border authorities; a Council of Ministers. Relationships involving Belfast, Dublin, London and the Scottish and Welsh assemblies are to be recast. The jail doors are to open for paramilitary prisoners. Sentence remission will be increased from 50 per cent to two-thirds, meaning half of Northern Ireland's 530 convicted terrorists will soon be released – the majority within two years.

It was this issue that threatened to scupper the deal. Ulster Unionist MPs, also dissatisfied with measures on the decommissioning of terrorist weapons, challenged Mr Trimble. He showed his mettle and swatted aside the group, led by Jeffrey Donaldson, a potential leader.

Agreement was sealed only with the intervention of President Bill Clinton, who had spoken through the night to participants.

The Irish Prime Minister, Bertie Ahern, remembered his mother, Julia, who

A blessed Good Friday – and after

died, aged 87, last Sunday. Mr Ahern, still wearing a black tie, admitted it had been a difficult week. He said, 'I am sure my mother would have been pleased that we made so much progress.'

George Mitchell, the former US Senator who had grasped the poisoned chalice as talks chairman, said, 'I am delighted. I really am.'

The political leaders seemed stunned but later delivered their own spin. Mr Trimble said, 'What everybody in Northern Ireland has won today is a new deal that will give everybody the opportunity to participate in a unique political arrangement.'

Mr Adams, also fighting some rank-and-file dissent, said the fight to unite Ireland would go on. 'This is a phase in our struggle. That struggle must continue until it reaches a final goal.'

John Hume, expected to be deputy first minister in the new assembly, said, 'Only once in a generation does an opportunity like this come along, an opportunity to resolve our deep and tragic conflict. This time we must succeed. We have to seize this opportunity.'

But 80 miles away in Londonderry, a family was burying this year's fifteenth terrorist victim. Trevor Deeney, aged 34, a stepfather to four children, is the latest of 3,500 victims of the Troubles. As a new era beckons, Northern Ireland hopes he is the last.

The Deal:
- Elected Northern Ireland Assembly of 108 members
- Controlling executive commitee made up of 12 ministers
- Release of paramilitary prisoners to be accelerated
- A British-Irish Council bringing together representatives from the Scottish Parliament and Welsh Assembly with counterparts from Belfast and Dublin
- Reform of the Royal Ulster Constabulary
- Promise of decommissioning. •

22 May 1998
Anthony McIntyre
'We, the IRA, have failed'

In the H-blocks of Long Kesh prison camp, when victory for the IRA seemed a foregone conclusion, 'doing time', despite the harshness of prison life, was relatively easy. Conviction sustained most of us. Our view of the world was simple, perhaps simplistic. Britain had no right to be in our country. It seemed as daft to us for British soldiers to die – as John Cleese once said – to keep China British as it was to keep Ireland so.

Part of the time spent in prison was under the leadership of the late Bobby Sands. He led us in an era when the British state had yet to get the measure

A blessed Good Friday – and after

of the IRA. And like many others who joined him in prison protest, he was arrested at a difficult time for Republicanism. The Republican movement was in a state of strategic turbulence, desperately trying to anchor itself in the wake of a truce described as 'disastrous' and 'virtual surrender' by leaders such as Danny Morrison and Martin McGuinness. The strategic alternative was to wage a long war.

As an IRA volunteer aged 18, in prison for the second time, I was unaware of much of this. It seemed there was a war to be fought and enemies to be killed.

I and others succeeded on both counts. On a cold January morning in 1977 in Belfast's Crown Court, with my mother gazing on in stunned disbelief, Lord Chief Justice Lowry informed me that I would serve at least 25 years for ending the life of a member of the Ulster Volunteer Force. I laughed at him, prompting tabloid headlines of 'Laughing Killer Jailed for Life'.

Sectarian attacks by young Protestant kids initially prodded me towards the IRA. They had their Orange parades. We had our IRA – although quite where it was no one seemed to know. But it was comforting to 'feel' it was there and would 'settle up' on our behalf at some time. And now I was part of it.

Membership gave me the arrogance of the damned – I did not care what the Lord Chief Justice said. I was immune from his concerns. As readily as I had 'settled up', I prepared to settle down for the long haul.

And a long haul it proved to be – 17 years of it. But the British had cause to fear Republicans and went to great lengths to defeat us. They could not hope to buy us off. So they put our leader in a coffin after 66 days on hunger strike and sent him to his grave at the age of 27. And it was upon this that I was forced to reflect when I witnessed the present Republican jail leader being allowed to attend the Sinn Fein Ard Fheis.

Padraig Wilson, like Bobby Sands, was and is a selfless volunteer. His integrity is beyond dispute. But I did not share the euphoria of delegates at his presence. He was not there as a result of an amnesty reluctantly conceded, but was allowed to attend because the British wanted to bolster their strategy in Ireland by securing a Yes vote for the Stormont Agreement at the Ard Fheis.

In that sense the conference was less a case of chickens coming home to roost than of turkeys celebrating Christmas. In trade union terms the Republican leadership told those it represents that it had secured them a six-day week and lower wages. That the body of the hall did not storm the podium in anger at the Ard Comhairle is an indication of just how defeated the original Provisional Republican project is.

Danny Morrison's recent piece in the *Guardian* was an exercise in putting a smile on the face of the corpse. To claim, as he does, that the IRA did not win but had not lost either is demonstrably wrong. The political objective of the Provisional IRA was to secure a British declaration of intent to withdraw. It failed. The objective of the British state was to force the Provisional IRA to

A blessed Good Friday – and after

accept – and to respond with a new strategic logic to – the position that it would not leave Ireland until a majority in the North consented to such a move. It succeeded.

I concur with Danny Morrison's hope that the war is over. But it would have been over 20-plus years ago, and in less ignominious fashion, had the post-truce leadership not insisted on fighting to an inglorious conclusion. And then we would have been spared the twin sorrows of one jail Officer Commanding dying to resist British state strategy and a second, through no fault of his own, appearing to legitimise it. •

11 April 1998

Conor Gearty*
Britain's finest attempt to solve the problem

After yesterday's breakthrough, it is finally possible to be a rational optimist on the future of Northern Ireland. The politicians have surprised us all – and perhaps most of all themselves – by the scale of their achievements after days spent in exhaustive but honest debate.

Presiding over the British side, Tony Blair and Mo Mowlam deserve to be spoken of in the same breath as Gladstone, for the energy, commitment and tolerant openness in the way they have dealt amiably with the seemingly intractable, and for having enthusiastically prised open the minds of the deeply prejudiced.

Of course, they have built on the work of John Major and co-operated with successive Irish administrations. Others, such as Gerry Adams and John Hume, have naturally had pivotal roles. But what we saw unfold before us yesterday was the finest attempt by a British administration this century to solve not (as it is commonly called) the problem of Irish nationalism, but rather the problem of Ireland's British unionism.

In his hour of triumph, Tony Blair has been chided for being unduly obsessed with David Trimble and his cohorts, but here is a Prime Minister who knows his British and Irish history.

No force has had greater destructive impact on UK politics over the past 120 years than Ireland's unique brand of loyalty to the crown. It ravaged Gladstone's Liberal Party in 1886. A romantic commitment to its absolute indestructibility helped transform Salisbury's all-powerful Conservative Party into a self-styled Unionist rump. Asquith's attempt in 1912–14 to deliver what we would now call Irish devolution provoked a seditious conspiracy across the United Kingdom.

---

* *Conor Gearty is Professor of Human Rights Law, King's College, London.*

A blessed Good Friday – and after

Lloyd George's solution in 1921 may have brought the Union a temporary victory in Ireland, but it was only at a cost of sacrificing three-quarters of the island and three generations of Northern Irish Catholics. They were transformed into a silently suffering 'inferior race' hidden in a nation that had the effrontery to persist in proclaiming itself the home of civil liberties and the rule of law.

When these people finally said enough, in the late 1960s, the resumed failure of Ireland's Unionism left blood on the hands of a succession of British premiers, mocking in their own backyard their delusions of sovereign power.

This is the vice of history from which Mr Blair and Ms Mowlam seem triumphantly to have extracted their country. This initiative is more likely to succeed than so many of the failures of the past because it has started from the right premise. The predilection of British policy in Ireland has long been for centre-based solutions, gatherings of the decent trying to solve by reason the turmoil created around them by the 'extremists', the 'terrorists' and the other irreconcilables supposedly contaminating politics with their criminal lust for violence.

Such an approach has inevitably always meant little change and more political violence. It was into this tradition that the Sunningdale failure fell, as did an earlier assembly of the great and the good, the now forgotten Irish Convention with which Lloyd George first tried to solve the Irish problem in 1917–18. He quickly learned his lesson, cut out the middle men and dealt directly with Michael Collins and the IRA to get the treaty that brought Britain a half-century of Irish peace.

Under the patient tutelage of John Hume, who like Parnell appreciates the significance of the violence that he nevertheless morally abhors, successive British administrations have finally followed Lloyd George's second precedent and brought all the politicians together, even those whose violence has not been sanctioned by the state. This settlement is their second big reward, their first being the paramilitary cease-fires that made it possible. But the price has been the contemplation of a deal that would never have been dreamed of by the centre parties acting alone and would normally be anathema to Unionism.

Despite this, the settlement has every chance of sticking. It is a triumph for the art of creative negativity. The Unionists in Ireland have been perpetually dedicated to the status quo, saying no at every critical moment in their community's history. This process has survived through astute dependence on such negativity, its guiding principles being the 'triple lock' and 'consent' (a polite word for veto). To Trimble's immense credit he did not balk at the manoeuvring and lapse back into the juvenilia of 'doing what we know best, saying no'. •

A blessed Good Friday – and after

11 April 1998

Leader
A blessed Good Friday

These men and women did noble work. Tired after 30 hours without sleep, their fatigue from 30 years of war proved greater. In the name of the people of Northern Ireland, they reached out to their deadliest rivals – and made peace. It took the deaths of more than 3,000 people, the serious wounding of some 30,000 others, but yesterday the two sides of that long and bloody conflict joined together to declare, 'Enough.'

The Easter snow never let up, the air outside the castle buildings stayed bitter and frigid – but still Sinn Fein's chairman described it as 'a beautiful day'. And so it was. Inside the Stormont building, men whose adult lives had been filled with talk of armed struggle and no surrender were now sharing a joke, paying warm tribute to each other. Usually hard-faced men came to speak, only to find a catch in their voice. One delegation was spotted in the middle of the night, its members quietly hugging each other. The emotion was earned, as was the universal declaration that Stormont had witnessed history in the making. There are important caveats. But no one should lose sight of the scale of the achievement. After three decades of conflict – and an antagonism that has endured for centuries – Unionism and nationalism, loyalism and Republicanism, Protestants and Catholics may finally have found a way to live together. This is no mere pact between governments, nor some worthy accord among moderates; it is not a rerun of Sunningdale or the Anglo-Irish Agreement. This is an agreement backed by those who represent the men of violence, standing at opposite extremes. Gerry Adams was smiling yesterday, apparently with the blessing of the IRA army council, but so were Gary McMichael and David Irvine, the men who speak for the convicted killers of hardline loyalism. It is as if the Middle East peace process had brought together Hamas and the Jewish settlers of the West Bank: it is an extraordinary feat of diplomacy. The politicians yesterday counselled against euphoria, rightly warning that the task of reconciliation has only just begun. Prudence would suggest waiting a while before handing out plaudits. Even so, it seems right to credit those who pulled off what so many – until very recently – said was impossible. In Northern Ireland, John Hume, Gerry Adams and David Trimble have all earned a place in history. Mr Hume for having the courage to stand with Sinn Fein early, encouraging them to choose politics over warfare. Mr Adams led the Republican movement away from violence and towards a compromise on its core doctrine of a united Ireland; Sinn Fein has now formally accepted the partition of Ireland – a historic break. Mr Trimble proved the most obstinate negotiator in the last moments yesterday, but he showed political strength too, persuading a party which has

A blessed Good Friday – and after

made intransigence into an article of faith to compromise. The Ulster Unionists' acceptance of the new ministerial council of the north and south grants the Republic a governmental stake in Northern Ireland for the first time. Until now Unionism has regarded the South as an alien, if not enemy power.

Outside the province, London and Dublin can allow themselves a weekend of congratulation. Bertie Ahern buried his mother on Thursday, then headed to Belfast for two sleepless days cajoling and arm-twisting the parties towards an agreement. Tony Blair was pivotal, luring David Trimble back to the peace table just when the entire effort seemed doomed. All that was possible thanks to the dogged, indefatigable work of his Secretary of State, Mo Mowlam. Her human touch has attracted much criticism these last months, but now she is vindicated: she has succeeded where every predecessor has failed. Thanks in part to her, Tony Blair has won the prize that had eluded every British PM since Gladstone. It is the crowning achievement of his first year in office.

Failure is a possibility. But so, now, is success. The people of Northern Ireland at last have an opportunity to live their lives in peace. It is a time for gratitude, and even the odd private prayer. For this was a blessed Good Friday. •

....

22 May 1998
John Mullin
Agony of an act of faith

Anne Slaine, aged 58, from Cookstown, County Tyrone, lives an ordinary life. Today, she is called on to make an extraordinary decision. Mrs Slaine, a retired occupational therapist, is one of Northern Ireland's silent majority. They are people with no time for extremists, and who keep their own counsel while getting on with their lives.

A mother of two and grandmother to five, Mrs Slaine is a Protestant, though her faith was dented when Reg, her husband, drowned while they were on holiday at Portrush on the Antrim coast nine years back. She has always voted Ulster Unionist.

Analysts believe Mrs Slaine and those like her hold the key to Northern Ireland's future when they vote in today's referendum. They say women over 40 who are Unionist supporters are the most reluctant group when it comes to embracing the Good Friday Agreement. Some people made up their minds immediately. But up to 20 per cent of Unionists are still thought to be undecided. Today, they will make the difference between the deal's success and failure.

Mrs Slaine is typical of them in all respects, bar one: what happened to her only son, Paul. She admits that has caused her agony as she weighs up what to do. As she sips coffee in the White Gables Hotel in Hillsborough, County

A blessed Good Friday – and after

Down, she explains her concerns. She thinks her story is unremarkable. Perhaps, though, the values it illustrates offer an insight into the dilemma facing tens of thousands.

'My mother and father were Elizabeth and Tom Greer. They always had Catholic as well as Protestant friends. That was always the way. He was a hardware merchant in Cookstown, and my brother, John, five years younger than me, ended up taking it over. It's closed now.'

Two days after Christmas 1963, she married Reg and moved to Omagh 'because Reg saw a job going as an organist at St Colomba's'. They had two children. Niki, now 30, is married with a 10-month-old son, Jamie. Her brother, Paul, is two years older.

The family was relatively untouched by the Troubles, complacent even. Mrs Slaine was shocked by atrocities, but there were so many. She believed the nationalist community was treated badly. She was still getting over the death of her husband after 26 years of marriage when she was in Amsterdam as principal at a vocational college for the young disabled. On the television news, she saw the remains of a police car, ripped apart by an IRA bomb in Newry, County Down. She watched as the photograph of RUC constable Colleen McMurray, aged 33, flashed on the screen. Her son was in the RUC, and he often worked with Mrs McMurray. She phoned home in a panic, to discover Interpol had been trying to track her down. It was March 1992.

Paul, who had joined the RUC four years earlier, was fighting for his life. He had lost both his legs, a finger, and they feared for his right arm. He had serious head injuries, a lacerated throat and needed 66 pints of blood. He is 32 now, a father of four, and back at work in the RUC. He is an ebullient man, helped through his crisis by his wife of 12 years, Allison, a psychiatric nurse. He staves off the bitterness, but he cannot forgive. The terrorists who killed his partner and almost murdered him have never been caught.

Mrs Slaine, proud of how her son has coped, says, 'There are parts of the deal I like. I think that after so many years of direct rule we are going to have some say in our own destiny with the assembly. But I look upon Yes as somehow letting Paul down, and those people who have suffered at the hands of terrorists who will now be able to walk the streets. The issue of the release programme for prisoners is the real problem, and it is for a lot of people.'

She rejects Tony Blair's guarantees that Sinn Fein will be excluded from the proposed power-sharing executive if the IRA fails to hand in its weapons. He will, she says, be unable to deliver.

'I have agonised so much about it. I listen to the radio all the time and I watch a lot of television. I hear one politician saying why I should vote No and agree with him, and then listen to the other side and change my mind. Maybe I'm easily swayed. If my generation doesn't bite the bullet now, we are simply deferring it for another generation. At some stage we are going to have to talk to people we do not want to talk to, that we feel we shouldn't be talking to.

A blessed Good Friday – and after

But it has to be done. I took part in a radio show last week and spoke of my fears of betraying my son. A schoolboy was the last to speak on it. He told me to think about whether I would be betraying my grandchildren by voting No, and that had an important effect on me. On balance, I think in my conscience I must vote Yes. I hope I do not live to regret it. It is a leap of faith.' •

25 May 1998

John Mullin
Adams told: it's time to deliver

David Trimble, leader of the Ulster Unionists, last night signalled the next phase in Northern Ireland's political transformation when he demanded a clear pledge from Gerry Adams, the Sinn Fein president, that the IRA was finished with violence for good.

Mr Trimble, buoyed by an impressive 71.1 per cent vote for the Good Friday Agreement, said it was vital now that Sinn Fein realised there was neither support nor justification for undemocratic methods. The Yes campaign was backed by at least 95 per cent of nationalists.

Mr Trimble said, 'The time has come for Mr Adams to deliver. It could start off with a clear statement that this squalid little war is over; that there is a commitment to peaceful means; that there will be no return to violence.'

Northern Ireland voted 71.1 per cent to 28.9 per cent in favour of the agreement. The turnout was 81 per cent and the result was announced on Saturday. Voters in the Irish Republic also ratified the deal. About 55 per cent turned out, backing the deal by 94.4 per cent to 5.6 per cent. It was the first all-Ireland poll since 1918. The results came on the two-hundredth anniversary of the 1798 rebellion, when Protestants and Catholics joined forces against their English oppressors.

Mr Adams yesterday repeated his demands to meet Mr Trimble, who so far has refused to speak to him. Mr Adams wants to talk to him about this July's annual Orange march at Drumcree, near Portadown, County Armagh. He wants Mr Trimble, whose Upper Bann constituency includes Drumcree, to use his influence to stop it.

The march has sparked violent clashes for the past four years as the Orangemen tried to march down the nationalist Garvaghy Road there. There are fears this year's trouble will be the worst yet.

Mr Adams refused to talk about decommissioning until after Drumcree. The Government made it a priority to ensure that the elections for the 108-seat assembly took place before the marching season, for fear it could spark enough unrest to wreck the poll.

Mr Adams said, 'You talk to me about decommissioning. Talk to me about

A blessed Good Friday – and after

that after 12 July if these parades go ahead. Talk to me about it after the Tour of the North in Belfast. Talk to me if the RUC hack their way down the Garvaghy Road.' He added it would be no big deal for the Orange Order to reroute the parade to avoid nationalist areas.

The independent Parades Commission, set up this year to rule on contentious marches, was poised to announce last month that it was planning to refuse the Orange Order permission to march down the road. Tony Blair intervened and told it to postpone the report, fearing it could badly hit the referendum campaign.

Mo Mowlam, the Northern Ireland Secretary, infuriated nationalists last year after the RUC forced a route through for the Orangemen. Police removed protesters who tried to block them. That followed violent clashes the two previous years between police and loyalists when the RUC had tried to stop the march.

Mr Trimble, himself an Orangeman, is on weak ground at Drumcree. He won the leadership of the Ulster Unionists in 1995 after his hardline stance in backing the Orangemen's right to march there. The Orange Order is opposed to the Stormont deal. It indicated to its 70,000 members in Northern Ireland to vote against it.

Mr Adams, who said the significance was that the guns were silent, appeared to be attempting to deflect attention from decommissioning of terrorist weapons. It is the one issue that threatens the working of the assembly and the power-sharing executive.

Mr Trimble is in difficulties over decommissioning. The agreement binds parties only to using their influence to try to ensure all paramilitary weapons are handed in within two years. Although Mr Blair tried to reassure Unionists terrified at the prospect of Mr Adams and his deputy, Martin McGuinness, sitting in government without the IRA beginning to hand in its weapons, there are no guarantees. Sinn Fein will insist on its places, while the IRA has signalled there will be no decommissioning.

The British and Irish governments have pledged to have decommissioning schemes in force by the end of next month. Canadian General John de Chastelain, one of the three co-chairmen of the multi-party negotiations, said yesterday he was not looking for the sides to make a public handover. But he expected them to get rid of their guns. •

A blessed Good Friday – and after

17 August 1998

Rory Carroll
A dynasty ended at 3 p.m.

Until 3 p.m. on Saturday the fields around Omagh had for 100 years given the Grimes family what they wanted most; roots, a place to raise their young and stay together. Such was the success of their dairy farm that neighbours joked about the family becoming a dynasty.

No one will make the joke again. Saturday's bomb ripped out three generations; Mary, aged 65, the matriarch: Avril, 30, her daughter: and Avril's three children. Only one of them, 18-month-old Maura, will appear on the casualty list for Avril was pregnant with twins. The family was Catholic.

Yesterday a convoy of cars with ashen-faced relatives churned the muddy path to the Grimeses's farm, on top of a hill in the townland of Cooley, one mile from the village of Beragh, seven from Omagh.

The deaths of Avril and her infants had yet to be confirmed but hope was draining with every minute. Mick, the patriarch, was unable to speak. He could only sit in an armchair and mourn his wife and prepare to mourn his daughter and grandchildren.

Only two days ago he was his typical gregarious self, cracking jokes and planning his next project. A prosperous farmer and the publisher of the local magazine, he was an important man in Beragh, the closest they had to a first citizen. If something needed sorted, he was your man. Mary kept a good home and all the children turned out well. In their world, they had it made.

What sounded like a clap of thunder could be heard on the hill on Saturday, but work continued until a radio newsreader, hesitantly, said there was talk of injured.

Workmen yesterday resumed hosing the yard and looking after the animals, but inside the house the Grimeses just hugged and cried. Few had slept the night before. One of Avril's brothers emerged briefly, his eyes and voice raw: 'We can't talk. Nothing's been confirmed yet, we've got to wait for confirmation.'

Listed as missing it was too much to believe his sister and niece had died with his mother.

Dark haired, pretty, Avril was vivacious and had thrown herself into community work, youth clubs and charity fund-raising. She had a good word to say about everyone, said one farm employee, suddenly appalled he had avoided the present tense.

His colleague, younger, added: 'Lovely, that's the word for her, lovely, like her mother. Loads of energy, always doing things.'

Avril married young and became Mrs Monaghan, but didn't move far, just

A blessed Good Friday – and after

down the road to Augher. She had three children before Maura, but this pregnancy would produce her first twins.

It is not known why Avril was in the centre of Omagh on Saturday: possibly to show Maura her first festival, possibly to buy school uniforms for her other children. Mary often went shopping downtown, picking up bargains in Dunne's Stores. Neighbours said she originally came from Cork but settled in the opposite end of the country after falling in love with Mick.

Though spirited, they were not the sort of women to flout the police during a bomb warning. They would be sensible and follow the advice, so like hundreds of others they were herded towards the bomb.

Tears streaming down his face, one man said it was the most savage end. 'That's what I do to cattle, I herd them into the slaughter-house. But Jesus save us, to happen to Mary and Avril?' •

17 August 1998
Jonathan Freedland
The bomb hit right where it was placed – at Omagh's heart

Like every place whose name has entered the unholy canon of atrocity – Guildford, Warrington, Cookstown – Omagh has seen a procession of dignitaries come to mourn. A helicopter chops overhead, then there they are – standing before a microphone: John Prescott, Gerry Adams, Mary McAleese, Tony Blair. The words are also similar, so utterly useless really, that after a while they all merge into a blur. It's not their fault, no one can say anything. Even the promise of a cross-border security summit, announced last night, sounds like Canute raging at the waves.

In all this, Omagh is no different from any other town visited by the tornado of terrorism. The pictures from here probably look the same as last week's from Kenya and Tanzania, but for Omagh this is not just another atrocity. The people of this small, polite market town have not seen it all before. Even if this was not the worst ever act of violence in the 30-year history of the Troubles – which it is – it would feel like it in Omagh. Because, this time, it happened to them.

Sean Loughran knows Omagh better than anyone, lived there all his life – and, besides, he runs the Campsie Bar just by Market Street. He heard the blast, and ran right into the carnage. He was looking for his son, Paul, aged just nine.

'I couldn't believe it, I was standing in bodies.' A water main had burst and water was gushing everywhere, unleashing rivers of blood; not as metaphor, but as fact. 'The bodies were floating past me, but you couldn't even tell that's what they were,' he says, and his voice is choked – as if he could sob a river of tears.

A blessed Good Friday – and after

A video shot by an amateur cameraman in the centre of Omagh captures the full horror

He saw arms, legs and so much blood – but still no sign of Paul. He rushed to his home and – thank God Almighty himself – there was the lad, waiting for him, thinking the very same thing. 'Da, I'm here!' the boy said, and as he hugged his son tight, Loughran felt a relief sweeter than he'd ever known.

But there was no sleep. At 5 o'clock yesterday morning he was wide awake, talking to himself – the first time he's ever done it. He can't bring himself to go to the Omagh Leisure Centre, converted now into the Incident Centre, where families huddle around notice boards waiting for word of the injured and the dead. 'I don't want to hear the names, because I know them all.'

The politicians struggled yesterday because the old script no longer applied. Sure, Gerry Adams did his best, condemning this action, committed by what everyone assumes is a Republican splinter group, in language he never applied to the Provisional IRA: 'I am totally horrified by this action. I condemn it without any equivocation,' Mr Adams said. Tony Blair also spoke of how the bombers would not win. 'They are not going to destroy the chance of a decent future for people in Northern Ireland.' But neither could deploy the old formula, of calling for a peace process. Because Northern Ireland already has one, and it has yielded all that anyone could ask: there has been an Accord, sealed on Good Friday, a referendum and even elections to create an Assembly which is already up and running. The war has been effectively ended with the

32 The Guardian Year '98

A blessed Good Friday – and after

approval of Sinn Fein and the Ulster Unionists, the Irish and British governments, and the people of north and south – and yet a bloody act of war has been committed.

Northern Ireland is now being tested again. Will they all unite against the handful of rejectionists who are bent on thwarting the march toward reconciliation? Or will they turn on each other? With Unionists blaming Gerry Adams for a bomb which was as surely an attack on his brand of Republicanism as it was on Market Street.

But these questions are far from the minds of the townsfolk of Omagh. They are still looking for their dead. They are like the parents asked to identify a son by just a shoe and a set of dental records. They are like the pregnant woman who looked on the scene of devastation last evening and clutched her belly, as if fearful that the tornado might strike again. •

17 August 1998

Henry McDonald
Among the victims – and the lucky few

The Skelton family make only two trips a year into Omagh town centre during busy Saturday afternoons. One just before Christmas, the other in mid-August when they buy uniforms for their children going back to school. Kevin Skelton had only just left his wife Philomena and daughters Paula (18), Tracey (15) and Shauna (13) in Kells outfitters – the main shop selling school uniforms in Omagh – when the bomb went off.

'I heard the explosion and ran into the street. It was as if the entire shop had fallen out. Then I saw my wife, she was lying in the rubble. She was face down, her clothes had been blown off her. I felt for her pulse but there was none,' said a distraught Mr Skelton. Two of his girls escaped unscathed in the blast but Shauna had to be taken to the local hospital where they fitted a brace to her jaw due to facial injuries she sustained.

'I knew Philomena was dead but I still had to go out and officially identify her last night at half past nine. There are no marks on her face. But her legs, there were large lumps out of her legs,' her husband said.

Mr Skelton, a prominent Gaelic football referee in County Tyrone, met his wife when he was just fifteen. They married four years later. Philomena would have been celebrating her fortieth birthday on 1 September.

Seventeen-year-old Brenda Logue had recently asked her neighbour Sean McAnespie for work on his mushroom farm near Lough Macrory, a Republican strong-

A blessed Good Friday – and after

hold a few miles outside Omagh. Yesterday morning Brenda lay dead in a makeshift morgue at a nearby army camp outside Omagh. She had left her mother and grandmother in a shop to see why people were fleeing when she was caught up in the full force of the blast. Her father Tommy, a truck driver, was given news of her death yesterday but said, 'I knew all along. I knew because the front of the shop was blown out and nobody could survive that.'

Brenda was a popular, outgoing girl who played in goal for her village's local ladies GAA football team, St Theresa's. Yesterday her family broke down inside Omagh Leisure Centre which was being used as an incident centre where information was collated about the dead and injured. The Logues, including her youngest brother as well as her twin Cathel, had to be assisted out of the building by Red Cross volunteers after the grim task of officially identifying Brenda was completed.

Sean McAnespie watched from a distance inside the Centre while his neighbours were helped out. 'She was a fun-loving type of girl, she would have done anything for anyone. She asked me for a job recently; she was willing to earn her keep. She was a first-class girl,' said Mr McAnespie, who is also a Sinn Fein councillor for the area where Brenda Logue grew up.

Many of the dead and injured come from villages like Louch Macrory and nearby Carrickmore – both areas with a strong support base for Sinn Fein. Rumours about who had been killed were flying so thick and fast that the living, the survivors, were included on original death lists.

A local publican, J. Maguire, was caught up directly in the explosion. Many people who visited the Leisure Centre yesterday were astounded to see him alive. Mr Maguire has owned The Cosy Corner bar at the bottom of Market Street (where the bomb went off) for the last sixteen years.

His neighbour Elizabeth Rush, who owns the fancy-goods shop next door to his bar, was killed in the explosion. He described his miraculous escape. 'The walls just came down around me. People were lying about everywhere yet when I got up I realised I was not even injured, but Elizabeth next door was dead. Shortly afterwards it was reported around town that I had been killed. But as you can see here I am.'

Mr Maguire is one of the lucky few. The walls of the Omagh Leisure Centre are plastered with the lists of names of the hundreds injured in the atrocity. ●

Peter Mandelson presents the Guardian *editor Alan Rusbridger with the Newspaper of the Year award*

'A thorn in the side'

'A thorn in the side'

28 February 1998

Owen Bowcott

Guardian wins accolade for record sixth time

For a second year running, the *Guardian* has been chosen as Newspaper of the Year in Granada's 'What the Papers Say' awards. Alan Rusbridger, the editor, received the award from Peter Mandelson, the Minister without Portfolio.

'Under the Tories, it was a paper of opposition and, since 1 May, it's been a thorn in the flesh of the new government too,' the judges said. 'But the award centres on one classic piece of journalism – the unravelling of Jonathan Aitken's web of deceit. The *Guardian* faced a potentially ruinous court case, not to mention the prospect of impalement on Aitken's sword of truth. But the paper's investigative team was ingenious, their lawyers supportive and the editor held his nerve.'

The *Guardian* has now won the Newspaper of the Year six times, more than any other newspaper. •

13 November 1997

Simon Hoggart

A dragon with a red rose in its mouth?

William Hague twiddled with his tie. Then he rubbed the side of his nose. A brief knead of the right ear, on to the cheek, under the nostrils and back to the tie. He'd given himself an all-over massage fully clothed. His nerves must have been awful. Faced with the scandal over Formula One tobacco advertising he had the perfect opportunity to destroy the Prime Minister's credibility, for 24 hours at least.

There is a film called *The Goalkeeper's Fear of the Penalty*. But it is nothing to the Penalty-taker's Fear of the Open Goal. Take Gareth Southgate. What is he remembered for now? For a lucrative pizza ad! (But you get the point.)

Mr Blair began. 'I will set out the position with enthusiasm and relish!' he said. He then set out the position in such a dry and indigestible fashion that it could have used a bucketful of relish, preferably a powerful and emetic chutney. There had been discussions, draft directives and legal questions. There were

36 The Guardian Year '98

'A thorn in the side'

different options, 'including legislating through subsidiarity or a period of derogation'.

A period of derogation! Was there nowhere the man would not stoop to bore us to death?

Behind him, cheering, were the massed ranks of Labour's Bleeper Brigade, summoned to give their support, instructed what to say. It was like the XXII Congress of People's Deputies in the Great Hall of New Labour.

Mr Lawrie Quinn (Scarborough) rose to say that it was time to ban foreign donations. Deputy Quinn had been furnished with his views by the Central Committee, then lost the place and had to frantically leaf through his notes to discover what he thought.

The Tories laughed immoderately.

The Prime Minister then turned out to agree with everything Mr Quinn said. Why, there would even be a full inquiry into the question of party funding.

Given the Tories' record, Mr Hague could hardly raise this topic, any more than Richard Branson can complain about late trains. Instead he asked about the threat to snooker sponsorship and angling. A few Tories stirred uneasily. They knew they were on marshy ground, but were they really outraged at the threat to world darts, or Rothmans championship cribbage?

The Prime Minister did what he usually does and blamed the Tories. He may be the last person in Britain to think they are a credible political force.

Mr Hague said that the tobacco row was yet another broken pledge. 'I'm not accusing the Labour Party of being paid to break their promises – they break them for free all the time!' It was a good shot. But in politics, unlike sport, when your opponent scores, you simply pretend that he hasn't.

Mr Blair scoffed: 'He's walked up to the penalty spot and booted it over the bar!'

But then the sombre figure of Martin Bell, in a suit that was not merely white but bleached like a dead whale's bones, stood up and said: 'The perception of wrongdoing can be as damaging to public confidence as the wrongdoing itself. Have we slain one dragon only to have another take its place, with a red rose in its mouth?'

Mr Blair looked deeply pained. Before we kill this metaphor for good, Mr Hague had smacked a fine shot, the Prime Minister managed a fingertip save. •

The Guardian Year '98

'A thorn in the side'

15 November 1997

Leader
Let the donors be revealed now

It is not just the end of the honeymoon. It is more serious than New Labour's worst week in government. Something much more critical is at stake: the loss of Labour's huge bank of public goodwill. Nothing is more important to governments than public trust. Yet Labour's handling of its U-turn on tobacco sponsorship is squandering this precious asset. Here is a government which was elected by a public outraged by Tory sleaze and crying out for open and honest administration. Yet since the U-turn on Labour's pledge to ban tobacco promotion last week, there have been nothing but evasion, half-truths and false denials. First they denied they had received any donation from the Formula One boss, whose motor races were to be exempted from the tobacco sponsorship ban after a meeting with Tony Blair. Finally Labour was forced to acknowledge a donation, but only later was its true scale revealed: a cool £1 million. Then they claimed they had turned down the offer of a second donation, only for it to turn out there had been no second offer after all – only a move by Labour fund-raisers to negotiate one. New facts keep emerging each day, but rarely thanks to Labour.

Information is released grudgingly, on a drip-by-drip basis, when it is clear journalists have discovered a new slant. No wonder all the talk of 'cash for favours'. Labour behaves as though there is something to hide. The last 10 days have deeply damaged the Government. As Martin Bell reminded the Prime Minister, the perception of wrongdoing is as damaging as wrongdoing itself. Despite the Prime Minister's statement to the Commons, many questions remain unanswered. Suddenly, there are no ministers available to provide the answers to *Newsnight*, the BBC *Today* programme or Channel 4 news. The public health minister is not even able to get to an anti-smoking awards ceremony. The Government is behaving like an opposition, but governments cannot dodge issues. They have to be faced. Instead the spin doctors have continued to duck and weave when they should have been trying to lance the boil. Most of the blame rests on Tony Blair's shoulders. He was wrong to exempt Formula One from the tobacco promotion ban. No one has talked more about the need to face hard choices. The Prime Minister chose the wrong option, as yesterday's medical research report documented: young boys

38 The Guardian Year '98

who watch motor-racing on television are twice as likely to become regular smokers.

What should happen now? Ideally, the Government should recommit itself to a total ban on tobacco sponsorship. But even more important is the issue of public trust. This can be restored only by an immediate disclosure of the donors. Not just their names but the amounts. It is in the party's own interest to take the initiative and not wait for the Neill Committee to recommend such an approach. Imagine the fuss if it is left to the press to unveil a second donor in need of a policy change who has made a huge donation. If there is nothing to hide, Labour has nothing to fear. If there is something to hide, then far better for it to be disclosed by Labour than the press. They are a young government and would be forgiven if they were open and honest now. What would not be forgiven is a cover-up. Let the donors – and their donations – be revealed. •

11 December 1997
Anne Perkins
Cuts outcry humiliates Harman

The muted cheers as Harriet Harman sat down at the end of her big speech said it all – the Social Security Secretary was deemed to have failed. 'No passion,' said one of many disgruntled Labour backbenchers who had been looking for a justification to back the Government and vote for the lone parent benefit cuts.

In a speech received in a silence broken only by hostile interventions from her own side, Ms Harman said that two key questions had been raised by MPs during the debate: did lone parents have higher costs than couple families, and would the Government's proposals discourage them from taking up work?

Lone parents did have one major extra cost – child-care, she said, which was why the Government was developing a national child-care strategy: 'Every parent will have access to out-of-school care for their child in their community.'

For more than three hours Ms Harman had sat impassive as the rebellion caught fire behind her, spreading from the newly ex-Scottish Office minister Malcolm Chisholm to parliamentary aides, to backbenchers.

'It hardened all the time,' Audrey Wise, a leading rebel, said afterwards, 'with people who had been going to abstain deciding to vote against, and others, who stayed in the chamber listening to the argument, deciding to abstain.' She declared, 'We are speaking here for children, children who are already poor.'

In a series of impassioned contributions, Labour MPs argued it was unacceptable to penalise the poorest in the country by cutting lone parent benefits. Most humiliatingly, there were more speeches in defence of the policy from Tories than from the Government back benches.

'A thorn in the side'

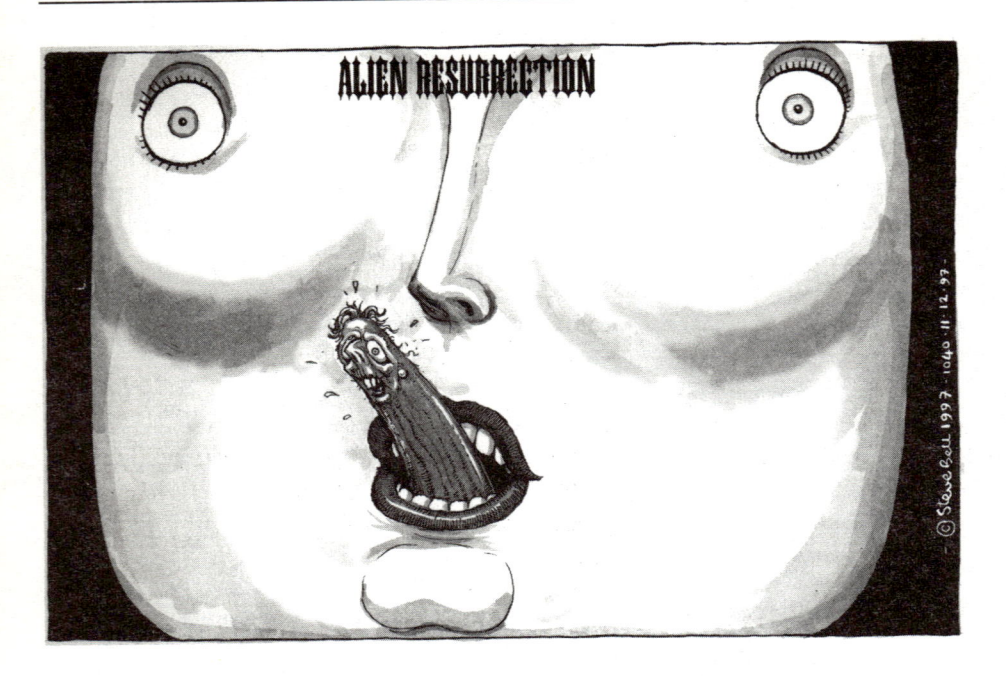

Liberal Democrats and nationalists joined the rebels as new figures showed that lone parents in work rather than on benefit would be just £10 a week better off, not £50 as Ms Harman has insisted.

In the first of a series of passionate Old Labour attacks on New Labour, Ms Wise told the House, 'I think we are entitled to say that these measures are not in accord with Labour values, they are not economically necessary.'

Her friend and colleague Alice Mahon, who knew her speech setting out her opposition to the cuts would bring her the sack as a parliamentary aide, said she had done all she could to change the Government's mind in private. Describing the cuts as 'punitive and cruel', she said, 'I believe the money's available to reverse the cuts.' She added, 'The Government's lost the argument, but it's too stubborn to back down.'

Gordon Prentice, who had already resigned as a PPS in order to speak out against the cuts, said, 'This is an insane loyalty test where my colleagues are being asked to support the Government even when they know it is wrong.'

Leading left-winger Ken Livingstone said, 'Rather than take on single parents, when are we going to take on someone bigger than us?'

But Peter Snape, MP for what was the marginal seat of West Bromwich, told the rebels, 'Those of us who live in marginals heaved a sigh of relief when we heard the commitment to stay in Tory spending limits, because we knew they wouldn't be able to lie their way back into office the way they did in 1987 and 1992. I'm afraid we've made our bed, and we must lie in it.'

For the Conservatives, who decided to encourage the rebels by voting with the Government to underline that Tories backed the measure, Simon Burns attacked the Government for reversing its position on the cuts. 'This debate shows up that the Government really is guilty of the utmost hypocrisy.' Rubbing salt in the wound, he went on, 'I have considerable respect, even though I don't agree with their view, for those Labour backbenchers who have had the courage, the consistency and the decency to stick by their principles both in opposition and now in government.' •

11 December 1997
Simon Hoggart
Floundering in offshore drift

The Commons was in ferment. A minister few had heard of had resigned. Rumours foretold a mass extermination of others of whom nobody at all had heard. Their 15 seconds of fame was due.

Members of all parties came to the Chamber planning to give Harriet Harman a good festive kicking. ('Deck the halls with bowels of Hattie, tra la la la . . .')

But Prime Minister's Questions came first. Why bother with the scullery maid, they thought, when the Master of the House was around? They proceeded to inflict on Mr Blair the worst session he has suffered since May. It would be hard to underestimate the sheer revulsion, the horror and shame, many Labour MPs feel about what a Labour government is doing over single parents' benefit. The whips – the 'goolie-crushers' – sat glowering sourly on the front bench.

Mr Hague pointed out that the Tories would be voting with Labour. People vote in the Commons for many strange reasons, but I can't recall a time when a party supported the Government purely to show how much they despised it. If I may paraphrase the Tory leader, his argument was: we are voting for the cut because we are heartless capitalists who would happily sell their children for medical experiments in Mexico if it would make bigger tax loopholes. You, however, pretend to be on a higher moral plane.

Mr Blair said he was wrong. Or rather, he said, 'I'm sorry, but he is simply wrong,' the word 'sorry' being used not to express regret but to imply 'you silly little person'.

Mr Hague returned with several examples of people who are now ministers saying, before the election, that they would not cut benefits.

'I'm sorry, but that is simply not correct,' said Mr Blair, again.

The Government was offering these women more choice, better child-care, greater opportunity, lots less money (well, not the last bit, but you knew that's what he meant). Mr Hague had clearly won the exchange again. Paddy Ashdown delivered the sucker punch. If the Government closed the offshore tax loophole

'A thorn in the side'

used by the very rich – a reference to Geoffrey Robinson – it would save twice as much cash as it was lifting off single mums.

'That is simply not correct,' said Mr Blair, once more. But it is. I have on my desk an official Labour document which says, 'We must end . . . the continuing misuse of offshore trusts,' and claiming this would save £120 million (from Mr Robinson alone, perhaps).

His voice leaden with contempt, Mr Ashdown asked how a Labour government could ask the poor to pay for the poor, while the rich could still duck their taxes.

When one backbencher incomprehensibly compared the Liberals to the Teletubbies, Mr Blair snarled that Tinky Winky would make a better economic spokesman than the one the Liberals had, and the whole House went 'Whoa!' because they saw then just how rattled he was.

When John Townend, a right-winger, said, 'While the Prime Minister says, "Put your trust in me", his ministers put their trusts offshore,' it wasn't just the Tories who whooped with glee.

As the debate itself began, Labour backbenchers, including Audrey Wise and Ken Livingstone, spoke with a dark, controlled rage, far more sinister and unnerving than anything they might have thrown at the old Tory enemy. It's a cliché to say that Mr Blair's honeymoon is over; yesterday may suggest that the divorce proceedings have begun. •

24 December 1997
Leader
Has baby, so must travel

Report on Welfare-to-Work applicant 'M' 25/12/00: an unusual case. The claimant, who doesn't have a surname, has shown enterprise in coming quite a long way for her first Gateway interview but may not be eligible for expenses under the Travel to Interview scheme since the journey seems to have been done by donkey. She was accompanied by her partner, who, she claims, is a carpenter though he doesn't have an NVQ or indeed any other qualification. She is adamant he is not the father of her child. But as she refuses to say who the real father is, she can't be recommended for Income Support until she can provide documentary evidence.

Nor can she be recommended for Housing Benefit. They are living in stables with no evidence that rent is being paid. Unless she can prove otherwise, one must assume she is taking advantage of one of the local Crisis at Christmas housing projects. Even this may be under false pretences, as there are reports that she has a real home elsewhere (suggest follow-up by Nazareth case officer).

The child looks well looked after and is resting in a back-to-basics manger

'A thorn in the side'

in the manner of straw wrapped in rags. Since it is no fault of the child's, perhaps a small clothing allowance would be in order. The mother is in good health and there is no obvious impediment to her looking for a job. She might be eligible for Parent Plus job search assistance and Child Care Disregard if a carer can be found, as long as the gold and myrrh found nearby aren't part of her assets. Her work incentives will necessarily be increased when news of the Herodian scheme for tackling youth unemployment gets more media attention. Meanwhile, I told her that the best thing would be to take heed of the new Government's caring philosophy and take up her bed and walk. •

---

20 January 1998
Hugo Young
A spin on the truth according to Gordon

The diaries of Richard Crossman, Barbara Castle and Tony Benn, the collective *locus classicus* for the behaviour of old Labour governments, display one striking contrast with the conduct of the new Labour Cabinet under Tony Blair. They chronicle rows, betrayals, insoluble problems and paranoid anxieties of the 1960s and 1970s that stand proxy for government at any time and almost any place.

The serpentine figure of Harold Wilson makes his manipulative progress through all their stories. As with Wilson, so with Mr Blair: reading the leader's intentions remains a task at the undelegatable centre of all ministers' lives. But there is a fateful difference between the generations. The old diarists describe a world in which the arguments and paranoia are, for the most part, personally driven. They're acted out in Cabinet, and if they leak into the public arena, this tends to be through the principals themselves. There are few intermediary lackeys. The doctrine of collective responsibility is challenged by such pre-emptive manoeuvring, but the argument is about policies and is conducted by visible, accountable politicians. In those days, you knew, like Our Man in Havana, whether you were getting the fat or the lean.

The deformity of the Blair Cabinet is that this has ceased to be. Senior ministers take responsibility for only part of what is said in their name. They've constructed a world of meta-politics occupied by their truth doctors, one of whose first achievements was to twist that blunt, exact depiction of themselves into the more beguiling notion of spin. Neither Crossman nor Benn had need of truth doctors, whose special contribution is less about truth than about deniability. But these people are close to ruining the life and work of Gordon Brown.

'A thorn in the side'

To Mr Brown's truth doctors, operating in the half-world of manipulation and deniability, truth itself is of small importance. They half help his recent biographer, they half read the manuscript of the book, they half deny they've done so, they half authenticate the outcome, while pretending wholly to repudiate any notion that the work has anything to do, on their part or his, with Brown's positioning *vis-à-vis* the Prime Minister. In October, they half ruined the launch of Britain's stance on the single currency. The principal may not entirely drive them, but he can't live without them. One half longs for the days when disagreements were fundamental and ministers' ventures into battle strictly their own.

There is no disagreement between Brown and Blair. That is the first absurdity of the rift that has been made between them. There certainly is a rift. The Brown biography, by recycling events of four years ago, has opened a rift, because its very publication, and the half-help with which it has been truth-doctored, reveal it to be a gesture by which Brown has apparently chosen to present himself as a rival to the Prime Minister. But, give or take some acceptable differences of nuance over Europe and welfare, there is no disagreement worthy of the effect all this is having – which is to reduce the potency of the Government by perhaps 25 per cent. A ridiculous and futile consequence.

The second absurdity is the unspoken premise on which this falling-out rests, namely that Brown remains a rival, even a potential threat, to Mr Blair's ascendancy – rather as Jim Callaghan and Roy Jenkins were seen as potent challengers for Harold Wilson's seat. In the Wilson case, this possibility was real enough, an ever-present part of political truth, as the diarists chart. But in modern times, it's a hallucination. Blair's mandate was so huge, and his personal association with it so complete, in regions far beyond the Labour Party, that the very idea of a rivalry with his Chancellor that might result in a challenge to his position could be entertained only by those so close to politics that they have lost all connection with reality.

There's one circumstance in which this might change. Unlikely though it is, a developing policy disagreement between Blair and Brown could make the malign work of the truth doctors a lot more damaging. If Brown, who still believes that what he is doing has an umbilical link with Scottish socialism, were to take a party-pleasing stance against the neo-Thatcherite direction Blair is seen to favour on welfare reform, his position would become untenable. It might even be imaginable, if the economy takes an Asia-induced downturn, that an old-fashioned Labour argument about priorities would begin in which Brown made a smart move to the left. At present, the position is tenable enough. Mr Brown is a brooding, difficult character who has more than an ordinary ministerial quotient of power-thirst and the widest opportunities to slake it. He has the political equipment to be a great Chancellor, and, at the intellectual level, an adequate relationship with his boss. We come back, however, to the truth-doctoring trade.

The Treasury is the extreme case where truth doctors have taken over government. They are the coterie which has, to an important extent, replaced the collective. Joint responsibility, still less fraternity, gives way to atomised groups of political advisers whose principal task is not the advance of the whole government but the triumph of their separate patron. Not merely are they remote from the collective, they sometimes exist for the prime purpose of fragmenting it. Several ministers have their truth doctors: and the philosophy of New Labour, in government as in opposition, puts heavy emphasis on perception. But none surpass those in the Treasury, once the home of institutional sobriety on information matters, in defining their work as the exaltation of the truth according to Gordon.

The Government is damaged by this, unnecessarily. But so is Brown, who seems unwilling or unable to stop it. I think he is unwilling, because he is unable to relinquish the belief that this might be the way to make himself more important than the Prime Minister. Or so the doctors, having no other purpose in life, are telling him.

Here we have another argument for reconsidering the merits of proper collective government. The collective needs to assist the Prime Minister in getting a grip on the Chancellor, one of whose secondary aggrandisements has been to offend so many of them. When the Home Secretary, the Foreign Secretary, the Education Secretary and the Deputy Prime Minister all mistrust the Chancellor's cabal, and are wary of the truth being doctored against them, the time has come to stop complaining and send Dr Charles Whelan undeniably packing. ●

16 January 1998
Bel Littlejohn
I'll never speak of my marriage to Roger Pook

I've made it a lifelong rule never to speak about my first husband, now a senior Labour Cabinet minister, and I'm very sorry, guys, but . . . I've no intention of breaking that rule now. Don't you think I've suffered enough? It was 30 years ago, and I've just about managed to put those dark days behind me. So please don't expect any vengeful revelations in this column about the little red squirrel whose amorous activities drove me to hell and back.

When I was approached by Linda McDougall to contribute an interview to her *Westminster Women*, I straight away wanted to know whether her book was authorised. She told me that it was entirely unauthorised, so I told her there was no way I would contribute less than four full-length interviews. I made it clear that I had no wish whatsoever to rake over old grievances, that the mixture

'A thorn in the side'

of infidelity, arrogance and cruelty that my ex had visited upon me during our brief marriage should not be used against him now, and that I would demand his total anonymity within her pages.

Any physical description should be kept to a bare minimum (red hair, horrid beard, mad bulging eyes, overblown sense of own importance, an aggressive little stoat in bed and out) and the man in question would only ever be referred to by the code-name 'Roger Pook, Secretary of State for Abroad'. With these provisos – the last thing I want is to wreck his career, or to draw attention to his gross unsuitability for high office – I granted Linda barely a dozen full-length interviews over a six-month period.

I told her that I first met Roger Pook on an Arbroath dance floor in 1969. In those days, he was no more than a feisty local councillor, but already one could detect tell-tale signs of a ruthless ambition at play. These were the early days of flower power, and many of his fellow males had arrived with flowers in their hair and garlands of inexpensive seasonal blooms around their necks. But Pook was determined to outshine them all. Early in the evening he had journeyed up and down the dance floor, furtively distributing weedkiller from a watering can on to the surrounding male foliage. Within 10 minutes, he was the only guy in the hall with flowers still in his hair. And so, dammit, I just had to go and fall in love with him, didn't I?

When Roger Pook asked me to dance, I found myself unable to say no. 'In the Year 2525' by Zager and Evans was playing on the turntable. Shouting over the music while flapping his arms to and fro, he detailed all the ways Zager and Evans had got it wrong. 'For all their undoubted tunefulness,' he yelled, 'these two don't seem to realise that by the year in question an ethical foreign policy combined with a reformed welfare state will make ample provision for the truly needy while preserving our position as a major player on the world stage.' Still in my teens, I was carried away by such rhetoric, and when he started elaborating on his schemes for a reorganisation of the state pension while we boogied on down to the Stones, I knew I was smitten.

Within a month we were honeymooning at Kirkcaldy, very handy, as Roger Pook enthused, for the Kirkcaldy racetrack. Yup, the old story is true. For Pook, the exercise of power was a powerful aphrodisiac. Even in those early days when he was only vice-chairman of the Town Parking Committee, he would arrive back from a council meeting, having just forced through a motion entailing over 50 yards of double yellow lines in a built-up area near the town centre, his top pocket laden with condoms.

Within the local Labour Party, he established a reputation for ethics second to none. The moment he was elected council leader, he made Arbroath a nuclear-free zone and issued a proclamation banning President Lyndon Johnson from entering the Arbroath council chamber until he had called an end to the Vietnam War. When the war did indeed stop just a few years later, Roger Pook pushed through a motion congratulating the Arbroath council for its role in bringing

'A thorn in the side'

an end to a decade of senseless violence. But outside the council chamber, Pook proved a very different character. It was while standing in the rain at the No. 3 bus stop in Arbroath High Street, ready to embark on an important VIP fact-finding mission around the Galashiels Town sewage works, that Roger Pook, now a parliamentary candidate, announced, coldly and brutally, that I was not to accompany him. He would instead be taking his long-standing secretary, Miss Dolly McNaughtie, who, he informed me, had excellent shorthand skills and better understood the pressure on a public figure. As that No. 3 bus set off with the two of them in it, sloshing me with rain from a nearby puddle, I vowed there and then never to go public with my revelations of life with the Rt. Hon. Roger Pook, the cocky little runt. •

10 April 1998
Michael White
And the groom wore a green anorak

The Foreign Secretary, Robin Cook, and his fiancée, Gaynor Regan, yesterday made New Labour history when they sacrificed a sure-fire Fleet Street photo opportunity in favour of Old Labour privacy by staging a dawn raid on Tunbridge Wells register office.

Instead of tying the knot, in what was a second marriage for both Mr Cook and his diary secretary, in their grand country house at Chevening, near Sevenoaks, Mr and Mrs Cook opted for the register office and what aides called 'a private event free from media intrusion' – 10 days earlier than planned.

To make sure they would evade the Fleet Street paparazzi, they also arranged at the last minute not to be married at 5 p.m. yesterday, but before normal matrimonial opening hours, at 8.30 a.m. Building works and a skip outside the door helped spoil any lurking photo opportunity.

But while the Foreign Secretary outflanked the media, he was unable to escape the prying eyes of the construction community. Builder Robert Harman saw the party arrive. 'It was just the two of them and two men. I think the men were witnesses, although one of them, who was wearing a kilt, looked like a minder. Mr Cook was wearing a green anorak-type coat and she was wearing a dark suit.'

His colleague, painter Allan Oakeshott, said, 'When they came out, he [Mr Cook] punched the air.' Air, incidentally, that remained confetti-free.

'Robin and Gaynor are delighted to be man and wife. I hope they will be left alone to enjoy the short break they deserve together,' said Mr Cook's constituency agent, Jim Devine, understood to be 'the man in the kilt'.

'A thorn in the side'

The wedding party then repaired to Chevening, set in 3,000 prime acres, to celebrate. Mr Cook let it be known he would be paying for the food and drink out of his own pocket.

His wife of 28 years, the Edinburgh hospital consultant Margaret Cook, told Channel 5 news: 'No comment, but I suppose I wish them well.' Since her dramatic separation on the eve of a family holiday, when the *News of the World* broke news of Mr Cook's liaison, she has given waspish media interviews about the hopeless immaturity of middle-aged men – and threatened to do more in the weeks ahead.

The new Mrs Cook, aged 41, and her husband have also been hurt by media attention, including the dubious accolade of a *Private Eye* cover.

Conspiracy theorists at Westminster could not decide whether the Cooks were attempting to upstage the Northern Ireland peace process or, on balance more likely, to marry while media attention was focused on Belfast. •

30 January 1998
Michael White
Blair & Co. do hate the *Guardian*

The 400-strong crowd in the Vauxhall Recreation Centre were as well scrubbed as the hall itself. Free tea and biscuits beforehand, free wine after, a touch of corporate sponsorship inside, a handful of Trots outside.

All very New Labour and a credit to the Blair–Kinnock revolution which gradually brought it about. Most pleasing of all, the ticket-only Labour audience for Tony Blair's second 'welfare roadshow' – a good cross-section of the New Britain – was respectfully affectionate towards their leader, but not fawning. Idealism was clearly being tempered by rationality, the questions on the Government's welfare reform plans were probing, but no one asked for miracles.

Mr Blair is plainly keen to squash what he called Labour's 'Yeah, but . . .' tendency – people who seem to discount the Government's successes and keep moaning. This was where the night's discordant note came in. The Prime Minister bashed the Tories, fair enough. But whenever he got the chance – twice – he also bashed the *Guardian*.

Asked about a John Gray article, he said he admires the LSE professor but, 'I don't spend a lot of time reading the *Guardian* nowadays. I prefer to read a Labour paper.' The audience tittered nervously. Ten minutes later he dismissed another recent article by Professor Gray – which detailed welfare cuts inherited from the Tories – as 'complete nonsense'.

This abuse is short-sighted and stupid, but Mr Blair, his ministerial allies

'A thorn in the side'

and officials do it all the time. He accused the paper of mischief-making at this week's NEC. His spokesman, Alastair Campbell, regularly berates the *Guardian* at lobby briefings. They both tell people to read *The Times*. Challenged to justify a Blair appearance in the *Mail*, Mr Campbell, who sometimes behaves like a chippy school drop-out (but actually went to Cambridge), told the *Guardian*, 'Your news coverage has moved into full betrayal mode. Statistical facts are now "black propaganda", spread by "desperate spin doctors" as part of a "frantic damage-limitation exercise". The facts are lost, just as the facts on lone parents were lost in your coverage.'

But Mr Blair was glad enough to hurl the *Guardian*'s cash-for-questions findings at William Hague during Question Time this week. What's more, none of them ever lambasts the Murdoch or Rothermere press for their mischief or mistakes (we all make them; so do ministers) or their eagerness to spread Robin Cook's private life endlessly across their pages.

Why does he do it? Because Labour activists read the *Guardian*, which is broadly supportive of Labour's goals, but — like the Luton audience — not slavishly so. New Labour news managers love control. The *Guardian* is hard to control (even by its editor!); other, more top-down papers are more easily squared.

In every country in which Mr Murdoch operates (and minimises his tax bill) he is a power broker, speaking power, not truth, unto power through his diverse media outlets. The Blairites have charmed Lord Rothermere and made a Faustian bargain with Rupert. They think they have a good bargain. Murdoch's career is littered with such illusions. Unfortunately, all governments need media whipping boys, especially those obsessed with presentation which think events are giving them a rough time (they ain't seen nothing yet).

The BBC is an easy target, so is the *Telegraph*, which guarded its own independence from John Major. The once-loyal-but-dumb *Mirror*, now guided by ex-Murdoch henchman, Kelvin 'Gotcha' McKenzie, looks like becoming a problem for Labour. Meanwhile, there is always the *Guardian* to kick. In geopolitical terms, it is a strategically placed, medium-size friendly power with which Mr Blair can afford to quarrel.

Labour leaders have always bitched about the *Guardian*'s influence, but never so openly or, dare I say, maliciously. Yet it is safe to predict that when the Government's fair-weather friends have sailed away, the *Guardian* will still be providing broadly sympathetic coverage. •

'A thorn in the side'

3 March 1998

Armando Iannucci
Faustian pact shock horror uncovered in Tony Blair's attic

I've been working in newspapers for 25 years now, covering Downing Street intrigue since Ted Heath was a prime minister in short trousers, but nothing has proved to me as extraordinary as my horrific discoveries of the last two weeks. It all started ignominiously enough at a champagne reception the Deputy Prime Minister had laid on for Fleet Street transport correspondents, to thank them for writing about freight. The reception room at Number 10 had been booked and at 8 p.m. 44 of the most powerful van enthusiasts in journalism were downing cocktails in the company of John Prescott and celebrity actresses who had been on trains in the past 12 months. At 9 p.m. Tony Blair came in to see if the gathering was worthwhile and circulated heartily among his minders. By this time, my gut needed emptying so I made for the door. Thinking a toilet would be not far along the corridor, I quietly looked in through a series of portals opposite. One revealed a primitive but inviting staircase furtively disappearing up into a small, dank opening some 100 feet aloft. Suppressing my gut, I climbed. As I ascended, a feeling of cold, dark fear poured over my body, a sense of shame and foreboding I had not experienced since my daily meeting with my commissioning editor. I rose higher, and the air chilled me like an icy flu of terror. For I knew I was crossing the threshold of evil.

And in seconds, there I was in Tony Blair's attic. It had recently been insulated and refloored in a durable pine. Fresh wiring had been installed and a sensible number of double sockets placed around the room, some of them at waist level, which was a thoughtful touch. A bag of old tennis racquets lay in the corner.

In every respect, it was a perfectly normal young prime minister's loft. In every respect save one. For my eye soon chanced upon the whole miserable bundle of ignomy that sat horridly in the corner, of whose appearance I can only now summon up the will to type. For there in front of me – and may God strike me from the National Union of Journalists if this is not my true word – there in front was assembled a collection of newspaper front pages containing some of the ghastliest headlines I've ever had the misfortune to witness. Acres of rank personal abuse sat framed before me: BLAIR 'EVEN WORSE PM THAN CHAMBERLAIN' SAY EXPERTS was the kindest, from *The Times*. The *Independent on Sunday* declared, BLAIR CHIEF CLOWN IN CABINET OF FOOLS. TWATTY BLAIR was on the front of the *Express*. LABOUR COULDN'T WIN AN ARGUMENT WITH A DEAD MAN ran the *Telegraph*. WE IMPLORE YOU ALL NEVER TO VOTE LABOUR AGAIN ponced the *Guardian*, while another journal ran with

'A thorn in the side'

TOE-KNEE BOLLOCK-HAIR: JOIN THE *FINANCIAL TIMES*' CAMPAIGN TO GO UP TO THE PRIME MINISTER AND KICK HIM IN THE CROTCH. Central to the display was a copy of the *Sun*, clearly dated for that very morning, although it bore no relation to the front page I remembered in the newsstands. My recollection of the original layout had been of something along the lines of a photo of the Prime Minister and his family cheerfully receiving a basket of pigeons from some Ukrainians, with a headline declaring, MY COO-COO CA-CHERIE-OO: BLAIR THE PEACEMAKER GETS FEATHERED – THANK-YOU FOR IRAQ-EFFORTS. But what I saw here now was an appalling travesty of that day's uplifting coverage. It was a grotesque photo of the Prime Minister's three children doctored to make it look like they were covered in blood smears, bird droppings and the occasional feather, with the accompanying headline, IT'S TIME TO GIVE 'EUAN' AND YOUR KIDS THE BIRD, MR BLAIR! THE *SUN* SAYS TO THE PRIME MINISTER: STOP DROPPING YOUR CHILDREN INTO EVERY PHOTO OPPORTUNITY LIKE EGGS FROM A HEN'S ARSE. A side panel had cartoon faces of Tony and Cherie in the form of a couple of fried eggs in a pan, with the subheading, LET'S TURN THE HEAT UP AND DEMOCRATICALLY BURN TO DEATH THESE YOLKS AROUND OUR NECKS.

Shuddering at what I had seen, I instantly recoiled from the room and fled back to the transport shindig downstairs. Breathlessly as I rushed into the room, I stumbled into the Prime Minister's chest and looked up. After what seemed an eternity's silence, but which was actually only four minutes, he spoke.

'That look on your face,' he said. 'That look of abject terror, of an ashen flannel of fear pressed across your brow. I know that look. I know you have chanced upon the worst sight you have ever beheld. And yet it is but one tenth of the awfulness I have known these past months. And I cannot let the public witness it. The slightest glimpse of the diabolical copy in my attic must never be revealed. When I first knew of it I . . .' And here he broke off in a troubled, piercing sigh that chilled the liver. '. . . even if I had to get on board the most demonic of forces, then so be it. Each day these front pages come in the morning, before dawn breaks. And when they arrive, according to the deal I have done with . . . with the castle of hell . . . they go straight up to my attic, and by some force I do not wish to understand, the pages that reach the newsstands carry a refreshingly positive spin on my government's achievements.' And then he turned to his Press Secretary. 'Look at Alastair. See that broken look on his face? That's the look I recognised on yours. It's what happens to a man who stares into darkest terror once a day.' I looked at his Press Secretary, who had just received the next day's newspapers. He was ashen with sick. Over his shoulder, I could just make out a front page of the *Mirror*, showing Blair as a penguin roasting on a spit. Before I could read the headline, they both walked away into a small side-room with some candles. And then they were gone.

Later that morning the *Mirror* ran a story about how grateful London Zoo

'A thorn in the side'

was for Tony Blair's intervention in securing them more funding for their aviary. And I am now more frightened than any man alive. •

28 February 1998
Alexander Chancellor
Dome and dumber

Relaunching the Dome at the Royal Festival Hall on Tuesday, the Prime Minister (I call him 'Prime Minister' because I know he would rather I called him Tony) told us all to stop complaining and to 'seize the moment', so we might 'say to ourselves with pride, "This is our Dome".' He sounded a bit like Henry V on St Crispin's Day. 'It's easy to say, "Don't do something,"' Mr Blair went on. 'It takes very little courage to say no to a new idea.'

In reality, of course, courage doesn't come into it. You either think a thing is a good idea or you think it's a bad idea, and then you say what you think.

But what sort of courage does it take to stand up to this popular Prime Minister? On Monday, the day before the Festival Hall rally, the *Sun* announced a sudden shift from Domoscepticism to Domophilia. In a leader entitled 'It's Domeday', the *Sun* boasted that it had been 'the fiercest critic of the £800-million project'. 'Like most of our readers,' it went on, 'we believe the money could have been better spent on schools and hospitals.' But, now that the Dome had 'passed the point of no return', griping about it would achieve nothing, the *Sun* said. 'Instead, we should all get behind it and ensure its success.' (Also on Monday, the *Independent* made the same U-turn, saying that praising the Dome was 'a much more testing intellectual challenge than going for the easy, negative cynicism which so disfigures modern journalism'.)

Next day, the *Sun* roared into action with an announcement that it had renamed one of its woman reporters 'Mandy Millennium' and asked her to be its 'Dome Dame'. 'I've been appointed Britain's first millennium correspondent,' Mandy Millennium wrote in an open letter to *Sun* readers. 'Yesterday I had a meeting with Dome guru Peter Mandelson to discuss my new role and pass on my hotline number for the latest developments.' The *Sun*, of course, has been in Mr Blair's pocket since before the election, when Rupert Murdoch told it to be, but still, it was surprising to see it jump to attention in public quite so smartly.

Having participated up till now, with regard to the Dome, in the 'negative cynicism which so disfigures modern journalism', I have reviewed my position in the light of Mr Blair's appeal and have decided that it should remain exactly the same. This may show a lack of courage and vision on my part, but I simply do not get the point of this absurd project. Its cost is unbelievable – £780

'A thorn in the side'

million, compared with, say, the £60 million that was spent on the architecturally much more remarkable new Guggenheim art museum in Bilbao (which contains, incidentally, the world's largest gallery). Peter Mandelson says that since 'all eyes will be on the Greenwich Meridian on 31 December 1999, it would have been a telling comment on ourselves if all we had to offer was bunting and 300 acres of contaminated wasteland'; which means he must have forgotten that Greenwich has long contained one of the finest architectural ensembles in the world, for the conservation of which the Government resolutely refuses to spend any money at all.

I am in sympathy with shadow 'Dome Minister', Francis Maude, when he worries about the Government's high-falutin' rhetoric on the subject. Take Mr Mandelson's press release last weekend: 'The Dome will be like a gigantic mirror for the nation. The reflection I want to see is of a nation intensely proud of its past and its achievements, its ingenuity and creativity, its bravery and its sense of justice and fair play. But more than that, I want the Dome to capture the spirit of modern Britain – a nation that is confident, excited, impatient for the future.'

When one reads that kind of thing, it seems inconceivable that such a project could have been dreamed up in the grey old John Major days of cricket and warm beer. Maude believes it has been hijacked by New Labour for party-political purposes, and he is right, in the sense that it has been 'rebranded' to conform to New Labour's rebranded country and has been adopted by Mr Blair as the 'grand project' with which he wishes to remain forever associated, as Georges Pompidou is with that other Richard Rogers creation, the Pompidou Centre in Paris, and François Mitterrand with the Louvre pyramid.

It is amusing to speculate what the Dome would have contained if Mr Major had remained prime minister: exhibits on the history of English beer, perhaps, or on how to make a cricket bat. There would probably have been a typical English village, with people giving lessons on thatching and building dry-stone walls. There might even have been a celebration of traditional country sports. One can be pretty confident there wouldn't have been a recumbent model of a naked person – woman or man – larger than the Statue of Liberty. Visitors are supposed to enter this silver-painted colossus through a door at the back of the waist and leave it from the right heel, having walked about in its innards, thinking about how their body works and asking themselves if they are abusing it. In the section called Dreamscape, you will recline with 14 others on a sort of floating bed and ask yourself whether you attach enough importance to rest.

The British have always prided themselves on their pragmatism rather than

The Guardian Year '98

'A thorn in the side'

fancy notions. The Great Exhibition of 1851 had the interesting and comprehensible purpose of 'wedding high art with mechanical skill'. The Festival of Britain was to celebrate the country's restored vitality after the Second World War, and it left behind it an admirable concert hall. The Millennium Experience seems to have found its purpose in the marketing of obscure concepts. Its official motto is 'Time to make a difference'. I will offer a prize to anyone who can tell me what that means. Well, on reflection, I won't, for I already know it means nothing.

From the start, we have been told that the 'experience' would be somehow about 'time', which seemed a fairly obvious cop-out since it was celebrating the millennium and taking place at Greenwich. But 'to make a difference'? That is just a phrase lifted from the vocabulary of American politics. When asked why they are seeking election to public office, American politicians nearly always reply that they think they can make a difference. (British politicians, to their credit, are more modest.) If the expression is empty in the political context, it is even emptier when applied to an enormous great Dome full of people marching through the guts of an androgynous giant. But it exemplifies New Labour's wholesale adoption of American political values.

Another explanation of the Millennium Experience was offered by Michael Grade, who said that he saw it as 'a living and breathing Internet'. Despite all my efforts to master this exciting new medium, I really will give a prize to anyone who can explain that. I am beginning to fear that if Messrs Blair, Mandelson and Grade are allowed to continue talking such gibberish, the whole nation will sink into a deep and inescapable trauma. •

21 April 1998
Jonathan Glancey
Nice wallpaper, shame about the paint

Now, what was it that Derry Irvine, m'Lord Chancellor, was saying about B&Q earlier this year? The gist, you will remember, was that a redecorated Gothic Revival apartment on the river side of the Palace of Westminster sporting hand-printed Pugin wallpaper at £350 a roll was not exactly the sort of home a peer of the realm and his lady wife would, or could, cobble together from weekend jaunts to the popular edge-of-town home-decorating store.

Well, you could have fooled me. Yesterday, the press was allowed to nosy inside the Lord Chancellor's home, now that the wallpaper (all £57,233 worth of the precious stuff) has been pasted up, the dining table (a snip at £14,000) has arrived from Edward Barnsley of Petersfield, and three Gothic beds have

'A thorn in the side'

A 'suitably fey Narcissus' in Lord Irvine's apartments

been installed at £49,773, the job lot. Choice and pricey stuff you would be right in thinking and no, B&Q does not stock hand-tooled Pugin wallpaper. Yet something has gone amiss with the detailing in Derry Towers; it looks as if the Lord Chancellor really did send some flunkey out to a home-decor warehouse with a long shopping list.

The ceilings are the giveaway. Not only do they look as if they have been given a thorough coating with swirly white Artex plaster (the stuff that looks as if it's been squeezed from a tube of ready-made icing sugar), but they are pitted with horrid little brilliant white downlighters. Naff or what? Other spotlights serve to highlight dreary paintings, and yet others are used (or abused) to supplement the bright light dazzling from blindingly shiny brass chandeliers.

There are moments in this house where sunglasses are needed to hide the glare. And some of the tackier details.

Try not to look at the ungainly, bog-standard panel radiators disfiguring the oak panelling in the corridors. Ignore, if you can, the nylon cords that raise and lower Gothic blinds in the double-glazed window-frames. Spare yourself the sickly orangy-sort-of-terracottaish-salmon-pink paint smothering the walls from the entrance lobby to the Lord Chancellor's private study at the far end of the apartment.

As for fitted carpets, my dear! And what about the unhappy use of brilliant white emulsion at the point where the £590,000 spent to date appear to have run out. Or the flashy electronic light switches. The tacky beige plastic bedside phone is just one last nail in the decorator's coffin.

'A thorn in the side'

None of these aesthetic blunders, however, can compare to the biggest fright of all. Come with me, if you dare, to the River Room and behold a trio of gross, marbleised MDF plinths, complete with built-in mini-spotlights, on which some vulgar, and even obscene, Victorian statuary has been put on display.

Here is a suitably fey Narcissus, and there a naked man with a bristling moustache and gym-toned body fondling a beautiful naked child of indeterminate sex. This dubious piece by one Edward Stephens is called *Shielding the Helpless*. Perhaps, but any Scottish nanny worth the salt on her morning porridge would have had it removed.

It is, in fact, extremely funny and an example of the naked bad taste that abounds throughout an apartment that one gawper compared to a rather sad railway hotel somewhere north of Perth, only not as good. This sniping and cynical comparison is helped on its way by the relentless prints of famous and not-so-famous bearded Scotsmen that line the orangy-salmony walls.

Augustus Welby Northmore Pugin, architect of the Palace of Westminster, was a brilliant decorator. The wallpaper and much of the furniture, original and revived, are superb, but while one applauds the efforts of the Lord Chancellor's department to restore the apartment, awkward compromises between old and new, unlikely clashes of colours and low-rent details add up to a fusty hodgepodge. Very uncool.

And Pugin, never a designer to mince words, would have set fire to the whole caboodle and insisted m'Lord Irvine start again. •

29 July 1998
Matthew Norman
A year in the life of Derek Draper

July 1997

At last, the literary pretensions of my friend Dolly Draper, the former Mandy Mandelson office boy, have been realised. Dolly's *Blair's Hundred Days* is not yet published (by Faber and Faber), but the first extracts have already appeared in the *Sunday Times*. The paper paid £55,000 for serialisation, and well worth the money it is too. Among several entrancing revelations, for instance, Dolly discloses that Camilla Parker Bowles has had meetings with Mandy, at Carla Powell's London home ... and any doubts about the accuracy of Dolly's claim were dispelled yesterday by a categorical denial from Downing Street.

'A thorn in the side'

February 1998

These are joyful days for New Labour and Groucho stalwart Dolly Draper. He has just become a director at GPC Market Access after the sale of Prima Europe, and as a result, the *Financial Times* reports, he is £400,000 better off. As old friends, we immediately phone to suggest he takes the Diary out to an expensive dinner. 'The Ivy?' he asks. 'I think that might look like I'm trying to corrupt you. We'd have to go Dutch.' Well, might he like to help with the wallpapering costs of the lavish Diary office? 'You're all pretty enough without wallpaper from me. By the way,' he adds, 'it's not a windfall. I worked hard for it.' And on that stern note, he is gone.

March 1998

The influence of Mandy Mandelson spreads across the planet. Indeed, according to his former office boy Dolly Draper, it has now reached Outer Mongolia. Dolly reports that a certain Mr Enkhbayar, leader of the Communist Party there, visited Whitehall last week and proudly told all he met that his party has dispensed with the red star. The new symbol for Mongolian Communism is the red rose. 'We hope one day to govern for the many, not the few,' said a spokesman when we called. 'But as we say in New Mongolia, there are tough choices ahead.'

21 May 1998

Not all New Labour people have lost sight of their manners, and Dolly Draper, the party's very own Arthur Daley, swiftly returns a pager message. Pronouncing himself 'extremely well', Dolly reminds us that the FT reported that he received £400,000 from the sale of the Prima consultancy. He is mystified, however, by the disappearance, from his *Express* column, of the strapline 'inside the mind of new Labour', insisting that his finger remains on the pulse. If so, his story in this week's *Spectator* should be read with interest. In it, Dolly claims that Rupert Murdoch is about to perform a spectacular volte-face and become a passionate advocate of Emu. So does Dolly have the ear of Murdoch? 'No,' says Dolly. 'In fact he'll be quite annoyed.' If Dolly is right, he has one of the scoops of the decade: the last big obstacle to monetary union will be removed, and British history will be changed for ever.

May 1998

Mischief-makers at the BBC are putting together a programme on the chemistry between Old and New Labour entitled *Living with the Enemy*. 'They want an Old Labour person to follow me around for a week to see if I've sold out,' Dolly Draper told the *Telegraph* on hearing he may get a starring role, 'but I don't

'A thorn in the side'

want anyone too smelly.' Nor, we suspect, will he want Jimmy 'King of the Gorbals' Wray, MP for Glasgow Baillieston, who, you may recall, shook the stuffing out of the young protégé at conference two years ago for declaring, 'I make the policy to get you elected.' Mr Wray pointed out then, 'The working class doesn't give a f*** for people like you.' There must be some (fragrant) Old Labour folk out there who don't share this opinion. The Diary appeals to them to come forward.

July 1998

The news of Dolly Draper shocks me to the point of paralysis and I take to my bed with a fit of the vapours. That Dolly, the high-minded ideologue known to Diary readers as 'New Labour's very own Arthur Daley', has been flogging government secrets . . . that Dolly, the man of honour who once went to ground owing Faber and Faber £1,000 on a book deal, is unmasked as a mercenary who speaks of 'stuffing my bank account at £250 an hour' . . . that Dolly, the reticent soul who once told veteran Glasgow MP Jimmy Wray, 'I'm the man who makes the policy', would have bragged about his access to the levers of power . . . well, who could possibly have seen it coming? Now poor Dolly's been suspended by his lobbying firm, and sacked by Rizla Rosie Boycott from his *Express* column. Don't you worry, Dolly, there's always a berth for you here. Just give us the word and a regular slot will be yours. The money's not great, but it's cash . . . and no need to put it through the till, my son, know what I mean? •

Tony and Gordon on song

Tony, Gordon and the invisible man

Tony, Gordon and the invisible man

15 July 1998
Leader
Brown's blockbuster: it's a stunning statement

Gordon Brown appeared to have pulled off the impossible yesterday. He promised sharply increased spending on education and health of socialist proportions yet within a tight fiscal framework that would be the envy of any sound-money Tory. He is planning to raise education spending by an unexpectedly large 5.1 per cent a year over the next three years (in real terms), compared with an average of 1.4 per cent a year during the 18 years of the last government. It may look less impressive averaged over the whole of this Parliament (including the first two years of near-freeze), but it is real money nevertheless. And it will have been achieved without any of the increases in income taxes which many critics said were needed.

Spending will be front-end loaded, starting at £3 billion more next year, leading to £10 billion in the third year, creating what could be the country's first pre-electoral boom based on education spending as opposed to excessive consumption. No one can now doubt what Labour meant by 'education, education, education' – even if teachers would be wise not to expect much of the surplus to spill over into higher wages. The Chancellor is planning a similar 4.7 per cent rise in health spending over the next three years, compared with 2.5 per cent a year during the last Parliament. Extra spending is being tied to performance, so it doesn't leak out into what are regarded as less desirable objectives (including inflation-busting pay settlements). What is more, this increase in spending is taking place against predictions – validated by the National Audit Office – of a steadily growing budget surplus totalling £30 billion over the three years. In cash terms, this is bigger than the freak surpluses produced by an over-heated economy at the end of the 1980s.

Where's the catch? The sharp increase in priority spending is at the cost of cut-backs in such other sectors as defence, agriculture and trade and industry, where the squeals won't be loud enough to be heard. This will achieve an overall growth in current spending (everything except capital expenditure) of 2.25 per cent a year, roughly in line with the hoped-for growth of the whole economy. This is unlikely to scare the City, which will be very impressed by the looming budget surplus after so many years of deficit. Of course, these plans could fall apart if the economy slides into a recession during the next few years. This could happen if the succession of interest hikes, associated with the over-valued pound, turns the planned slow-down into something more sinister.

There are two other potential weaknesses. Gordon Brown may be hard pushed

Tony, Gordon and the invisible man

to keep the lid on public sector pay, which is rising at only 2.5 per cent, compared with 5.9 per cent in the private sector. It will take all the Chancellor's guile to target some extra resources into priority areas (such as scarce teachers) while preventing industrial unrest among other disgruntled public sector employees. Mr Brown's plans could also run into trouble if hospitals, schools and other institutions fail to agree to the improved performance criteria the Chancellor is insisting on as a quid pro quo for extra cash. In that event, will he really withhold the money? We shall see. These reservations apart, Mr Brown has delivered an extremely impressive Comprehensive Spending Review which appears to fulfil nearly all of the high targets he set himself.

Even the most optimistic social policy experts were rubbing their eyes in disbelief yesterday at the Government's unexpected generosity. This month's promise from the Prime Minister at the fiftieth birthday party of the National Health Service for sustainable year-on-year real increases was fully realised. The 4.7 per cent real increase over each of the next three years in England will compensate for the squeeze over the last two years, pulling up the average for this Parliament to 3.7 per cent, compared to the 2.5 per cent over the last Parliament.

The extra money for education will mean more money for pre-school children, nursery-school children and further-education institutions, which, with sixth-form colleges, now account for 60 per cent of our 16- to 19-year-olds in education. The new money has come just in time with two-thirds of FE colleges in debt. It will also make it easier for ministers to meet their target in reducing class sizes in primary schools.

On both pensions and child benefits the Chancellor signalled his readiness to look after the poorest. There will be a minimum income guarantee, ensuring the 2 million poorest pensioners on income support get increases not just above prices but also above earnings: £2.5 billion in the next three years.

There will be those in Old Labour who will undoubtably criticise the Chancellor for daring to plan for a big budget surplus when there are still desperate needs to be fulfilled. But most people will be stunned by the deft way he is combining high spending in key areas with help for the poor and a budget surplus. If Treasury claims that there are no 'smoking guns' turn out to be true, yesterday's statement could be a defining moment for New Labour – and for Gordon Brown as well. •

Tony, Gordon and the invisible man

2 May 1998

David Marquand

The magic lingers on as Blair faces hard choices

A year after New Labour's landslide victory, the purpose, nature and significance of the famous Blair project are as mysterious as they were on that magic May morning when the last government was sent packing. We know what the new regime is not; we don't yet know what it is. Patently, it is not socialist. It is not even social democratic or social liberal. It has abandoned the tradition once exemplified by such paladins of social democracy as Willy Brandt, Helmut Schmidt, Ernest Bevin and Hugh Gaitskell. It has also turned its back on Keynes and Beveridge. It is manifestly unshocked by the huge and growing disparities of income engendered by the late-twentieth-century capitalist renaissance. Like the Thatcher governments before it, New Labour espouses a version of the entrepreneurial ideal of the early nineteenth century.

It disdains traditional elites and glorifies self-made meritocrats. It is for widening opportunity, not for redistributing reward. By the same token, it has no wish to undo the relentless hollowing out of the public domain or to halt the increasing casualisation of labour – white collar as well as blue collar – that marked the Thatcher and Major years. It is more tender to the employers than to the trade unions, more anxious to court Rupert Murdoch than the *Guardian*, and more wary of the European social model than of the contemporary American mixture of hyper-individualism and social authoritarianism.

Yet the widely held notion that New Labour stands for the continuation of Thatcherism by other means is hopelessly wide of the mark. There are at least four crucial differences between the new regime and the old. Thatcherism was exclusionary; New Labour is inclusionary. Margaret Thatcher was a warrior; Tony Blair is a healer. Where she divided, he unites. Where she spoke of 'enemies within', he speaks of 'the people'. New Labour speaks and acts as though it embodies a national consensus – a consensus of the well intentioned, embracing rich and poor, young and old, suburbs and inner cities, black and white, hunters and animal rights campaigners, successful and unsuccessful. In place of the Thatcherite cold shower, it offers a warm bath, administered by a hegemonic people's party appealing to every part of the nation. This may have nothing in common with social democracy, but it is the nearest thing to Christian democracy that modern British politics has known. And Christian democracy is light years away from Thatcherism.

The second difference is more complicated. Like its predecessor, the new regime is for individual achievement, not collective action. But it has a radically

Tony, Gordon and the invisible man

different conception of the forces that empower achievers. For the Thatcherites, the vehicle of mobility was the undistorted market. For New Labour, talent has to be nurtured before it arrives at the marketplace; and state intervention has to nurture it. The social vision is closer to Thatcherism than to any other tendency in post-war British history. Individuals compete. There are winners and losers. New Labour has no patience with whingers or shirkers. But the political vision is far from Thatcherite. Underpinning the individualistic, mobile, competitive society is a dirigiste workfare state which would have warmed the cockles of Beatrice Webb's heart.

That leads on to a third, more paradoxical, difference. Like the Thatcher and Major governments, the Blair government looks across the Atlantic for inspiration, not across the Channel. It shares the prevailing American view of the global economy and of the relationships between states and markets within the global economy. That is why it is suspicious of the European social model, why it shares its predecessor's commitment to flexible labour markets and low social costs, and why it sees the French socialists and German social democrats as suspect deviationists rather than as fraternal exemplars.

Unlike the Thatcherites, however, it also takes the European Union as a given, and seeks to run with the grain of European integration – including monetary integration. The paradox is that, as the Thatcherites correctly spotted, part of the purpose of the EU is to Europeanise a solidaristic model of the society and economy, drawn partly from the continental social democratic tradition and partly from the (also continental) tradition of Catholic social thought. By the

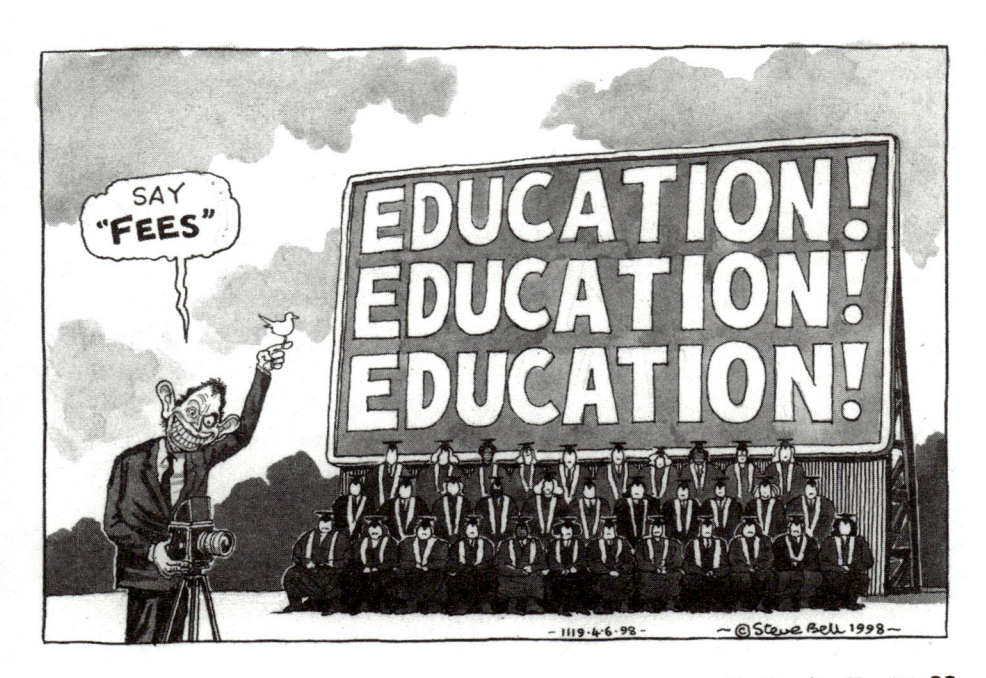

Tony, Gordon and the invisible man

same token, part of the purpose of monetary union is to defend that model against the pressures of the global marketplace, to create a supra-national space in which to protect the European social market from creeping Americanisation.

New Labour, in short, is facing both ways. It is for Americanisation. Although it has not said so in so many words, it is also for the supra-national space. How it will behave if and when it enters the space remains a mystery.

The fourth difference is more paradoxical still. In theory, the Thatcherites were for a minimal state. In practice, they assumed that centralisation was the only possible vehicle for marketisation; that if they were to hobble or crush the manifold institutional and cultural obstacles to their free-market utopia, they would have to make the maximum possible use of the powers which the ancient British doctrine of absolute and inalienable parliamentary sovereignty confers on the government of the day.

In 10 years, the Thatcher governments transformed the political economy and the public culture. The new, low-tax, business-friendly, union-spurning, Murdoch-courting Labour Party is a tribute to that transformation. In a more pluralistic polity, with the checks and balances that most modern democracies take for granted, nothing of the sort would have been possible. New Labour, by contrast, has embarked on the most far-reaching programme of constitutional reform attempted in this country this century.

To be sure, New Labour's constitutional commitments contrast sharply with its approach to governance. Beneath the new regime's inclusive style and hegemonic ambitions it is not difficult to detect a propensity for arm-twisting and heresy-hunting. But that merely underlines the paradox in New Labour's constitutional programme. Before the election I feared that its reforming zeal might fade away once New Labour bottoms were safely ensconced on the Treasury bench in the House of Commons. I now think I was wrong. I also think the implications of the Government's constitutional agenda go further than most commentators have realised. The combination of devolution for Scotland, Wales and Northern Ireland, elected mayors, domestication of the European Convention on Human Rights, freedom of information, House of Lords reform and a referendum on proportional representation points the way towards a profound transformation of the British state.

The process of constitutional change will almost certainly generate a dynamic of its own, carrying the transformation further than its authors intended or expected. This is true in several areas. At present, the Government's approach to House of Lords reform is defiantly minimalist. The voting rights of the hereditary peers are to go and the House of Lords is to become the biggest quango in the land. I do not believe that it will stick. Once the reform genie is out of the bottle, the proposition that a second chamber of placement is a significant improvement on the present one will be laughed out of court. With the hereditaries under sentence of execution, the Conservatives have nothing to lose and a great deal to gain by outbidding the Government in the reform

Tony, Gordon and the invisible man

stakes. If they have any sense — and it is a mistake to assume that they are bound never to have any sense — they will argue for an elected second chamber. Even if they don't, others will.

The long-term implications of devolution are much more radical. The home-rule tide that swept through Scotland in the 1980s was uniquely Scottish. (As the devolution referendums showed, Wales saw nothing comparable.) Yet the forces that set the tide in motion had something in common with the forces that destroyed the Conservative Party in the deindustrialised cities of the north of England.

When Newcastle sees a Scottish parliament sitting in Edinburgh — when it realises that a Scottish chief minister is dealing directly with the Brussels commission, cosying up to the German *Länder* and lobbying potential Japanese investors with an authority unmatched by any sub-national politician south of the Border — it may well decide that it deserves an assembly too. And if devolution leaks southwards into the north of England, as I suspect it will, there will be still more alternative power centres, challenging the hegemony of the metropolis and articulating values at odds with metropolitan economic orthodoxy.

Electoral reform is also likely to put some disruptive cats among the New Labour pigeons. It is a truism that the iron cage of the first-past-the-post electoral system forces parties that aspire to govern towards the centre ground. New Labour is itself a product of the iron cage. The one unanswerable argument of the Labour modernisers was that they offered the only passport to victory. But once the cage disappears, the party game is played by different rules. Not only are minority parties fairly represented; much more important, the pressures of electoral competition no longer squeeze out dissenting views.

It is, of course, impossible to tell how proportional representation would affect the British party system. The one certainty is that there is a sizeable collectivist constituency in this country, to the left of the Blairite Labour Party, which still clings to the social democratic values that Labour used to embody and which no one now represents. I can't believe that it will remain unrepresented if and when the electoral system becomes proportional.

Even if I am wrong about this, there is no doubt that PR would loosen up the system. In doing so, it would bring minority tendencies in from the cold, propel British politicians towards a politics of pluralism, negotiation and coalition building and make single-party hegemony on the Thatcher model unfeasible.

Blair therefore faces a dilemma to which there is no resolution. He has the sense to see that, if he is to turn New Labour's temporary success into permanent hegemony, he needs to keep the Liberal Democrats on board. But he can keep them on board only by offering them PR. And if they get PR, permanent New Labour hegemony will be impossible.

The implications of all this are startling. The Blairites' right hand seems not

Tony, Gordon and the invisible man

to know – dares not find out – what its left hand is doing. The Thatcher paradox – liberal economics combined with Tory politics – has been followed by the Blair paradox: economic continuity combined with political discontinuity. That second paradox, I believe, holds the key to the mysteries that still envelop the new regime.

Its origins lie in the confusions and contradictions of the Thatcher years. In the name of economic liberalism, the Thatcher governments made war on traditional institutions and traditional elites. The victims of the Thatcher blitzkrieg included not only such bastions of traditional Labourism as trade unions and local authorities, but the elite universities, the BBC, the *noblesse oblige* Tory grandees, the bench of bishops, the higher ranks of the Civil Service – all the interlocking networks that made up the old establishment.

By May 1997, the *ancien régime* was in disarray. The fundamental doctrine of absolute parliamentary sovereignty was under threat – from Brussels, from Strasbourg, from Luxembourg, from uppity judges at home. On a deeper level the essentially imperial structure of status, authority and consent which had carried the *ancien régime* through two world wars, the coming of democracy and the installation of the welfare state had crumbled along with the empire itself.

Monarchy-baiting had become one of the favourite sports of an awesomely vulgar tabloid press. Julian Critchley's garagistes had taken over the Tory Party; Barings was brought down by a young Cockney without a university degree. Britain had at last experienced the long-awaited bourgeois revolution. It had become a land fit for Richard Branson.

The only way to stem the drain of legitimacy which had helped to undo the Thatcherites was to reconstruct the state on lines appropriate to a modest, post-imperial, late-twentieth-century European country of the second rank. This is what Blair and his colleagues are now doing; this is what they have to do if they are to root the state which they aspire to govern in popular consent.

For the moment at least, the New Labour coalition extends from the dispossessed of the inner cities to the corporate elite – from Diane Abbott to David Sainsbury; from David Blunkett's constituency of Sheffield Brightside to Gisela Stuart's Edgbaston.

In its triumphant heyday the Thatcher coalition was held together both by ideology and by interest. The New Right themes of choice, enterprise and individuality spoke at least as loudly to aspirant former Labour voters as to traditional Conservatives. Privatisation, deregulation and cuts in direct taxes did as much for their pockets. None of this is true of New Labour's coalition. Despite the talk of a third way, it has not yet acquired a distinctive ideology, and it is divided by a sharp gulf of interest.

The central fault line in modern post-industrial society is that between the winners and the losers in the global marketplace. The lion's share of the extraordinary productivity gains associated with the current capitalist renaissance has gone

Tony, Gordon and the invisible man

to the owners of capital, to a new techno-managerial elite and to a handful of stars in the increasingly global entertainment industries.

Confronting them are the losers: the anxious middle classes, threatened by proletarianisation; the increasingly casualised working class; and the burgeoning underclass. That fault line runs through the New Labour coalition. As the story of the Clinton administration shows, well-intentioned populism cannot bridge it.

Yet it would be wrong to end on a sour note. Last May's magic has not yet worn off. The Government can draw on an enormous fund of goodwill. It has more room for manoeuvre than it appears to realise, more options than it is willing to acknowledge. Sooner or later, it will have to resolve the paradoxes that face it but it can do so in a variety of ways. No iron law prevents it from accepting the pluralistic implications of its constitutional programme, the solidaristic implications of its Europeanism or the redistributive implications of its commitment to social inclusion. For those who cherish the core social democratic values of justice, freedom and solidarity there is everything to play for. •

20 December 1997
Matthew Engel
A very private wedding

As you would expect when a former British Cabinet minister gets together with a former civil servant, the wedding took place in private. It was followed by a night at a secret location as the prelude to a honeymoon at an undisclosed destination.

None the less, a supposedly reliable source announced yesterday afternoon that, at 2.38 p.m. precisely, William Jefferson Hague had married Ffion Llywelyn Jenkins in the Chapel of St Mary Undercroft in the Palace of Westminster. The source added that there had been a sharp intake of breath when the bride walked up the aisle; that no one had fluffed their lines; and that the new Mrs Hague had not promised to obey the leader of the Conservative Party. That, at least, is in keeping with the mood of the rest of the country.

Mr Hague has done what his party expects of him as a first step towards changing that mood by finding himself a bride with good looks and teeth, an apparently sound constitution and no obvious mental instability.

About 170 people attended the ceremony and the reception in Speaker's House. Since Sir Leon Brittan was at the more glamorous end of the guest list, this was not Camelot.

When the Conservative politician Duff Cooper married the beauty Lady Diana Manners in 1919, thousands are supposed to have lined the streets. A crowd did gather outside St Stephen's Entrance yesterday. But, excluding the media

Tony, Gordon and the invisible man

and passing tourists who stayed just long enough to discover what the fuss was about, the grand total of gawpers appeared to be seven.

There was a lady from the East End, who was at the Royal Golden Wedding last month as well; another from Guildford; two South African girls who had seen Mr Hague on TV with the strippergram girl; a Tory lady called Kathleen; and a couple from Swansea, staying with their daughter in town. The woman turned out to be a member of the Labour Party.

When the couple emerged on to the pavement, to pose for the photographers beneath the gargoyles, there was a cheer. (One person cheered.) There was an intake of breath here too, though, because Ffion did look stunning. The source described what she was wearing as a sheath dress, with a drape neckline and short train. It was an uneasy photo call, mainly because the train was long enough to fall into puddles, and the couple stayed as near to the steps into the Commons as they could. He kissed her four times, the longest kiss lasting four seconds.

Further facts emerged later. The ceremony lasted over an hour because it took place in both English and Welsh. There were, according to the order of service, two readings: the First Reading and the Second Reading (though no committee stage). The source, for mysterious reasons, declined to say what they were.

The best man was a college friend called Nick Levy. Ffion did not wear something old, new, borrowed and blue, because she is not superstitious. And she will be Mrs Hague at home but Miss Jenkins while at her arts sponsorship work.

Her main job now, however, is to produce some children in plenty of time for an election in 2001 or 2002, preferably with her looks rather than his. This is in keeping with the ancient Conservative myth that politicians need to be safely married with children. This seems to have been strengthened rather than weakened by the premiership of Edward Heath, even though the electorate made him prime minister without knowing a damn thing about his sexuality.

Among the presents were a photograph album from the Blairs and (which the source did not mention) a subscription to *Gay Times* from the homosexual group OutRage.

Few other details were released. We don't even know the contents of the groom's speech. But doubtless he said he was a very lucky man. Funny thing is, he appears to be right. ●

Tony, Gordon and the invisible man

30 May 1998

Ewen Macaskill and Lucy Ward
Twelve months for the invisible man to start making a mark

William Hague returned from Bosnia yesterday. You didn't know he had been there? Not many people did. Not a single line about the visit has appeared in the press, nor even a few seconds on television or radio.

The Leader of the Opposition spent the week speaking to British troops and meeting warring politicians – but failed to get any of it reported. The inability to generate publicity reflects the general lack of interest in Mr Hague and the Conservative Party. A strategic decision to keep a low profile was taken after he won the leadership last year. He has achieved that, but, to the chagrin of those around him at Westminster, it is even lower than intended. Apart from Prime Minister's Question Time, he can spend most weeks as Westminster's invisible man.

Things are no better in the constituencies. Tories are forced to take comfort from the fact that, when Mr Hague goes out on the road with his private secretary, the former athlete Seb Coe, the under-thirties ask who the 'old bloke' is with the Tory leader. The over-thirties are just mystified by the baseball-capped man next to the former Olympic runner.

The problems are reflected in opinion polls, where Mr Hague's standing is dreadful. A Mori poll this week showed his personal rating fell in the last month from –15 to –25. However, defending the leader's record, one of his frontbenchers insisted there was little Mr Hague could do in the face of the euphoria that embraced Labour after the general election – except keep his head down.

Undeniably, though, he got off to a disastrous start. Plonking a baseball cap on his head to try to give himself a youthful appeal is an image that still haunts him – the first thing Tories mention when asked for a list of his mistakes over the last year. Although he is only 37, one of the youngest British party leaders ever, he has long had a middle-aged mentality, and donning a baseball cap or going to the Notting Hill Carnival will not change that. On the first occasion he looked nerdish, and on the second patronising.

Worse was to follow. He misjudged the public mood when asked to respond to Princess Diana's death, his measured comments contrasting with Mr Blair's 'People's Princess' soundbite. His defenders say that, in fairness to him, he did not know her and his response was genuine; he had not appreciated that the British public had developed a taste for public, even if synthetic, grieving.

Tony, Gordon and the invisible man

He and his party have proved cack-handed in lots of areas, failing to exploit Labour weaknesses in the Bernie Ecclestone tobacco sponsorship affair, and then over the Sierra Leone arms-export affair. And, excruciatingly, on the day the Good Friday Agreement was signed, his Northern Ireland spokesman was in Africa, unavailable for comment for a week.

On the broader front, a Tory MP sympathetic to Mr Hague defended him, insisting there was little any politician could have done post-election. 'Our misfortune was to have won in 1992. We lost so much credibility in those years. The public were disgusted with us. It is going to be hard to win them back.'

Mr Hague made a good choice in picking Archie Norman, who transformed the fortunes of the Asda supermarket chain and is now a Tory MP, to draw up a plan for party reform. 'We have gone from being the least democratic party in Britain to the most,' a Hague aide said yesterday.

The party's poll rating is extremely low, not having risen above 31 per cent and often having fallen below that, with only 26 per cent this week. But the party did at least fight Labour to a draw in the council elections.

Nicholas Budgen, the Eurosceptic Tory MP defeated in Wolverhampton at the last election, points out that Baroness Thatcher also had low poll ratings while in opposition and in office – until the Falklands conflict. The new leader, he believes, has made too few formal speeches spreading the Tory message.

At a personal level, Mr Hague's debating skills have helped him do well at PMQs. Neil Kinnock seldom got the better of Lady Thatcher, nor John Smith of John Major – although Mr Blair had a good strike record against him. But Mr Hague has frequently got in hits, and done even better in set-piece debates: not bad for a politician whose only previous experience was as Welsh Secretary, the most junior member of the Tory Cabinet.

On the matter of low public profile, the Tory leader is fond of remarking, 'I'm bloody well known in Yorkshire and I'm bloody well known in Wales.' Central Office underlines the point that, where he has lived and worked, he makes an impression and wins trust.

One of the main continuing criticisms of him is that he has so far not come up with a set of alternative policies, other than his anti-single currency stance. But one of his advisers said yesterday the party would have been pilloried if it had come up with a new set of policies straight away.

If Mr Hague fails to turn his party round at the general election, a successor is waiting. A new-look Michael Portillo, complete with a conscience, should be back in Parliament. •

Tony, Gordon and the invisible man

18 March 1998
Hugo Young
Labour is working, working, working

Gordon Brown's first full Budget would show, said Tony Blair, what New Labour was all about. From it we learn that New Labour is all about work, work and work again, with fairness added and aspiration thrown in. The providers of work are equal with the takers, and the Government's central task is, by every imaginable means, to encourage both sides to play their allotted role.

In an hour of utmost earnestness, Mr Brown showed the dedicated imagination he has been training for years to apply. Work has acquired ideological status. Ask what has replaced equality in the party bible and you have your answer. It was a profound, rooted performance, just as much so – but how very different! – as the last time this happened: a Labour Chancellor delivering his first Budget after the wilderness years.

In 1974, reaffirming the politics of the Left, Denis Healey spoke for two hours 20 minutes, and his speech – according to his memoirs – 'was received with rapture by the Labour movement as representing the first step in that "irreversible transfer of wealth and power to working people and their families" which we had promised in the election'.

This time the promise is to non-working people, and there is no such thing as the Labour movement to register its feelings. A little while later, negotiating an incomes policy, Healey spent 'eight days in continual discussions with TUC leaders', another category wholly absent from the New Labour perspective. The Blair–Brown world unveiled yesterday is about work of the people, by the people, for the people, as long as the people are defined to include every class of earner and provider across the income scale.

The Budget was about incentivising the whole of society, irrespective of class. It was from the Labour – sorry, New Labour – benches that the first deep-throated growl of approval was heard, when Mr Brown announced the reduction of corporation tax and assorted similar pro-business measures. This had come to seem an entirely natural response, such is the speed with which this government has associated itself with the business imperative and succeeded in instructing the great majority of its MPs in the elementary economics of wealth creation and work supply.

There were, by the same token, no catchpenny words, not a single sop to the vestiges of opinion still surviving from the Healey era. The enormously important tax credits to be given for child-care, like the radical enhancements laboriously

Tony, Gordon and the invisible man

invented for the relief of low-paid working families, are a social statement for the modern era, not an obeisance to old gods: all about equality of entitlement to work, nothing about equality of wealth or earning or ownership.

Another way of putting this is to say that New Labour is all about encouraging aspiration, however lowly, rather than cushioning under-privilege, however chronic. This is what the welfare-to-work schemes in the Budget persistently home in on, and, along with the new money for public services, is what distinguishes the philosophy of this government from John Major's. The schemes have been conjured up with passionate enthusiasm, the money for health and education – and the vital small signal conveyed by free museum entry – handed out by real believers.

The New Labour ministers are, however, cautious about trusting themselves. The memory of 1974 obsesses them as a lesson in the catastrophe of profligate spending which then has to be grabbed back when the economy turns down. As a cage to confine them, they have therefore invented their 10-year fiscal plan, a domestic stability pact that is supposed to restrain the insatiable spending ministries. It's the second of the expedients which subcontracts their freedom – and the fate of their new ideology. For no incentives to work, however imaginative, will work if work itself does not exist. And this is now contingent on another body than the Treasury, the Monetary Policy Committee (MPC) of the Bank of England, which will make its own judgement on the Chancellor in deciding whether to raise interest rates, thereby affecting, perhaps decisively, the level of the pound, therefore exports, therefore work itself.

It is extraordinary to listen to a Budget, traditionally the key moment of economic management, that makes no reference to the vital question of the hour. Not a word about either the interest rate or the exchange rate. Which makes one see this sacred moment in a different light, as a long-term social pattern-setter more than an immediate economy decider.

That suits the strategic nature of Gordon Brown's approach to politics, not excluding the desire he shares with Mr Blair to set things up nicely for the next election. But one must understand, in the new dispensation, that in the short term the Chancellor is more accountable to the MPC than the MPC is to anyone.

If the hawks secure a majority on the MPC, the ideology of work will take a beating. It is also at risk from the actual functioning of the incentives that will be put in place. The small print of the schemes has yet to be thoroughly declared, and the behaviour of unworking people, presented with new marginal changes in the possibilities open to them, will only disclose itself over time. Reports on the welfare-to-work schemes over the last few months are, quite predictably, patchy. They call for collaboration, as well as hard-headedness, from the providers as much as the takers of work, and this philosophy – the very core of what Blair–Brownism most passionately believes in – has yet to penetrate every part of society.

Will it do so? In Healey's day, forecasting related to matters more measurable than human behaviour. The Treasury's under-prediction of the public sector borrowing requirement in 1974 amounted to £4 billion, a magnitude of error, the old boy writes, 'greater than that of any fiscal change made by any Chancellor in British history'. He vowed to do for forecasters 'what the Boston Strangler did for door-to-door salesmen: make them distrusted for ever'.

The faith of Mr Blair and Mr Brown is not in forecasters but in the people. They are their own prophets, of the faith that people can be made to want to work. But they don't control all the circumstances that make work, and can't guarantee who will be distrusted in four years' time. •

20 March 1998
Madeleine Bunting
Sell your soul to the company store: fine – but what about the family?

It was a budget all about work: how to get into it, how to stay in it while you have parenting responsibilities and how to create more work for other people. The Government is understandably preoccupied with work, because for nearly two decades, everyone else has been. The legacy of the 1980s – still with us – was that working long hours became a status symbol. The division between the overworked in work and the debilitated morale and self-respect of those out of work has haunted this country – and Europe – for nearly two decades.

But the final programme in the BBC series *Having It All*, on Tuesday evening, showed the consequences of our work-obsessed culture on marriages, children and family life. The consequences of what Brown unveiled in the afternoon were thus demonstrated in 'Juggling', which focused on three couples, each with their three children and two jobs. Those endless negotiations over who does what, work intruding on family life, the rushing from work to puzzled kids and back again. It was horribly familiar. The toll on marriages was obvious: too little time and too many things to arrange. Where did anyone have time to relax and unwind? One woman uncomplainingly admitted that after completing the night shift at the crisp factory, the ironing, cleaning, cooking and her husband's accounts, she might have 20 minutes to herself in the day. Another woman, reflecting on three children in five years while training to be a barrister, concluded that the one thing she had definitely learned was time management.

I know exactly what she means but groan all the same. Life is like a pie chart which we divide up, apportioning slices to employers, children and partners.

Tony, Gordon and the invisible man

Let me ask one heretical question in this wonderful world of work, work and more work: why? The obvious answer is: 'Can't afford not to.' But for many people, and certainly middle-class professionals, 'afford' is a flexible friend. What most people mean is that they have to work hard to sustain the kind of lifestyle they have chosen. Our consumer culture is relentless in its drive to make us consume more and more, and to do that we have to work more and more. This cycle of work and consumption can become absurd because what is lost in the equation is time: in recent months, I have replaced a video, dishwasher and microwave, but have yet to find the time to find out how any of them works.

Consumption and work are the two pillars around which we now structure our identity. As familial, communal and national allegiances have weakened and membership of organisations from trade unions to churches has declined in the course of the second half of the twentieth century, we have loaded our need for identity on to what we consume – which is how we project our identity – and on to our work. I consume, I work, therefore I am. Measure human identity in this way and unemployment not only makes you poor, it destroys your humanity.

What frightens me about this is the extent to which it has crept up on us all and how it goes unchallenged except by an odd assortment of religious thinkers, travellers and drop-outs who find themselves marginalised and ridiculed as irrelevant and unrealistic.

But it's dangerous. As we desperately search in our workplace for identity, and a sense of belonging, we become vulnerable to what Professor Richard Roberts at Lancaster University identifies as 'the key aim of effective human resources management which is the harnessing of personal identity in which boundaries between work and home are eroded'. Employers will 'retool' the personal identities of employees to meet their commercial objectives in training programmes which manipulate and accelerate the process of personal development and change. Successfully retooled, the executive – usually under 35 because older people are less malleable – enjoys an enhanced sense of identity which meets the needs of her/his immediate corporate environment. The career flourishes with a quasi-religious sense of fulfilment (explicitly encouraged by the corporation's co-option of religious language and concepts).

Yet to place your identity at the mercy of your employer is foolhardy. There is an obvious paradox in that, as we have come to invest more of our identity in our work, our workplaces have become unprecedentedly competitive and insecure; the result is acute anxiety and stress. And there is another reason to worry, an underlying and even more sinister development. Roberts describes the retooling as the application of Taylorism to the mental processes of the professional, managerial classes. What Frederick Taylor did in 1911 was lay out the management theory behind the Ford production line. The slogan of Fordism for the workers was 'leave your minds outside'. Every aspect of the industrial process was controlled by the manager; the worker simply performed a specified function. A bolt on a wheel 300 times a day.

Tony, Gordon and the invisible man

When you apply this to the professional, managerial classes, the principle is the same Marx used to describe the impact of Luther's Reformation, whereby religious authority is no longer external but internal – everyone has a priest inside themselves. So professionals become their own middle managers: they internalise the management tools of organising their task and measuring their performance. They internalise the fear and attempt to anticipate their employer's wishes. There is no room – even in your head – for rebellion or genuine autonomy. 'Consultation' is simply about providing people with sufficient time to listen, understand and then obey. All of this makes plenty of sense for the employer, who cuts out layers of management. It's a nasty, neat fit which is virtually impossible to break out of because it is self-reinforcing. Remember, Orwell's *1984* was as much about the totalitarian nightmare of managerialism as about that of communism. It impoverishes and jeopardises our understanding of who and what we are. It sets up a rat race (the expression sounds dated, so prevalent is the concept) which starts in primary school. We are in a performance culture ruthless on those who fail to perform (but by what criteria?). The pressure on a besieged family home-life to give relief and provide refuge is incalculable, and the strain is showing. •

Clive Harold introduces himself to Prince Charles as a former fellow pupil

A class apart

A class apart

5 December 1997
Alex Bellos
The prince and the *Big Issue* vendor: from classmates to a class apart

Once upon a time two little boys were friends at school. One grew up to become a prince and lived in a palace. The other fell on hard times and ended up sleeping rough on the streets. Forty years later they met again. Yesterday this fairy tale became reality when the Prince of Wales unexpectedly came face to face with an old schoolfriend who is now homeless.

Clive Harold, aged 49, stunned the prince as well as colleagues at the *Big Issue* yesterday when, during a royal visit to the magazine's headquarters, he introduced himself as a former pupil at Hill House prep school. He said the two were in the same class for two years and had even played football with each other at the school, in Knightsbridge, west London.

Clive then told the prince that he made a 'few mistakes' in his life and he had lost everything. For the last two weeks he has been selling the *Big Issue*, wearing a red scarf and Santa Claus hat. The old classmates shared a joke when Clive showed the prince his hat and offered to let him wear it. 'That's all I need,' came the reply, to shrieks of laughter. Clive had told the prince that selling the magazine had brought discipline back into his life. The prince told him, 'As long as you're all right, that's the main thing.'

Clive later explained that his father was a well-known financier who lived in a mansion in Launceston Place, central London. Of his schooldays he said, '[The prince] and I were in the same stream for about two years and I reminded [him] how we used to walk from the school to the Territorial Army ground near Sloane Square for football. He remembered that and he also remembered the headmaster giving us mint sweets. The prince did not remember me of course and I only remember him because we both had big ears and because he was obviously well known there. It is a long time ago and I cannot really remember if I was very friendly with the prince.'

The headmaster of Hill House, Colonel Stuart Townend, confirmed Clive had attended the school. He was the prince's classmate in 1956–7.

After leaving Hill House, Clive went to Millfield public school while the prince went to Gordonstoun.

'After college, I became a journalist and was writing showbiz pages on *Woman's Own* and other women's magazines,' Clive said.

Woman's Own confirmed he had worked for the magazine as a staff feature writer and gossip columnist between July 1981 and January 1983.

A class apart

He added, 'I wrote a book called *The Uninvited*, which went to number eight in the best-seller lists. I still carry a copy of it around with me. It is a sort of security blanket. Everything was going so well in my career. I was speaking with stars like Sylvester Stallone and I went to New York and Hollywood. I sold the film rights to my book in Hollywood but nothing came of it. I am still technically under contract to write a second book, but that's difficult at the moment. While things were going well in my career, my private life was falling apart. I realised that I had not given enough time to my family and friends. I suppose the booze got me in the end.' He added, 'I have been married twice and it was when my second marriage failed that things really fell apart. I lost my house and one day I woke up in a shop doorway in the Strand. I had lost everything.'

He said that with the help of the *Big Issue* he was regaining his confidence. He is now on benefit and living in a bed and breakfast. 'I have joined a writing class here and teach others to do what I should be doing.'

Big Issue founder John Bird said, 'The prince told me as he left, "It just shows you, doesn't it?" Today's meeting illustrates that anyone can find themselves on the streets, no matter what start they had in life.' •

27 December 1997
Tim Radford
A unique hoard emerges from history

They float, suspended in spirit, the embryos the world forgot. They are part of a unique collection gathered by hunting parties 80 years ago and they could be about to help answer some of biology's most challenging questions. The yet-to-be born sloths, anteaters, hedgehogs and other creatures come from collections by embryologists at a time when scientists researched with guns rather than cameras or field notebooks. There are 2,000 specimens and 80,000 microscopic slides of 6,000 vertebrate species in the Netherlands Institute for Developmental Biology in Utrecht, where they have been rediscovered by Michael Richardson, of the St George's Hospital Medical School in London.

The embryos include those of duck-billed platypuses and marsupials gathered by an Englishman, James Hill, in Australia and South America, and another huge assembly by Ambrosius Arnold Hubrecht from what is now the Indonesian archipelago.

'Hubrecht was quite rich and used to send shooting parties into the Dutch tropical colonies. He collected a lot of species. They cut them open and if they

A class apart

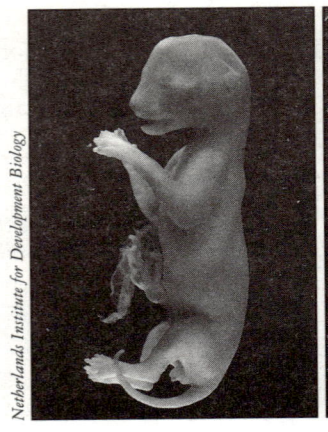

Cat embryo   *Flying lemur embryo*   *Anteater embryo*

were pregnant they would put the embryos in formalin and send them back to the Netherlands. It was a terrible slaughter,' said Dr Richardson. 'He didn't do much with them. He published some work on hedgehogs but on the whole these embryos have sat, unstudied and unloved, for 80 years.'

They were joined by a collection originally assembled by Professor Hill for University College, London. In 1957 – because there were fears the collection might be neglected – his daughter Catherine transferred them to Holland. It took her 10 years to catalogue them.

The collection is irreplaceable. Some of the species are nearing extinction, some are protected in the wild and many will not breed in captivity. So even after eight decades in pickle, they could answer a huge array of questions about physiological development and about evolution.

Dr Richardson finds the sloth specimens most remarkable: they look a little human, a little like extraterrestrials. The near-to-term embryos are remarkably like miniature versions of the adults they might have become. All present a challenge for the would-be photographer. Dr Richardson painstakingly fished out what he calls the 'dandruff' shed by the embryos from each jar, and then set the jars against a black background.

'You have to get the lighting right, to get shadows, otherwise you just get a white blob,' Dr Richardson said. •

A class apart

1 October 1997

Martin Wainwright
A teenager who could take no more taunts

Kelly Yeomans made her lonely arrangements with a bottle of painkillers after falling, along with her family, into the fatal role of easy meat for a gang of bullies. Tormented at school, where she left PE lessons in her games kit only when everyone else had gone, the puppy-fat 13-year-old gave up hope when even her home failed to provide a safe haven. Two days before she died, the council-owned semi off Derby's ring road was plastered with eggs and margarine, in a cruel mockery of cake making, while her persecutors – boys aged 13 to 16 – shouted abuse about lard and fat.

Up in the front bedroom the family keeps a favourite ornament, a large and elaborate glass fish. Kelly's mother, Julie, alternating yesterday between fond memories and complete despair, said, 'Kelly was cowering in there when a block of margarine came flying in through the window. It landed right on our fish.'

A smear of yellow margarine was still streaked on the half-rendered brickwork of the house as Mrs Yeomans described what amounted to a short-lived siege. She said, 'It was after that Kelly told us, "Mam and Dad, it's nothing to do with you but I can't stand it. I'm going to take an overdose."'

Police began interviewing a series of youths and their parents on the Allenton estate as preparations for an inquest got under way. 'Everyone knows who they're seeing,' said Hazel, Caroline and a string of other neighbours calling with flowers, cards and a big envelope for the street collection they had arranged. 'The trouble was, these were the only ones in Carter Street who took it, didn't come out and say, "You lot – piss off,"' said Hazel, a kindly woman who comforted Mrs Yeomans as a colour photo of Kelly, smiling shyly behind her specs, prompted tears. 'They knew they could have what they called their fun and get away with it.'

A 16-year-old boy, hanging about on the corner of Flint Street and Carter Street, where the Yeomanses have lived for 12 years, agreed that the gang had been 'out for a laugh'. He said, 'I don't think they'd a clue it could lead to something like this. I've heard they want to say they're really sorry to the family, but they're scared because of the police calling round.'

Like Allenton itself, a mostly neat estate with privately owned houses scattered about and a daily file of suited commuters walking through to the offices at the Rolls-Royce works, Kelly was not a friendless and abandoned misfit. She had her own circle at grant-maintained Merrill College lower school, including Marie

A class apart

Porter, a 15-year-old blonde unlikely to get shouts of 'fatty' or 'smelly' from boys.

'I think I was her best friend,' said Marie, bringing her own card and flowers. 'We tried to help her over the bullying she got. She didn't talk about it much but they didn't let her alone, did they, Sarah?' she added, as Kelly's older sister walked up. 'They had it in for your family.'

Sarah, who is 16, nodded and listed some of Kelly's regular ordeals. 'They dumped her trainers in the bin at school. Our mam gave her a favourite T-shirt and that went into the bin too. Someone put salt in her food and she hated trying to get away from PE without being seen.'

Kelly had also seen less of another group of loyal friends as work at the 1,000-strong college had taken more of her time over the past year. She had been a regular visitor to elderly patrons of the Salvation Army centre on Allenton, where she also played the tambourine in the band.

'She was a lovely girl, always wanting to help us all,' said Ada Dodsworth, aged 75, a regular. The Sally Ann's local major, Pamela Nott, said, 'Everyone who knew her spoke of her so warmly.'

Similar strong feelings came from the Yeomanses' neighbours, calling in a steady stream to comfort Sarah, Julie and her husband, Ivan, a former Rolls-Royce worker who tried in vain to wake Kelly for school on Monday morning. But the sympathy was mixed with resignation about effective ways to help a 'picked-on' target.

Patricia Russell, from Flint Street, who offered to take the children in for the night after Julie appeared in tears on her doorstep after the last attack, said, 'I told her the only answer in the end was to get the council in and start proceedings for harassment. Otherwise it just wasn't going to stop, ever.'

Last Friday's attack on the house, the latest in an intermittent series of incidents stretching back nearly three years, ended when police were called – the gang melting away just before the patrol car turned into Carter Street. But the willingness of neighbours to protect their own homes, by telling the youths where to go, had never extended to fighting back on behalf of others.

Four doors down from the stricken family, a yellow window bill in a pensioner's bungalow reading 'This property is protected by the Community Watch Patrol' gives the false impression of neighbourhood action. 'Oh, that's the council. It's one of their empty properties and they keep an eye on them,' said another Carter Street resident. 'Local people aren't going to go that far in tackling gangs like this. They know that they or their kids or their houses could be the next target.'

Derbyshire police said yesterday that the inquiry was concentrating on a small number of juveniles and could take some time. 'It isn't something we want to rush into,' said Detective Inspector Mark Cheetham. 'We're interviewing everyone in the surrounding streets and also offering support to the family.'

Governors at Merrill College and its principal, Mike Shaw, are also examining

A class apart

anti-bullying measures, although the school said that Kelly had not passed on her concerns to the staff.

Derby's housing director, Hilary Keenan, said full support would be offered to the family, including rehousing if that was what they wished. But the Yeomanses' neighbours are hoping to persuade the family to stay. Adding more coins to her street collection, Hazel said, 'They have got good friends round here and we think it's disgusting what they've been through.' •

31 January 1998
Rory Carroll
Two in a small, secret legion

It's a small living room on the ground floor, curtains drawn tight. The window looks out on a cul-de-sac with 18 houses and some parked cars. From the kitchen you can see the backyard, empty except for a wheelie bin.

Not much of a view, but it was not much of a life for Stephen Protaszczak. He and his twin, David, rose each day about 10.30 a.m., sat down in the living room and watched television, usually until past midnight. They did this for 20 years. Stephen virtually never stepped out of the three-bedroom house, never went to the pub round the corner, never walked one of the dozen or so stray dogs kept in the house and never saw a doctor until last November, when an ambulance took him, too late and unwillingly, to Luton and Dunstable Hospital.

He died, aged 38, of shock lung a week later, the result of a broken leg and malnourishment so severe he could move only by crawling even before he fell down the stairs. This week the coroner, David Morris, recorded a verdict of accidental death in which self-neglect had been a factor.

The television still flickers in the living room in the village of Sundon, near Luton, where David continues watching in between making trips to the kitchen to eat food prepared by his mother, Ethel Protaszczak, aged 68. The difference now is that each morning he walks the half-mile to visit his twin's grave at the St Mary the Virgin Church. Neighbours said that on Christmas Day they found him kneeling at the wooden cross in pouring rain, refusing entreaties to come indoors.

Why two boys chose to grow to middle age as recluses remains unanswered. Staff at Northfields Upper School in Dunstable, Bedfordshire, told reporters that the twins were good-natured, normal and liked. They were quiet and constantly together but gave no indication of joining the small, secret legion of people who retreat into their homes and turn their backs on the world.

David was born on 15 January 1959 at the family home in Dunstable. Stephen arrived one hour and 45 minutes later. Their mother and Ukrainian father,

A class apart

Petro, already had two other sons, John and Peter. The couple had two more children, Karen and Paul, all of whom went on to lead normal lives.

What happened to Stephen and David remains a mystery. Their parents divorced about the time they left school, aged 16. Peter and John stayed with their father while Karen, Paul and the twins moved with their mother to Upper Sundon. Karen and Paul got jobs and left to get married, but the twins stayed behind, growing closer, odder and ever more dependent on their mother. She cooked, cleaned and shopped, catching the bus into Leighton Buzzard and lugging back videos and food which was increasingly left untouched. The videos were devoured. Comedies mostly, the twins apparently veered from Frank Capra to Mr Bean.

Neighbours did not overhear much laughter, telling reporters, 'From the street you could hear them screaming at each other, no words, just garble. There would be all this crashing and banging of doors. Windows would get broken. Sometimes I would see their mother standing in the backyard after the twins had been rowing, just sobbing her heart out. I felt so sorry for her, but if you go round to offer help, you just get the door slammed in your face.'

It is a common refrain often heard from neighbours interviewed after a tragedy has unravelled next door. In the late twentieth century it tends to be coroners, not neighbours, who shed light on families who 'kept themselves to themselves'.

Karen Morgan lived in her bare bedroom for 14 years, in Clapham, London, seeing only her mother and ordering her through handwritten notes. She died with wasted muscles in 1996, aged 29. Desmond Lockwood died after locking himself away for 30 years from the age of 19 when he lost his job. He became a recluse who lived on ice-cream and tea and stared endlessly at the TV in his bedroom. Even a dynamic figure like John Patterson, the multi-millionaire founder of Dateline, was not immune. He was found drowned in his bath after the panic attacks became too much and he stopped going outside.

The impulses which drove Stephen can only be imagined. Did he ever gaze at the sky and wonder what it was like to be on one of the planes taking off from Luton Airport? Or observe a neighbour parking a car and wonder what it was like to drive? Or watch customers emerging from the Crown pub, 40 feet from his front door, and wonder what a pint of draught bitter tasted like?

The stimulation offered by TV the night the ambulance arrived ranged from *Friends*, *Baywatch*, Rory Bremner and the *Wogan Years*.

His father, Petro, a retired cement worker, insisted the twins led normal lives. 'Stephen ate food when he wanted to, like me. What the press say is rubbish, he ate food. He had an accident, that's why he died.'

The pathologist who examined Stephen's body left a different epitaph: 'Postmortem examination has shown ascites, pleural effusions and oedema almost certainly due to malnourishment.' •

A class apart

16 December 1997
Owen Bowcott
Olde England stages last supper

Collective dementia or defiant celebration of traditional British feasting? The black armbands worn for the occasion by the Worshipful Company of Butchers left little room for doubt. Their Farewell Dinner for The Roast Beef of Olde England delivered six courses fiercely at odds with the 'spineless recent government decision' on BSE in the final hours before midnight when Jack Cunningham's beef on the bone ban came into effect.

'Bullshot' vodka cocktails whetted the appetite at Butchers' Hall, near Smithfield Market in the City of London, followed by beef dripping on toast, ribs of beef, oxtail soup, a baron of beef on the bone and suet treacle pudding.

'What I object to is the removal of our liberties,' insisted Charles Boyd, whose company, Chester Boyd, provides traditional boardroom catering for City firms. 'Why can't people choose for themselves? It's not going to mean job losses for us but it's a quality loss, it's the end of roast beef. There's a distinct improvement if you roast meat on the bone.'

Butchers' Hall has suffered its share of setbacks during a history which can be traced back to 975. The building was demolished during air raids in both world wars. But the City Livery Company met the latest onslaught with a last supper radiating grim satisfaction. Candles on the dining-hall table were set in cuts of marrow bone, napkins were wreathed in black ribbons and guests were presented with tee-shirts declaring, 'The End of Roast Beef as we know it. RIP. 15th December 1997'.

'Every time there's a fresh warning, it's like a ratchet,' complained John Warde, a Kent farmer who was invited to the dinner. 'Each time a little more of the animal has to be got rid of, there's less in the price at the end. The Government hasn't consulted anyone but scientists and scientists are not practical people.'

Sipping a beef consommé-based Bullshot cocktail, the chef for the dinner, Peter Kerwood, said, 'You are more likely to choke on a fish bone than catch anything from a piece of beef. This is the last time you will see anyone eating oxtail soup under these "Maff-ia" rules.' In future, he suggested, a black market in beef on the bone could develop.

After the baron of beef had been paraded around the hall by uniformed waiters bearing a ceremonial meat cleaver, and the meal consumed, departing guests were presented with a T-bone steak and the promise that 'this will not damage your health'.

A class apart

MENU
Aperitif: Bullshot (beef consommé with vodka and spices), plus canapés including bread and dripping, and bite-size ribs of beef with mustard sauce
Starter: Oxtail soup, served with chestnuts
Main course: Baron of beef (a pair of roast sirloins on the bone)
Dessert: Treacle pudding made with suet

....

11 March 1998
Owen Bowcott
'Have you heard of CJD?'

Clare Tomkins enjoyed life to the full, loved animals, was looking forward to getting married and had been a strict vegetarian since the age of 13. But over the course of six months, she degenerated into a tormented patient racked by spasmodic head movements, whose hands and feet turned inward. She could not walk unaided, cowered in fear from members of her family and 'howled like a sick, injured animal'.

Yesterday her father, Roger Tomkins, described in harrowing detail the agonies endured by his terminally ill daughter and the effect her wasting condition is having on the family's life.

Relatives of other victims wept as the BSE inquiry listened in hushed silence to Mr Tomkins, an engineering company director, recall how Clare gradually succumbed to the human equivalent of the disease, new variant CJD (nvCJD). Clare, now aged 24, is bed-bound, doubly incontinent and requires round-the-clock nursing and an automatic pump to clear accumulating saliva.

Mr Tomkins and his wife, Dawn, from Tonbridge, Kent, first noticed in October 1996 that Clare was behaving oddly when she returned from a holiday with her fiancé, Andrew Beale, in an uncharacteristically depressed mood. Just 5ft 2in tall, she began to lose weight, dropping from 7st 3lb to 6st. She also complained of a nasty taste in her mouth.

She became increasingly depressed, was crying for no reason and could no longer face her job in the pet department of a local garden centre. Her fiancé, fearing the relationship was causing her distress, broke off their engagement but later restored it when he realised the extent of her devastation.

The following year Clare's ability to walk began to suffer and she started falling over and complaining of dizziness. 'She complained of a numbness in her lips. She began to complain of double vision. She also complained of pains in her knees. Her memory was beginning to fail, so that she could not remember events that occurred only hours before. My wife and I also noticed that Clare began to make unusual facial expressions.'

Clare's handwriting, which had been large and flamboyant, was first reduced

A class apart

to a quarter of its normal size and later became an indecipherable scrawl. She was treated with antidepressants by her GP but became childlike in her reactions and developed a nervous laugh. She appeared continually anxious, breathing heavily and was unsteady on her feet.

'We were always optimistic. We always felt there was going to be a light at the end of the tunnel,' Mr Tomkins told the inquiry. She was admitted as an in-patient to a private clinic. There her therapy involved not seeing her parents for two weeks, but her condition deteriorated rapidly and the psychiatrist soon doubted his diagnosis that she was suffering from acute anxiety.

Treatment at several hospitals, involving being sectioned under the Mental Health Act and electro-convulsive therapy, followed before she was referred to St Mary's Hospital in Paddington, London.

Finally, in August 1997, after a biopsy test on her tonsils, doctors confirmed that she was suffering from a 'prion encephalopathy'. Mr Tomkins told the inquiry, 'I asked what that was. "Have you heard of CJD?" the doctor replied. That was the moment when the theoretical light at the end of the tunnel began to close down.'

Although a vegetarian, Clare had eaten sausages and burgers as a young child and had also worked with pet feed in her job.

'You go through a process of bereavement,' Mr Tomkins said, 'imagining everything without her, but then I can go upstairs and hold and cuddle her, but some day I know I will no longer be able to do that. When alone I too cry, because of my feelings of sheer frustration and despair: frustration because I cannot do anything to help my daughter recover from her illness and despair because I know that Clare will in time succumb to an untimely death.' •

....

11 June 1998
News in brief
Mother dies after daughter

A father who lost his daughter to Creutzfeldt-Jacob disease seven weeks ago was yesterday mourning the death of his wife, Dawn, aged 52. Roger Tomkins, 52, was with her as she lost her seven-month battle against ovarian cancer early on Tuesday.

In April their daughter, Clare, died from CJD, the human form of mad cow disease, despite the fact that she had been a vegetarian for nearly 13 years.

At the family home Mr Tomkins said, 'Dawn was very ill in the last weeks of Clare's life, yet she dug very deep into her own resources to be there for the end and the funeral. I think it left her very weak and she went rapidly downhill. She died in my arms.' •

The burnt-out Jolly Brewer

Jean's war

Jean's war

10 November 1997
Nick Davies
A last stand for sanity

Leeds is the second largest metropolitan area in Great Britain, one of the busiest hives of financial and legal activity outside of London. It has the West Yorkshire Playhouse and the Headingley Cricket Ground and the Leeds International Film Festival; it has a city centre full of Victorian pride, all funked up with pedestrian precincts and riverside chic; it boasts that it has more parkland and open space per square mile than any other city in the country; and, most important, in the 1990s it has been the scene of an economic boom that has generated 20,000 new jobs and more than £700 million in new investment.

It also has its share of problems. It suffers from crime and unemployment. In the spring of 1995, nearly 30,000 men and women were out of work, 7.5 per cent of its workforce. Leeds reasonably could claim to contain just about all of ordinary life in Britain at the end of the millennium.

Just to the north-west of the city centre, near the University of Leeds and the General Infirmary, there is an area called Hyde Park and Burley. It is neither famously rich nor notoriously poor, neither overwhelmingly white nor particularly black, a place that appears to offer a cross-section of city life. It has its middle classes, elderly people, single mothers, black families, Asian families and, most of all, young people whose lives have been shaped here.

Outwardly at the time it was an unremarkable place. There was the long, straight stretch of Hyde Park Road where Patisserie Valerie advertised oven-warm croissants, and the old back-to-back terraces huddled together in tight-knit families, all sharing the same name. And, finally, there was the council estate itself. This was Hyde Park and Burley.

Something was wrong here. The narrow back-to-back houses to the west of Hyde Park Road, for example, looked now just as they would have done 100 years ago — slightly scruffy, quietly colourful, busy with men and women going through their daily routines — but there was one odd little difference. Almost all the ground-floor windows were scarred with thick iron grilles. A lot of the doors were too. Like leaded lights and Viennese blinds in the posh new houses on the nouveau-Barratt estates, grilles appeared to be almost compulsory extras for every home here.

Who would pay for an iron grille? Presumably someone with something to fear and most likely the object of this fear was crime. Even so, an iron grille was an expensive fixture. So it wasn't going to be bought by the victim of a single crime. Each of these grilles must mark the exasperated victim of a series of crimes. But could that be right? Why would these houses attract criminals in such numbers? From the Antiques and Collectibles shop at its western end,

Jean's war

whose face was masked by a dense steel grid, past the burglar alarm which screamed like a demented cat near the junction with Autumn Grove, the line of houses with barricaded front doors made the whole road look like Coronation Street in Harlem. There was something else. The shops were dead. Jan's Salon – closed. Di Clementi's general store – closed. The printer's shop – closed.

And then there was the writing on the walls. The abandoned shops offered a canvas for the graffiti artists, although not for love hearts pierced by arrows but for a hand that wrote a more essential message: 'Kiss it, bitch.' And over and over again: 'Fuck the police . . . Fuck the law.' A police car prowled quietly around the corner from Hyde Park Road and slowed to a halt in the car park in the middle of the close. Silence. Two thick-set policemen in uniform stepped cautiously out of the car and made to walk along the pavement. Their feet had barely touched the kerb when a fistful of brick soared out of nowhere and hurtled through the air towards them. They ducked. The brick exploded in fragments on the road behind them. Somewhere behind the houses, there was the sound of footsteps running.

Jean Ashford had a story to tell. She wasn't too sure quite where it began, though the ending was clear enough. It was all about her, but it was also all about Hyde Park – or any other place like it. In a way she supposed that it started one evening a year or so ago, when she found herself walking past the pub that used to stand on Hyde Park Road, almost exactly opposite Hyde Park Close. The Newlands, they called it, though Jean Ashford had never heard any good reason for the name. 'Badlands' would have been more like it. It was about six o'clock. She could see two lads on the other side of the road. She recognised them straight away: Jimmy Clarke and Dean Boyle. Jimmy was small, with thick mousy hair which tumbled down across his forehead. He looked quite boyish and innocent – he was only 16 or 17 – but she had seen what he could do before. The other one, Dean, looked the way he acted. He always reminded Jean of a rat; he was a skinny, mean-faced little lad with his hair cropped so short that it looked like a shadow on his skull.

Jean dropped her eyes and hurried her step. She would just ignore them. Only 20 yards and she'd be past them. 'Foogin' grass.' It was Dean's voice. Her heart started to thump. She'd just ignore them. Only another 10 yards. 'Hey! I'm talkin' to you. Hey!' She was almost level with them now, eyes down, head down, hands clasped together in front of her, walking as fast as she could without losing her dignity. They were crossing the road. She could see them out of the corner of her eye. Keep walking.

Too late. He was on her. It was Dean. He had one hand on her throat, gripping. She flinched. He twisted her round and pushed her hard against the wall of the pub so that the back of her head thumped against the brickwork. He had both hands on her throat now and he was shoving her backwards. 'I'm gonna get ya. I'm gonna burn ya foogin' house down. D'ya hear?' Her neck was hurting. And the back of her head too. She was afraid she couldn't breathe. 'I'm

Jean's war

gonna foogin' murder you. I'm gonna come round your house when you're asleep and I'm gonna foogin' murder you.' She could see his little black eyes right up in front of her face. He was almost shaking with hatred.

There was a shout from across the road, a man's voice, telling someone to clear off out of it. It was Mr Mangan, who lived opposite the pub and had two great big Alsatians. He was opening his gate and the dogs were with him, he was letting them out into the road. Dean and Jimmy turned and vanished. Mr Mangan came across and asked if she needed help. He thought they had been trying to mug her but Jean knew what it was really about. She knew the whole story, and that had all started a lot earlier.

It had started years and years ago, in the spring of 1972, when Jean Ashford had moved into Hyde Park with her three young children. Jean was happy to be there. She had been born in Leeds, a couple of miles away, in Beeston. Then she married and drifted away for several years; but when her marriage broke down she had wanted to come home, to be close to her parents, and she had been lucky to get this brand-new house in St John's Close.

It seemed a very fine place. The council had bulldozed all the tattered old housing to make way for this new estate and the houses were lovely. Hers had three bedrooms and a big kitchen. She wasn't saying it was perfect – the garden was just a patch of mud, and it was hard work bringing up the three children on her own without very much in the way of money – but it was a good street, a good mix, and, since the tenants were all new at the same time, everyone soon got to know everyone else. The children ran in and out of the houses, playing on the grass or going up to the swings on Woodhouse Moor. Jean liked it. Hyde Park was like a self-contained town. It had its own football teams, its own churches and clubs. She hardly ever had to go into Leeds.

The change came slowly, almost invisibly, like waves wearing down a cliff. Years passed before she had to admit that something was wrong. The children had grown up, Jean was into her mid-fifties and a grandmother. It must have been around 1989 or 1990 that she first noticed it: a little raft of places that she had come to rely on as part of everyday life in Hyde Park suddenly seemed to sink out of sight.

The community centre up at Belle Vue was one of the first to go. There were all sorts of activities up there and the local youngsters used to go there to play pool and listen to music. Suddenly there was talk of trouble. Parents were saying that they didn't want their children going up there any more, that there was drug-taking and vandalism. Some said it had something to do with the black boys who went there – it was true that more black families had moved into the area. The upshot was that the white children stopped going there and pretty soon afterwards, for some reason, the whole place closed.

Then there were the churches – three of them suddenly went. The United Reform Church, which used to have a lot of activities for local people, shut up shop without warning and the building was sold to the Muslims for use as a

Jean's war

mosque. The Catholic church, Sacred Heart, closed down for good. Apparently, there just weren't enough people going to the place. That one was sold to the Muslims as well and it became the Grand Mosque for the whole of Leeds. And then the Hyde Park Methodist Church, on the corner of Woodsley Road and Belle Vue, closed down as well.

It felt as though her familiar world was starting to crumble at the edges. It worried her, but there was something else that worried her even more – the people. There was violence on the streets, people being mugged or stabbed or bashed. The small children wouldn't go up to Woodhouse Moor any longer. They said they were scared. Some of them wouldn't go outside at all. The old people wouldn't go out at night.

Jean couldn't understand what had happened. She would see these little gangs of youngsters hanging around the car park on Hyde Park Close, smoking and spitting and doing nothing, just looking for trouble. Jean knew most of them, the McGibbons and the Hooks and the Clarkes and the Boltons. Half of them seemed to be related to each other somehow, like some kind of clan. She couldn't help feeling there was something really wrong with them. They were only kids, some of them only 10 years old, but they'd stare right through you as if you were nothing to them, just meat.

There were drugs in Hyde Park. She'd seen the dealers selling the stuff on the pavement outside the Newlands pub, and she'd heard that there were big dealers who came down from Chapeltown to sell there.

She looked around her now and could hardly believe some of the things she saw people getting up to. She'd be sitting at home, minding her own business, and she'd suddenly hear a rush of footsteps and one of the little gangs of youngsters that hung around in the Newlands would come racing down the steps at the end of St John's Close, carrying armfuls of record players or radios or computers. They had obviously stolen them, and they used this maze of footpaths around the estate to escape. She'd be asleep at night and be woken by the sound of kids joy-riding stolen cars around the area with the engines roaring and the tyres screaming. Sometimes she'd wake up in the morning and find a car burnt out in the car park – the kids had used it and then just set it alight for fun.

Just across the road there was this young man – Chad, he called himself – who was selling drugs from his front door. Jean could see him clearly. Well, he made no attempt to hide it. Jean could see all these strangers coming up and knocking at the door and handing him money while he handed them little packets.

She got sadder and sadder at the sight of it all, but at some point she made a decision. She decided to fight back – for her children, or for her grandchildren, or just because she had always been inclined to stand up for herself and she couldn't bear to see things getting any worse.

Her fight eventually became a war between two worlds: between one that

Jean's war

believed in living in peace and harmony in a community to which everyone belonged, and another that believed in nothing. Like many other wars, it began quietly.

Jean Ashford tried to recruit reinforcements for her fight by writing a questionnaire, asking everyone in the area for new ideas to help the place. It took her a week to cover the whole patch and then only a few people replied. They had some useful thoughts: somewhere for the children to play safely; somewhere to get reliable legal advice; somewhere for black people to go. But when Jean circulated the results it all went dead.

It was disheartening but she didn't give up. She couldn't. The estate was getting worse and worse. There was an epidemic of burglary now. Jean and her friend Anne used to be on the phone to each other half a dozen times a day: 'Have you seen what they're doing now? Have a look. Quick.' The police seemed powerless. Sometimes, when they tried to drive into the estate, these kids would attack the patrol cars.

The first time the kids tried to get into Jean's house, she was sitting reading newspapers in the front room when she heard this tremendous kicking at the back door. Jean jumped up, ran to the door and let the dog out on them. She saw three or four of them running off towards Hyde Park Close, flicking V-signs and swearing over their shoulders. They were just kids, kids she knew – her neighbours.

They soon came back for another try and this time they found the house empty and took several hundred pounds' worth of things. A couple of weeks after that the youngsters were back again, and this time they took everything that was worth anything: the microwave, the old knitting machine, the TV and the video, her son's computer, her little collection of jewellery, a silver christening bracelet that had been worn by a baby daughter who had died. All gone.

One night, just as she was about to go to bed, Jean looked out of her window and saw a little gang of lads coming from Hyde Park Close and instantly she thought to herself that something bad was about to happen. The next thing she knew, there was a loud banging outside; she looked out of the window again and saw the same little gang trying to kick in the door of the neighbouring house. She rang Anne and by the time she got down into her back garden Anne's husband was already there, shouting at the lads to clear off. She saw them going off down St John's Close – not running, not worried at all that they had just been caught attempting to burgle a home, but strolling together down the road with their hands in their pockets. One of them was waving a V-sign over his head. Another turned to yell some abuse – and that was a mistake. She saw his face clearly in the streetlight and she knew it. It was Jimmy Clarke, the brother of Beverley Clarke, whom Jean used to see through her window storing stolen goods for the lads.

Jean had had enough. No one had been arrested for any of the raids on her house or anyone else's and so she called the police and told them what had

Jean's war

happened. When they asked her if she had recognised any of the boys, she told them that she had. She made a statement, naming Jimmy Clarke. The police arrested him. She agreed to give evidence. That was how the trouble started.

For a few days, it was nothing worse than glares and threats from the gangs of kids and them all hissing 'grass' when she walked by. Then came that evening when she was walking past the Newlands and was grabbed by the throat and shoved up against the wall.

She went back to the police and made another statement, describing the attack outside the Newlands. The police charged Dean Boyle with assault and gave Jean a leaflet about witness protection. It meant very little to her. She couldn't go out of her house now without walking a gauntlet of threats. When the day came for her to go to court, the police sent two men to escort her. She sat on the bench outside the courtroom and found Jimmy Clarke and his mother sitting right opposite her, muttering abuse. She gave her evidence and Clarke was convicted. He got a conditional discharge and a £50 fine. Jean told herself it might have been worth it to see justice done, but it wasn't worth it for the punishment he got.

Now it was like living in a permanent blizzard of threats and abuse. Everywhere she went, people followed her and jeered. Jimmy Clarke's mother used to cross the road to spit at her. Sometimes she'd hit her target. Jean had heard of people starting fires by shoving burning rags through people's letter boxes, so she filled a bucket with water and stationed it behind the front door, where it might catch anything that they tried to push through. She kept her key permanently in the lock on her side of the front door in case she needed to escape in a hurry.

It all made her scared. But it also made her angry. They were pushing her into a corner. Either she ran or she stayed to fight. And she didn't really know what it was about her – you might call it pride, or maybe it was just her natural stubbornness – but whatever it was, she knew she wasn't going to run anywhere just to please people like this. She decided to fight on.

Jean contacted the police and they told her that the trouble was that they were short of real evidence of the crimes these people committed. They had thought about putting in an observation vehicle to record what was going on but they knew that if they put it anywhere near Hyde Park Close or the Newlands, where all the action was, it would be spotted within hours and burnt out. So Jean agreed that they could use her spare room to watch what was going on. She knew there'd be hell to pay if anyone found out but the police made sure that they slipped in and out at night. She watched them set up their camera and she brought them cups of tea and prayed that she was doing the right thing.

She tried once more to recruit reinforcements. Once more, she failed. She wrote a leaflet, inviting all the residents to a meeting. Only six turned up. Jean

Jean's war

knew the real problem: they were afraid. These kids didn't just burgle to get money; they would break into people's houses to teach them a lesson.

Superintendent Colin Haigh arranged a big meeting at Millgarth police station in the middle of town. This time, 17 residents turned up and agreed to try to help themselves. Haigh organised a confidential hot-line so that they could phone straight through to report crime without being identified as informants.

Jean felt that they were really beginning to move now. People were finally admitting there was a problem and looking for solutions. They talked about getting new streetlights and blocking off some of the exits from the estate to make life more difficult for the thieves. They talked about finding good new tenants and organising a football team, and Jean said she would start a credit union.

A few neighbours started to show some spirit. One was a lady in her fifties who lived alone and who had watched the stolen goods going through the estate, in and out of certain houses. One afternoon, she had a couple of tots of brandy, armed herself with a can of white paint and a brush, and went out on to Hyde Park Road, where she found a wall and painted a clear and straightforward piece of information for all-comers: 'Bent Goods This Way. Second on the Left.' Even better, Jean heard rumours that, behind the scenes, the police were up to something special. The brewery which owned the Newlands suddenly decided to get rid of the landlord, whose own sons had been arrested for drugs. Everyone reckoned that it was the police who had got rid of him, that they must have put a bit of pressure on the brewery. Now, they changed the name of the pub to the Jolly Brewer and they put in a new manager, a man named Bernard Sherry, who was described in the local newspaper as being 'a former hairdresser to the stars' on *Coronation Street*. On police advice, Jean set up a crime prevention evening and symbolically chose the reformed pub, the Jolly Brewer, as the venue. It turned out to be a mistake. People told Jean they wanted to come but they'd be scared to go to the pub. She told them there'd be safety in numbers, but when she turned up at the Jolly Brewer on the evening of the meeting she had to pick her way through groups of youths hanging around outside with hoods pulled over their heads. An inspector from Millgarth came with another officer but there were only five other residents and Jean ended up apologising for inviting them in the first place.

The kids hit back, smashing the pub's windows and smashing them again as soon as they were repaired. The pub put up boards and padlocks; the kids removed them and smashed the glass again. Bernard Sherry didn't seem to worry. There were a lot of rumours about him on the estate, mostly that he was an ex-policeman and even that he was allowing the police to use the pub to spy on the kids who were still dealing drugs in the street outside.

The kids were looking sullen and angry, strutting round the car park, flicking stones at passing cars, occasionally walking round to Jean's house to lob a lump of concrete at her gable or just to stare. Jean stayed well away from them. Then

Jean's war

one night someone went into the pub and told Bernard Sherry he was needed outside. When he got there, two young men told him he was a grass and attacked him with baseball bats. They broke his wrist and several of his ribs and put him into hospital.

A few days later, Jean noticed a little pile of charred rags and burnt matches just outside her back door.

By now the police had gathered enough intelligence to act and, at six o'clock one morning, they pounced on the estate, banging on doors and rounding up 16 of the kids. They took them to Millgarth police station and charged them with a total of 70 offences – burglary, car theft, robbery, possession of drugs, intent to supply drugs. A couple of nights later, not long before midnight, the opposition hit back, and this time they went all out for victory.

Jean was just settling down in the spare room to do some paperwork before she went to bed when she heard a lot of shouting and banging. She went to the window and saw people running, people with big sticks and dustbin lids in their hands. They seemed to be coming from every corner of the estate.

She went to her telephone and called her councillor, Gerry Harper. 'There's something going off,' she told him. 'I think there's going to be a riot.' At that moment, there was a bang and a burst of flames, and Jean realised a car had exploded in the street. She heard alarm bells. Now she could see flames reaching up towards the night sky from somewhere over in the car park. Something dreadful was happening.

She heard a new sound, a steady thumping, like a jungle drum, and she realised it was the sound of sticks being beaten rhythmically against the road. There was another bang – a deep, soft whoof of a sound – and a balloon of orange light burst into the night. That was the pub. They were burning the Jolly Brewer.

The sounds of battle rumbled through the night – shouts and muffled bangs, flames crackling, sirens, footsteps running. When Jean finally ventured out the next morning, the streets of Hyde Park were littered with the burnt-out wrecks of cars. There were police on every pavement, and journalists and gawpers were wandering from house to house. And on Hyde Park Road there were fire engines still spraying water over the blackened remains of the Jolly Brewer. It was burnt to a ruin.

That morning, the Chief Constable, Keith Hellawell, reviewed the damage and warned that gangs were tearing the city apart: 'We have lost a generation who are now in their teens and are being left to their own devices.'

That night, the opposition struck again. Just before midnight, Jean looked out of her window and saw people gathered outside her house, looking towards her. There were about 30 of them, most of them young men, most of them with their hoods pulled over their heads. Some of them were shouting the usual abuse and, as she watched, they started battering at the steps at the end of St John's Close, tearing up lumps of paving stone and running back to sling

Jean's war

them at her home. They were yelling that they were going to burn down her house.

Now she was frightened. That night, the police put a van at the end of her road. On the streets the next day, every face seemed to be snarling at her. She tried to ignore them but their voices still pierced through to her. So many threats – to break her legs, to burn her home, to kill her. There were notes through her letter box. And, once again, she found burnt rags by her back door.

Three days after the burning of the pub, the streets seemed quieter. Jean was looking after one of her grandchildren, Joshua, and had arranged to meet his mother, Emma, at the bottom of Woodsley Road. She strapped the little boy into his buggy and walked quickly down St John's Close, looking directly in front of her, somehow hoping that if she saw no one, no one would see her.

As she turned into Woodsley Road, two big lads came at her. These weren't boys, these were grown men in their twenties. One of them was particularly thick-set and strong. They were swearing, hissing through clenched teeth. She tried to walk by them, pushing Joshua in front of her. One grabbed her from behind, spun her round to face him and punched her in the ribs. She tried to double up but he was already punching her again. She had one hand across her midriff, trying to protect herself, but she had to keep the other on the buggy, clutching it for fear that, if she let go, Joshua would roll off down the hill into the traffic. Now they were both punching her and screaming at her. And thrashing their heavy black boots into her shins.

Vaguely, in the background, in another world, she was aware of people walking down Woodsley Road with their shopping bags, not stopping, not doing anything to save her. Then it was over. The two men turned and disappeared into the estate. Jean stood, doubled up, one hand still on the handle of Joshua's buggy, all alone in the street full of strangers.

She couldn't go home, not like this. She turned and pushed the buggy into the butcher's shop. She knew them there. As she came through the door, she half heard a woman say something to her and she opened her mouth to tell what had happened and, finally, she started to cry.

The police said she had to go. There was no way they could guarantee her safety here any more. That afternoon, they arranged for the council to show her another house in another part of Leeds. That night, plain-clothes police guarded her home.

In the papers, the then Home Secretary, Michael Howard, was reported as visiting the ruin of the Jolly Brewer and promising that the perpetrators would be brought to justice. But everyone knew there was no chance of that. No one was going to give evidence against them. Not any more. They'd won. They were children, but not the kind of children who had once lived here, not the kind of children who played games and enjoyed life and looked forward to growing up. These children were wild and hard and impervious to pain – theirs or anyone else's.

Jean's war

Jean had lost. She had lived there for 23 years. Now she had only 24 hours to move out. When the furniture van came to take them away, it had to be protected by a police escort.

This article and the one which follows are extracts from Dark Heart: The Shocking Truth About Hidden Britain, *by Nick Davies (Chatto & Windus, £16.99).* •

11 November 1997
Nick Davies
Talking to the Hyde Park Estate's angry young men

There was no sign of anyone. There was only that pricklish sensation that someone was watching. Only at the far end of Hyde Park Close was there any obvious sign of life. There were two of them. They looked about 16, both skinny, both wearing torn trainers, dusty jeans and baggy T-shirts, the uniform of city boys. They were sitting on the pavement with their backs to a red-brick wall and their legs splayed out flat along the pavement in front of them, dangling their hands in their laps. Neither of them spoke. Both were oddly still.

They must be the ones. Along with their mates, they must be the ones who had signed the walls and smashed the windows and broken down the doors, the ones who had battered Jean Ashford and burnt down the Jolly Brewer, the ones who lobbed bricks at policemen, the kids who ran riot in Hyde Park. This was their patch. It was as if they were guarding its gateway.

Minutes passed. From down the hill to their left came a shriek like a witch in flames, and a car swung into the bottom of Hyde Park Road and roared up the hill towards them, shiny and black and very, very fast. As it came level with them, it juddered to a halt so suddenly that its rear end bucked off the ground and landed alongside the driver with the front of the car twisted round to point directly towards the two figures on the pavement. White smoke churned up around its wheels. A lad with a Spanish look about him grinned out of the driver's seat and suddenly swung the car again so that it pointed back up the hill, its engine panting.

The two on the pavement eyed him, still not moving. Then one of them spoke. 'Thought you was gonna get a Bim.' A BMW.

The Spanish boy's eyes were as bright as his smile. 'Couldn't find one,' he called.

The engine started to yell again. He flashed a grin of madness through the window of the driver's door. 'I'll go find one now.' Roaring and squealing, the

Jean's war

car leapt off up Hyde Park Road, leaving behind a bitter smell and a long, black streak in the road. The two lads shrugged and went back to their silence.

They were the ones. They sat there and life passed them by, except that every so often they got up and declared war on it, burning and burgling and spreading distress. But why would they be like that? After all, this was not one of the notoriously bad parts of the city. This was Hyde Park, in the shadow of the university.

For a while, they refused to talk. They just shook their heads and stared at the pavement or looked away and wanted nothing to do with nothing. Then one of them said something about students: 'They're the foogin' problem round here,' he muttered. 'Students! I feel like ripping all their hearts out.'

Close up, he was even thinner than he had looked in the distance. He was not very tall, probably not much more than 5ft, he had coal-black hair so short it was like a shadow on his skull, and the skin drawn tight across the bones of his face was scattered with pimples and sores. 'Foogin' students,' he went on, shaking his head in disgust. 'They throw all their rubbish out in the streets. It's not healthy. Place is full of students. They're going through the streets in big groups, 20 or 30 of them, going through the streets together. They're taking the place over. It's all right for them. Students can get good jobs. Students can get good money. You see 'em coming down here with their parents in their cars. I foogin' hate 'em.' He paused and sniffed and turned away and, for a moment, it looked as though he would say no more. Then he went on.

He said he'd lived in and around Hyde Park since he was born and he'd probably be here for the rest of his life. He'd gone to the City of Leeds School, over the other side of Woodhouse Moor. He hadn't gone to school every day, he confessed, and he had passed no exams. He had never worked. He had never done anything. He shrugged and said he had nothing to do now. That was what really got to him, he said.

'Every foogin' day is the same round here. I can't think of one thing to do all day. There's no point going to town – you need money. I wake up in the morning. Sometimes I sleep till the afternoon. I come out. I call for my mates. I just hang around, wait for something to happen. That's the only thing there is to do in this whole area. Just hang around, just be there on the street, looking trampy, then go home. Every day is the foogin' same.'

'And smoke draw.' The other one spoke for the first time. He had a younger, fleshier face, lightly decorated with pubescent fur around his throat and chin and upper lip. 'You get charged out your head and then you just chill out.' Where would they get the money to buy their draw? It was the very skinny one who answered. 'I don't sign on. I can't, not allowed to. There's no benefits for 16-year-olds. Anyway, I don't want to sign on. Don't want to crawl to a bunch of people for foogin' £30 a week. I want a job. Don't matter what it is. A packing job, mechanic, don't matter what it is, long as it brings in money. See?' He started to stab the air with his right index finger. 'I want to have a

Jean's war

job, earn some money, save it up, get a girl, have a kid. Look at me. Will you look at me? I live like a tramp. I live like a foogin' animal. Don't I?' While he was talking, he had started to crouch forward from the wall, but now he sank back again so that he and his mate looked once more like two shadows on the pavement.

What about their parents? Did they work? Did they give them money? 'They got no money. Why they gonna give me money? No foogin' way.' The furry one leaned forward and spoke thoughtfully. 'My dad works but I don't really know what he does. I don't really live with him.' He rubbed his face.

But when they were younger, did they think they'd get work? What had they wanted to be when they grew up? 'Fireman,' said the furry one with a shrug. 'I wanted to be a fireman. But I can't do it. I've got no exams. I do want to go to college, but you have to pass a test. Don't ya? I'd do anything, me. I'd just go anywhere, to stop being bored.'

His skinny mate sighed and took a plunge. 'What I want to do, what I would like to do –' he was looking upwards with his eyes half shut – 'is to go up in an aeroplane and parachute down, come down from the clouds. I want to float. I want to foogin' fly. Down from the clouds. I've always wanted to do that.' For a moment he was alive, his face flushed with excitement at the memory of his dream, no matter how far away from his real world it might be, but then in the next moment, his energy had passed and he was slumped back inside himself again. There they sat: the boy who wanted to be a fireman and ended up an arsonist; the boy who wanted to fly free and ended up . . . well, like this.

And they still hadn't answered the question. What did they do for money? 'I foogin' rob students, don't I?' He almost shouted the words, as if he was showing an idiot to his own front door. 'Whaddya think I do? Look. Listen. The only way to get them out is rob them. If they don't like it, they can fuck off.'

Four or five others had strolled out of Hyde Park Close, evidently aware that something was going on, and had gathered in a group, staring down at the two on the pavement. They were listening, checking, starting to nod, trying to butt in, starting to talk now, muttering their agreement, returning to the one great reality of daily life. There was nothing to do and nowhere to do it.

So what did they do with their time? The answer came in a chorus. 'Twocking.' Taking cars without the owners' consent. It was easy, they said. City workers left their cars in Hyde Park on the way to their offices, so they were just sitting there, waiting for twocking. Break a window. Stick a screwdriver in the ignition. Burn it up.

One of the newcomers was wearing a battered baseball cap with a dirty kangaroo on the front and every time he opened his mouth to say something, he twisted the peak from his forehead round to the back of his neck, as if this somehow turned on his speaker. Then he swivelled his peak right the way around his head to indicate that he was coming to his main point. 'It's war against the

Jean's war

law. Innit? That's what it is. Innit? War against the law. Police round here, they take the piss ... Three Sundays on the trot, they come into our place, never found nothing, never charged me wi' nothing ... They done me for drugs, right. Some draw and some Es. But they were me girlfriend's. They weren't mine, right? They say we're lowlife. They're foogin' lowlife.'

They started to vie with each other with stories of their first assaults on the law. One reckoned he had set fire to a doctor's surgery in Chapeltown when he was seven; another said he'd put bricks on a railway line to try to kill people when he was five. There was an older lad, tall and thin with curly blond hair – he looked a little like the England cricketer Michael Atherton – who spoke for the first time and, although his manner was quiet and almost bashful, the others stayed silent while he said his piece.

'We're not animals. Our houses are pleasant and tidy. I've got a family, three kids and another on the way. I'm not skint, I can afford to raise them, because I have my ways of bringing in cash. Then I see families walking together and I look at them and I think they must have a job, and I would love to be just like them – go to work in the morning, have the weekend off, live a straight life. All I want to be is a family man. All I want is to support my family legally. I've had loads of jobs. When I first left school, I installed Skysat dishes. I was on £250 a week. Then they found out I had a criminal record, so they kicked me out. I've done scaffolding, but I kept taking days off to go to court. It's like you can't get away from it.'

The lad with the hat switched on again. 'War against the law,' he announced. 'That's what it is.'

Michael Atherton said people didn't understand that they hardly ever got caught – 99 per cent of them got away with 99 per cent of what they did. 'Look at the crime rate round here. Look at the number they catch. They think they're wired. I've done 15 months for burglary. That's all I've ever done. If they do get us for something, it's only one thing. Most of what we do, they never get on to.'

A car pulled up alongside them. A thick-set lad with red hair and a black T-shirt leaned out and said hello to no one in particular. The giant in jeans stepped over and peered into his car.

'How come you've got keys in your car?'

'It's my bloody car.'

'I never seen ya with keys before.'

'Couldn't find me screwdriver, could I?'

The lad with the furry face spoke up from the pavement. It was easy, he said. Burglary was really, really easy. And it was exciting, too. 'You get hypervibes,' he said. 'Specially if you're out your head.'

Michael Atherton didn't like all that. 'We don't just rob anyone. You don't just kick down any door. People think that because we're thieves, we're evil or something. I burgled a house two weeks ago and there were a woman, she

Jean's war

started screaming. We'd put the stuff in the car in front of her house and she pulled up in her car just as we were leaving. She were screaming, cos she knew we'd taken her stuff. I felt gutted. We all felt gutted. When we drove away, everybody went quiet. I felt like saying, "Very sorry, lady, please don't cry."'

The others nodded and agreed that they had rules. Even though it was not clear that they necessarily always obeyed them, they thought they did. This was a war against the law and they were all bound by its rules. But how serious was the war? Did they have guns? If they were going to fight a war against the law, did they need guns?

Michael Atherton nodded grimly. 'They see us as thieves, that's all. They are going to get fucking shot. If I need a gun, I know where to find it. Most of us do.'

Had they taken them out on the night of the riot? 'We didn't need to,' he said, and he smiled.

Then they talked about the great victory, the burning of the Jolly Brewer. The young lad with the furry face started, sadly recalling the joys of the old pub. 'We owned the Newlands [the pub's name under its previous landlord]. It were ours. It's our area, this. It were very dark there, it had all ripped seats and no decorations. It were like an old saloon and you could go in there and do what you wanted. You could smoke a joint. Everybody were on a good vibe. You could relax. There were a pool table and a jukebox. There was some bands some times. Karaoke. It were ours.'

The lad with the hat switched on. 'We went in there and we weren't doing no one no harm. It were better than lying on the street.'

'And they banned us from the place,' the boy with the fur continued.

Then they all pitched in: 'Nobody wanted that place to get burnt down. It only happened because of the law ... The new landlord were a grass and he let the law put cameras in there. They were filming us ... This is our area. They thought they were so clever, running around at night. We saw 'em the first night they went in ... It had to happen.'

And together they described how they had reclaimed their pub by destroying it. They had planned it. It wasn't obvious who the leaders were but it was clear they had sat down and planned the assault. It had started earlier in the evening when two police cars had come on to their patch. They knew there were houses the police had raided a few days earlier where they hadn't found the people in, so everyone knew they were looking to make more arrests. So they had stoned the police cars and beaten them out of the area. But they had known it wouldn't be long before they were back with reinforcements, so they had moved in quick.

They had spread the word to get everyone there and then they had broken into all the cars that were parked around the pub and shifted them into the middle of the road as barricades, to keep out the police and the fire brigade. Once they had got the whole area sealed off, they had set fire to some of the cars and then broken into the empty pub. They had grabbed anything they

Jean's war

wanted: bottles of booze, bags of crisps. When they had taken all they wanted, a couple of them had climbed on to the lowest roof, at the side of the pub, broken a couple of windows and set fire to the curtains. From the road, they had lobbed in a couple of petrol bombs. It had gone up fast. Within minutes, they reckoned, there were flames all across the top floor. Then they had set fire to the rest of the cars in the road, and Hyde Park had belonged to them. One of them had phoned the *Yorkshire Evening Post* to tell them what was happening. Another had grabbed a video camera to record the happy occasion.

And Jean Ashford?

'She were grassing,' said the skinny lad, from the pavement. 'There's nowt worse than a grass. She were putting all this police harassment on us. She should keep her nobby little nose out. If she didn't like the area, she should have moved out.'

It was chaotic and it was violent and the rules they wanted to keep were punctured with holes, but there was a kind of logic to it all. They had no money, no excitement, no status, no skills – except what twocking and burgling gave them. If they weren't breaking the law, they could only sit inundated with inactivity, almost physically paralysed by their own boredom. This war against the law gave them an income and it gave them a purpose. It gave them heroes and villains and something to excel at. And once they were committed to waging this war, there were certain necessities that flowed from it. They had to stop the enemy spying on them and so they had commandeered road blocks and organised an assault and successfully taken out the enemy's forward position. And then they had dealt with their traitors.

But not all of it was logical. They knew that themselves. There was a kind of chaos around them that had crept inside them, as if they had been force-fed on some sort of bitter bile which eventually started to seep through them, poisoning their everyday life. It was there when the skinny lad talked about students. He wasn't just talking about students, he was talking about everybody – everybody who had everything they didn't have, the people who had qualifications and jobs and cars and houses and families and futures. The students were just the most blatant example of the world that went on without them (like the advertising hoarding in Hyde Park Road with a huge picture of a £10 note and a bank's offer of cheap loans, but only for students).

They all had their own dreams, most of them very mundane. They wanted to go to college, to get a job or simply to have something to do all day. In real life, as they readily described, there were only two things to do – thieving and twocking. They wanted much more. Their lives refused to let them have it, so they became frustrated and hopeless and bitterly angry. And they fought their war against the law with a furious rage.

The lad in the black T-shirt stirred up the engine of his car, twisted round and popped open the back door. Several of the others, including the one with the furry face, climbed in. Where were they going? No real need to ask – off to work, off to the front line. The others started to drift away, back into Hyde Park Close.

The skinny lad was still spread out on the pavement, lifeless, but suddenly he leaned forward and started to speak with a passionate intensity, as if he were warning the world: 'Things are going to start getting rough round here. Students are going to start getting killed.' He stabbed his index finger into the air. 'Look at me,' he said, after a moment, holding his palms out to each side. 'I'm 16 and I feel like foogin' killing somebody.' He covered his face with his right hand, dropped his chin on to his chest and mumbled, in a voice that was heavy with the sound of defeat, 'This area's fucked up.' •

Boom Boom '98

Eclipse of the sunrise

Eclipse of the sunrise

13 June 1998
Alex Brummer
A defining moment

The lurch of the Japanese economy into official recession, for the first time in six years, is a defining moment for the global economy. Until now, the Asian economic problem has been confined to important but second-ranking countries from Thailand to Indonesia. But while the nations of south-east Asia have sunk into the mire, the economic performance of the richest industrial countries has been bowling along, apparently impervious to events on the other side of the world.

But in the new global economy of open markets and large financial flows there is no protection from a crisis of confidence. Japan's problem is that of the United States, Britain and continental Europe. The collapse of the yen, in response to Japan's banking and economic catastrophe, could rapidly provoke a series of further devaluations across the region and rapidly lead to volatility and a dramatic setback for Western stock markets. The monetary effects of Tokyo's problems could overwhelm the actual movement of goods and services across the continents. Unless Japan takes urgent and radical action to resolve its deep-seated difficulties, its next export will not be a wide-screen digital television set or a Toshiba laptop, but a worldwide slowdown that will damage Western standards of living.

The most direct impact so far has been on Western banks and stock-market investments in Asia – but these for the moment have been felt by a professional financial community, not the broader populace. However, all our pension funds, PEPs and endowment policies will have been indirectly hurt. That may soon change. Japan is the world's second largest industrial country and what happens there will eventually impact on every other country in the world. The first ripples are being felt in Asia. The slide in the Japanese currency this week from 140 to 145 yen to the dollar, with most market operators predicting 150, is a major source of instability.

The initial round of devaluations in Asia, which began a year ago in Thailand, was partly triggered by the weakness of the yen, with the Pacific countries feeling the need to lower their exchange rate to keep their goods competitive with those of Japan. The further devaluation now will put renewed pressure on the currencies and stock markets of countries across the region, including those like Singapore, Hong Kong and even China, which have avoided the worst. The conventional wisdom has been that Beijing will stick with its current exchange rate as a matter of 'face' and because it can afford to: the overseas trade sector represents less than 20 per cent of the Chinese economy. But as Japan is China's biggest trading partner, all those assumptions are off.

Eclipse of the sunrise

The capacity of events in one part of the globalised economy to upset those in another is already being seen in Russia. The attack on the rouble in recent weeks, the collapse of the key index of Russian shares by 16.6 per cent in the last week, the failure by the authorities there to sell adequate bonds to finance government activities — even with interest rates above the 50 per cent mark — demonstrate how easily the contagion spreads.

The severity of the problem in Japan cannot be underestimated. Although the Prime Minister, Ryutoro Hashimoto, has won support within his own party for an expansion package which is due to deliver growth, this will not begin to be implemented until July. Moreover, fiscal policy is notoriously slow to work its magic and Tokyo's hopes of restoring growth by the end of this year look remote. The financial sector of the economy is in deep difficulty, with several of the big banks technically insolvent, with the latest focus on the Long Term Credit Bank. Many of the companies the West has come to associate with Japan's business acumen, including Nissan, Mitsubishi Motors and Toshiba, have become loss-makers in the last year. Unemployment has reached a post-war high of 4.1 per cent and will climb further as the shake-out in the banking and construction industries intensifies.

Given the current crisis, Japanese companies are seeking to export their way out of difficulty. Local markets have collapsed because of the difficulties in Korea, Indonesia and Thailand, which means Japanese exporters are looking to Europe and North America. In the short run, this may help to ease the pain. But it is a dead-end strategy. The European Union already has strict agreements on Japanese motor exports to Europe, as does the US.

Nevertheless, overall exports to the US are soaring — fuelled by US domestic growth — in a development that is already leading to a rise in the American trade deficit with Japan and a sharply deteriorating US balance of payments position. As Japanese goods flood the US markets, the Clinton administration can be expected to face increasing protectionist pressure from Congress and there will be pressure on the US authorities to tighten policy, so as to deal with the trade imbalances. Moreover, the rebuilding of the Japanese banking system could have repercussions for the rest of the industrial countries, as American and European banks take defensive action to protect their loans in the country. •

....

6 December 1997
Andrew Higgins
Betrayal of the salaryman

In front of electronic panels flashing orange-coloured numbers cracks the calm of the salaryman, dispirited foot soldier of an economic empire in retreat. The figures, on display in Tokyo's financial district, relate not to the collapsing

Eclipse of the sunrise

share prices of Japan's brittle banks but to something far more fundamental – 18-hole golf courses.

The figures are provided by Eagle Golf, a broker of country-club memberships just down the corridor from a branch of the defunct Yamaichi Securities. They signal Japan's economic malaise. The prices of what were a fail-safe investment and status symbol are in a nose dive.

'The price keeps going down. Nothing goes up any more,' groaned Masami Fukushima, a life insurance manager and weekend golfer. 'The golden age of the golf club is over. It is finished.'

Like legions of other salarymen, Mr Fukushima splashed out during the 'baberu' or bubble-boom of the 1980s to buy a club membership. For 3.9 million yen (£18,000) he secured the right to drive out of Tokyo each weekend and fork out £150 in green fees for a round of golf. It was, he calculated, a sure-fire investment. His membership is now worth only 500,000 yen – less than 10 per cent of its peak value of 7 million. The price, set by brokers, has halved in a fortnight.

The despair of Japan's golfers reveals the rotten core of its economy and helps explain why its financial system is groaning under the weight of bad debts officially calculated at more than $200 billion (£135 billion), but thought to be far higher.

The immediate cause for gloom is the death of Yamaichi Securities. A string of banks has gone under and others will follow. Foreign deposit-takers report brisk business as Japanese shift money into what they hope are safer hands.

The roots of the crisis lie in a failure to control the boom or deal with the bad debts that have built up since the bubble burst. The air has gone out of the inflated assets that once made Japan feel so rich – and the rest of the world shudder – as Japanese went on a shopping spree, snatching New York's Rockefeller Center, chunks of Hollywood and symbolic foreign properties, such as the former headquarters of the Greater London Council. The calculations based on bubble-era prices are finally coming unstuck. In Ohtemachi, Tokyo's answer to the City, bookshops hawk self-help crisis primers and how-to bankruptcy guides. The bombast of boom-era tracts has given way to self-flagellation. Typical of the mood is a collection of essays, *Vanishing Japan*, and *Lazy Japanese*. For bankers seeking solace there is *The Sun Will Definitely Rise Again*.

Japan as a stumbling shadow is as alarming as the old caricature of an omnivorous Godzilla. It remains a potent force, but perceptions matter, particularly those of the Japanese themselves.

Amid the hype about Asia's tigers it was forgotten that Japan was the powerhouse. Its banks' loans, of $250 billion, dwarfed the $40 billion from the US.

Asian countries conquered by Japan during the Second World War face the prospect of a Japan in retreat. At a meeting last month of the Asia Pacific Economic Forum, prime minister Ryutoro Hashimoto said Japan could no longer

Eclipse of the sunrise

act as the region's 'locomotive'. Tokyo's Export-Import Bank this week said, 'Japanese investments in Asia have peaked.'

The old confidence has gone and there are fears that a more inward-looking Japan could mutate Asia's sickness into a global contagion. A sign of the virus spreading would be any move by Japanese banks and institutions to unload their $210 billion of US treasury bonds.

So important is Japan to the world economy that a wrong step could bring catastrophe. During a visit to Tokyo this week, the head of the International Monetary Fund, Michel Camdessus, spoke exuberantly about the travails of South Korea, Russia and Indonesia. Asked about Japan, though, he referred repeatedly to notes, measuring his words.

Japan is now ablaze with unanswered distress signals. A central pillar of Japan Inc. is under threat — the certainty that the state will prevail and ultimately provide. The shock is as much psychological as economic. Many now feel betrayed. The suicide rate among white-collar workers has risen by 16 per cent as the pressures of uncertainty mount.

'We were all educated in the value of loyalty to the company,' said Yoshikazu Ishikawa, a sacked manager. 'But we are losing this loyalty because the company betrays it.' So embarrassed are many job-seekers that they approach the eleventh-floor Tokyo Talent unemployment office as if entering a pornographic peepshow.

The question now is just how far insolvent banks and brokerages will be left to fend for themselves. Mr Hashimoto's government has already made clear it is pressing for taxpayers' money to be used to compensate customers.

While Eagle Golf struggled this week to sell country club memberships that nobody wants to buy, a branch manager of Yamaichi Securities was presiding over the wreckage of his career and, he said, his life. He laboured to keep up appearances, posting two staff at the door to greet customers with deep bows and numbered slips to fix their place in a queue of people eager to get their money back. It was a very orderly wake. 'The customers don't get angry with us. We often even get their sympathy,' said manager Noriaki Kohama. 'But I've lost my job. I have no future now. I feel very angry and very sad. The thing I care about most has gone.' •

30 May 1998
Nick Cumming-Bruce
Net closes on Suharto

The troops, tanks and barbed-wire barricades that guarded Jakarta's Grand Hyatt Hotel against rampaging mobs have gone, but the threat to the Suharto family's interest in one of the capital's ritziest hotels may be just beginning.

Eclipse of the sunrise

In a modest bungalow a mile away, a dozen lawyers and economists are working on a strategy to unravel the vast web of businesses and privileges amassed by former President Suharto's family and cronies during three decades of power.

'We will gather information from the public on everything,' Albert Hasibuan, a newspaper proprietor and member of the national human rights commission who leads the group, promises. His self-styled Commission of Concerned Citizens on State Assets will try to pull together a case for legal action. 'We will deliver this information to the attorney-general's office,' he says.

Only a week after the president resigned and before the group has even advertised its existence, faxes and letters are rolling in with details of alleged financial abuses by the former first family. One says the Grand Hyatt, part-owned by one of Mr Suharto's sons, has not paid taxes, courtesy of a 10-year exemption.

After the mob fury that targeted businesses identified with the Suhartos and their cronies, politicians and reformists are taking up the demand for retribution in a city where even street-corner child vendors are hawking photocopies of a list of the Suharto family's businesses.

'Everybody thinks this wealth should return where it belongs, to the people of Indonesia,' argues Yusuf, a student who took part in the occupation of parliament. 'We understand the Suharto wealth is very large and if we gather it back we may be able to pay off all our debts,' chimes in Sakyanata, an economics student. 'I want to see Suharto on trial.'

Mr Hasibuan's is only one of a series of investigations into businesses that control a huge slice of national wealth. 'In 1965 there was a purging of communists,' says one finance company executive, alluding to the bloody upheavals that brought Mr Suharto to power. 'In 1998 there will be a purge of first-family interests.'

'It's a way of achieving national reconciliation, it's going to become a very big issue and take a very long time,' says Bruce Rolph of Bahanna Securities. 'It goes right to the heart of what has happened in Indonesia and implicates a lot of important people.'

A minister for investment has promised to examine the tax breaks handed out to companies linked to the Suharto family. Far more sensitive is the promise by Indonesia's state oil and gas company, Pertamina, to cut away the web of corruption. Its management reveals that at least 120 companies among its suppliers and contractors are owned by the Suharto family and associates, a statistic that hardly begins to expose how the old autocrat's relatives fed on one of the financial arteries now keeping Indonesia's stricken economy alive.

Two of Mr Suharto's sons, Tommy and Bambang, had stakes in two companies that were allocated Pertamina's crude oil for export. Even their oil industry interests are only a fragment of the assets acquired by a family that in latter years was avidly courted by foreign corporations and banks. Michael Backman, an author, says he has identified 1,247 separate, active companies in which Suharto family members have significant shares.

But as the investigation gathers momentum, investigators may find they are heading into a financial, legal and political minefield. The queues that trailed this week from branches of Bank Central Asia, owned by a crony and two Suharto sons, reveal one of the problems. The rush of customers, some waiting three hours to retrieve the maximum allowed of about £30, marks a collapse of confidence that spells doom for what was Indonesia's biggest private bank. Like much of the rest of Indonesian business, many family enterprises are technically bust. Asset hunters will also have to pick their way through a web of companies and deals that on paper are legitimate. More difficult may be the decision how far to pursue the paper trail. Mr Suharto's business culture rewarded a wide circle of people. His successor, President Jusuf Habibie, was prominent among them.

Mr Hasibuan is under no illusions about the scale or sensitivity of the task ahead, yet he seems undaunted. Inquiries will focus not just on Mr Suharto's family and ministers but on those in the government who replaced him, he insists. 'Mr Habibie is on the list,' he confirms, adding bluntly, 'By investigating this we hope we can bring the president down.' •

....

21 March 1998
Alex Bellos
'The flames are huge like sails – an ecosystem is being destroyed'

The smell of burning fills the air. The sky is a white haze of smoke. 'Fire is coming,' says the Yanomami Indian, pointing into the distance, 'and we are afraid.'

Less than five miles away the jungle is ablaze. Plumes of smoke rise from the jungle canopy, making the normally lush horizon look like a line of factory chimneys. An entire ecosystem is being destroyed, and as the inferno gradually encroaches on the Yanomami reservation it is threatening the world's largest Stone Age tribe.

'We are afraid the animals will leave – the monkeys and deer,' says the Yanomami man, whose name, in his native language Ninah, is never revealed outside his tribe. Surrounded by members of his tribe at the Mucajai river, he adds, 'If they go we will have nothing to eat. We will die.'

Elders in neighbouring settlements had already started a sacred ceremony, he

Eclipse of the sunrise

said, only performed in the face of environmental catastrophe: snorting the hallucinogenic bark of the virola tree and entering a trance.

'We would do it here,' he said, 'but the man who knew the ritual died two years ago. All we can do here is hope for rain.'

The primary rainforest has never caught fire before because it is normally too wet, according to environmental experts. But it has not rained for three months, and the forest's edges are catching alight from one of the region's largest ever savannah fires, which is affecting up to 20,000 square miles. Although specialised firefighters have arrived from Argentina and the Brazilian army has sent reinforcements, the fires are not expected to be extinguished until the arrival of the rains, forecast for mid-April. Much of the blaze is in inaccessible areas and, surprisingly, Brazil lacks an airborne fire service.

'We lost control of this thing a long time ago,' the fire brigade captain, Kleber Gomes Cerquinho, said.

There are as yet no accurate figures of how much rainforest has been destroyed. Flying over the area, a front of smouldering forest can be seen at least 10 miles into the Yanomami reservation – only a few miles from the settlement on the other side of the Mucajai river. The wind appears to be moving the front deeper into the forest. As far as the eye can see, smoke billows out from under the canopy. The flames have turned tree leaves and branches an autumnal orangy brown. Through the branches one can see that all the vegetation on the ground has been destroyed, leaving a mat of black ash. Occasionally there are glimpses of small flames.

'This is very bad. The fire is burning the base of the trees. A lot are dying, so next year there will be more burning and it will be worse. You have started a process in motion which will destroy the whole forest,' said Professor Philip Fearnside of the independent Institute for Amazonian Research (INPA).

In January the fires were already out of control, and the Roraima state government declared a state of emergency. Yet farmers are still burning their land, despite television broadcasts telling them to stop. Only the outermost Yanomami villages are threatened as yet, accounting for a small percentage of the 20,000 Indians who live on a reservation the size of Portugal which stretches over the border into Venezuela. This year's savannah fire is believed to be the worst in almost a century. It is the combined result of a dry season prolonged by the El Niño weather phenomenon, strong winds and settlers burning their land. Farmers scorch land to clear it and because the ash is a useful fertiliser. The government estimates that 12,000 cattle have died and 15,000 families have been seriously affected. Near the village of Apiau, 50 miles south of the state capital Boa Vista, the fire has ruined many livelihoods.

Fernando de Oliveira was in his hammock when he heard a crackling sound. He found the forest at the end of his land in flames. Half an hour later his three-hectare plot of pasture was burnt. 'I've never seen anything like that in

Eclipse of the sunrise

my 37 years here,' he said. A day later, his land is black, polka-dotted with white ash strips.

His neighbour a few miles away shows the burnt bones of one of his cattle. Jaci Viera da Costa also lost all his cash crops – banana and cashew – as well as pasture land. His wife, Maria Elena, says the fires are all around them. 'At night the mountains look like an illuminated city. There are huge flames like sails.' Their 35 remaining cattle now graze 10 miles away. They are trying to replant the banana trees but it will be at least two years before life for them and their 10 children will be back to normal. 'I have lost everything,' Mr Da Costa says. 'My dream has been destroyed.'

From Apiau, a small village of 346 people, the sun cannot be seen through the haze until late afternoon. About 10 per cent of the local people have already moved away. Ten a day are turning up at the health post complaining of tiredness, headaches and breathing problems. The latest casualty, three-year-old Queriaz da Silva, was suffering badly. Her abdomen shook as her lungs took fast, short breaths. She pointed for the nurse to the places that hurt: her throat, head and back. Nurse Jurasy Maxima de Sousa said the village did not even have an inhaler. They had made a request to the state government weeks ago, but none had turned up.

In her corner shop Maria Reis said, 'The fires have destroyed everything in the area. The summer just never ends.' •

18 April 1998
Martin Woollacott
Unmasking tyranny

When the American correspondent Janet Flanner reported on the Nuremberg Tribunal, she could find no meaning in the proceedings that could be properly related to the enormous crimes before the court. The defendants were ridiculously preoccupied with internal quarrels over status, although occasionally united in sniggering over some supposed triumph by their lawyers, and those lawyers were in turn obsessed with upholding the niceties of legal codes which Germany had for years happily deformed and violated. They were, Goering apart, a trivial bunch. Nobody less likely to be able to answer the question of why those crimes had been committed could be imagined, except for the fact they had committed them.

Hitler, of course, was not there. But even had he been before the court, it still seems unlikely that 'answers' would have been available. Hannah Arendt famously did find a kind of answer to the Nazi enigma at the Eichmann trial in Israel, but it was an answer that took as its starting point the accused's lack of understanding and responsibility, except in the narrowest bureaucratic sense.

Eclipse of the sunrise

It is not the case, therefore, that the death of Pol Pot, which now seems pretty conclusively confirmed, and his 'escape' from the trial that was apparently being prepared for him, has cheated the world of a great source of enlightenment on what happened in Cambodia. He himself, in occasional remarks, spoke almost lightly of the killings as 'mistakes', and put down the failure of the Cambodian revolution to the Vietnamese, the historical enemies.

Could the tyrant have explained the nature of the tyranny? It is possible that, in court, the contrast between the public Pol Pot, a man of some charm and even humour, and the private man, who was both vindictive and cruelly schematic, would have been pointed up. But would that unmasking, had it taken place, do much to explain why Cambodian society entered a period of savage self-destruction after Khmer Rouge troops took the capital in 1975?

It is worth remembering that the actions of the Khmer Rouge then came as a surprise to many who afterwards wondered why they had not known better. They included some of the US diplomats and soldiers who, 23 years ago this spring, were talking, amazingly, of a coalition government in which both the Khmer Rouge and non-communist politicians would figure, or at least of a 'controlled solution' – an orderly transfer of power in the capital, honourable arrangements for the disarming of government troops, handover of the Central Bank and so forth. What ignorance and madness! Not much later, Phnom Penh had been emptied and every officer the Khmer Rouge could lay their hands on massacred. As for the Central Bank, its doors were soon to swing back and forth in the same wind which blew the now useless banknotes up and down deserted boulevards.

Those deceiving themselves also included some of the politicians who stayed on, a few in expectation that they might indeed have a role, others in the hope that they would at least survive. And they included many of the journalists, who knew unpleasant truths about the Khmer Rouge but, in anger at American war-making, tended nevertheless to romanticise the bare-chested fighters in the paddy fields.

A quarter of a century later, everybody does know better, thanks to the work of scholars like Ben Kiernan, David Chandler and Michael Vickers, to the reflections of rueful reporters like Sydney Schanberg, and to the testimony of Cambodians like Someth May and Dith Pran.

But the essence of what was then misunderstood bears restating. It was the power of ideas over people, the triumph of theory over flesh and blood. The simplified version of Maoism, already itself half-baked, which Pol Pot and his top men thought they were putting into practice in Cambodia, easily transmuted into a campaign of racial purification. All but the true full-blood Khmers, physically untainted by Thai, Vietnamese or Chinese genes, and mentally untouched by poisonous foreign notions, were to be purged, at which point a huge multiplication of national energy and power would be achieved, along with economic self-sufficiency and the defeat of Cambodia's enemy-neighbours.

Eclipse of the sunrise

The reporters vaguely thought they were faced with a would-be inclusive 'common front' national movement – something not too different from what they believed they saw in Vietnam – when what was coming down the road was a peasant blood-and-soil movement led by men at ease neither in the real peasant society of their parents or grandparents, nor in the little urban world of post-colonial Cambodia. When they put their fantasies into practice, real men and women died in their hundreds of thousands.

The leaders of this terrible campaign are, many of them, still with us. They include Ieng Sary, one of the Khmer Rouge's three founding figures, who defected to the government two years ago, and has even founded a political party, and such lesser men as Ke Pauk, a more recent defector, reckoned to be responsible for slaughtering the Cambodian Muslim community. They may soon include Ta Mok, leader of the Khmer Rouge rump, said to be negotiating with Hun Sen, the former Khmer Rouge commander who has run Cambodia since he tipped out his co-premier, Prince Ranariddh, last July.

And some of the ordinary men and women who ran their own private reigns of terror within the larger terror also survive. They were the back-country peasants who had all their teeth capped with gold once they achieved a certain position within the Khmer Rouge structure, interspersing their enjoyment of new privileges with regular sessions of torture and execution of which the victims were the 'New People' from the towns. That they eventually often became victims, either of Khmer Rouge witch-hunts or of that government's inhuman demands, or, after the Vietnamese invasion of 1979, of those they had terrorised, does not excuse their participation. What explains it, in part, was the horrendous division in Cambodian society, made deeper still by war and US bombing, between town and country. It was as if Cambodia resembled one of those binary bombs where two chemicals combust once acid eats away the partition between them.

With or without a Pol Pot trial, we understand enough about Cambodia to sense some connections between its pathology and that apparent in places like Serbia, Bosnia and Algeria. The Cambodia of Year Zero, seen at the time as a communist movement gone wrong, was more to do with a weirdly unrealistic form of regressive nationalism, combining the purification theories of its leaders with the anger and alienation of a largely rural population to produce terrible results. Although every case is different, and the world does move on, similar things can happen again, or are happening. It is an indication of how little, still, we know about these destructive forces that Bosnia and Algeria were almost as much surprises as Cambodia was in 1975. •

Eclipse of the sunrise

11 June 1998

Ian Traynor

Swiss were 'in grip of Nazis'

Switzerland's blemished wartime reputation suffered another blow yesterday when an American-Jewish investigation uncovered evidence of rampant anti-Semitism pervading all levels of wartime Swiss society and of a hushed-up government scheme to keep Jewish refugees out of the country. In a report that accused Switzerland of pandering to home-grown Nazi sympathisers – and triggered extremely angry denials from the Swiss government – the Los Angeles-based Simon Wiesenthal Centre also alleged that Swiss neutrality was all but notional during the Second World War since the country was in the grip of dozens of public or clandestine racist and anti-Semitic organisations.

'They practised no neutrality whatsoever,' said the author of the 128-page report, US historian Alan Schom. 'The extraordinary variety and number of associations and societies in Switzerland representing the extreme right – patriotic, fascist or both – during the Hitlerian era is most striking,' said the report, released yesterday in New York following exhaustive research in the Swiss national archives.

Such claims follow 18 months of revelations about the scale of collaboration between the Swiss banks and Nazi Germany. The debate has punctured the Swiss myth that they resisted Nazi pressure, and has led to a sober appraisal of the role of the national bank in selling and dealing in gold looted by the Nazis from Holocaust victims and Axis-occupied countries.

But the Swiss are now bridling at further attacks on their war record, which they feel they have done more than most to come to terms with. In an unusually heated reaction to the report's claims, the Swiss president and foreign minister, Flavio Cotti, rejected the allegations as 'untenable and perfidious'. 'This report insults an entire generation. It also defames the current Swiss authorities,' he declared yesterday.

Contradicting Swiss government assertions that Nazi sympathisers constituted a negligible minority during the war, the report said the country was saturated by organised anti-Semites. Mr Schom said there were around 40 such clubs and secret societies operating in more than 160 Swiss towns and cities. 'The Swiss were always for the Germans,' Mr Schom told US television. 'They thought the Germans were going to win the war.'

Yesterday's report highlighted the wartime government's dealings with the Swiss Fatherland Association, an obscure but powerful anti-Semitic and nationalist organisation of top businessmen and senior army officers which lobbied the government to keep out Jewish refugees.

On the fiftieth anniversary of the war's end, three years ago, the Swiss govern-

Eclipse of the sunrise

ment apologised for turning back tens of thousands of Jewish refugees during the war. It had also admitted some 27,000.

Yesterday's report said that Eduard von Steiger, the Swiss police and justice minister during the war, met anti-Semitic leaders secretly and repeatedly to co-ordinate plans for keeping out Jewish refugees. Citing Swiss minutes of the meetings in 1942 and 1943, the Wiesenthal Centre reported that Steiger assured the Fatherland Association that the government had decided on a 'fundamental slowing' of refugee admissions and asked the racists to tone down their anti-immigration rhetoric since government policy was quietly but effectively producing the results they wanted. Steiger insisted that the meetings and the policy be kept secret, the minutes record. He assured the lobbyists that 'more severe measures are in place against refugees at the border', but the association officials pushed for a more explicitly anti-Semitic propaganda offensive from the government, telling Steiger that 'whether one likes it or not, this is a question of race'. Steiger was quoted as telling the racists that a small number of Jewish refugees had to be admitted to prove the problems of living with foreign Jews.

While the steady drip-feed of revelations emerging in the past two years, mainly from US investigations, has focused on Switzerland's role, Ignatz Bubis, Germany's Jewish leader, said there had to be closer scrutiny of banks in Britain and the US too, because of their profiteering at the expense of Holocaust victims. 'It is emerging that there were accounts in Britain too, the same as in Switzerland, of Jews who sought to flee Germany but didn't survive. The British state cashed in these accounts,' he claimed. •

8 November 1997
David Beresford
Mandela's greatness lies in making a dream come true

A colleague who knows Nelson Mandela fairly well confided recently that the great man seemed to be going through what might be described as a late-life crisis, suffering angst about the meaning of his life. It is difficult to imagine a man adored by most of the planet, who played midwife to the birth of a nation, wondering what his life is about.

In a curious way I feel close to Mr Mandela, not as a journalist, but as a humorist. I have just escaped the burden of a weekly satirical column that has been running for three years in the *Guardian*'s sister newspaper in Johannesburg, the *Mail & Guardian*. 'Dear Walter' was an imitation of *Private Eye*'s 'Dear Bill' letters, addressed to Walter Sisulu, Mr Mandela's former aide, who now lives in retirement in Soweto.

Eclipse of the sunrise

The column started in the week of Mr Mandela's presidential inauguration. Several friends pleaded with me not to go ahead with it. 'Mandela's a saint; you can't make him a figure of fun,' they said. Rationalising that I would not be making fun of Mr Mandela but of those around him, I went ahead. Judging by the protests when I tried to stop it on previous occasions, and the brief appearance of an anthology on local best-seller lists before it sold out, it did not offend sensibilities.

Mr Sisulu was apparently a fan and Mr Mandela, asked by a cabinet minister what he thought of the column, replied cryptically, 'I draw political conclusions from it.'

Inevitably, after spending so much time writing about a man's life, one puzzles over his character. Recently I attended a lunch with the Chilean playwright Ariel Dorfman, author of *Death and the Maiden*, and was struck by his awe when he spoke of Mr Mandela. Intrigued by such hero-worship from a writer of political sophistication, I asked him what makes Mr Mandela great. He looked bewildered at the question.

Mr Mandela's reputation is one that is open to attack. His conduct of his family life seems to have been fairly disastrous. He trained as a lawyer, but gossip at the South African Bar says he was no great shakes at lawyering. He was the 'Black Pimpernel' but got caught, which is a no-no for pimpernels. He was commander of the African National Congress's military wing, but that was one of the world's less successful guerrilla armies and it certainly had not achieved much by the time of Rivonia. There was, of course, his glorious statement from the dock at the Rivonia trial – that sent him to Robben Island – but it remains unclear to what extent it was a collaborative effort.

Mr Mandela's reputation flowered during his time in prison. But it has continued to grow since his release, without any evidence of political talent other than a dogged pursuit of reconciliation. For a 'great democrat', he does not show much regard for the popular will. His loyalty to cabinet colleagues in the face of incompetence and scandal raises questions about his political judgement.

The 'Dear Walter' letters were, as I originally intended, more about the characters who crossed Mr Mandela's path. But the reaction of the characters to the man himself conjured up a picture of Mr Mandela which, it often struck me, was reminiscent of Chauncy Gardener, the hero of that work of comic genius *Being There*, by Jerzy Kosinski.

Chauncy, portrayed by Peter Sellers in the film of the same name, is a gardener who was adopted by a rich man as a child and spent his life in a mansion where television brought him his only 'knowledge' of the outside world. The rich man dies and Chauncy is cast into the street. Stumbling through life making enigmatic utterances, he is mistaken for a man of great profundity and the story ends with Chauncy heading for the presidency of the United States.

Mr Mandela, of course, is not the empty vessel that was Chauncy Gardener.

Eclipse of the sunrise

He is an intelligent man, but he is no philosopher king. He is an endearing man, but there are many of that ilk. He is, in the final analysis, a great man not because of his innate qualities but as the expression of the wishes of a people. Like Chauncy, he is the creation of the collective imagination – specifically, an expression of national identity deeply desired in a bitterly divided country. In fact it goes further, because the adulation he draws from the world reflects the wish to overcome the racism that has been such a blight on this century – to realise the dream of a community of mankind.

If President Mandela is feeling angst, he can perhaps take comfort from the thought that no life can be more meaningful than one which gives expression to such a dream. •

....

15 May 1998
Leader
Time to treat the gangrene of Third World debt

There is no greater sore on the conscience of the world than its procrastination in the face of the crippling debt problems of the Third World and sub-Saharan Africa in particular. Even after reading the harrowing experiences and statistics we have published this week as part of our series 'The New Slavery', it is still difficult to really comprehend the mindless depredation that lies behind them. That is why the *Guardian* is backing debt forgiveness as a vital campaign for the millennium. How can we really know what it is like to be an impoverished peasant working for most of the year to clear off part of the interest payments on international debts you will never be able to pay back and which were often incurred by former regimes siphoning off much of the fruits for themselves? We can read the bald statistics – developing countries' debts to the West have soared from $600 billion (£370 billion) in 1980 to $2.2 trillion today – without

Eclipse of the sunrise

being fully able to grasp the human tragedy behind them. We have reported many instances of failed economies – but the 'success' stories are mortifying as well. Like Guyana, which, 10 years into an IMF programme, has earned plaudits from that organisation for paying back $1.7 billion to its creditors, yet without managing to repay any of the capital, leaving 45 per cent of the population below the poverty line. If this is success, spare us the failures.

The reasons poor countries developed this financial gangrene are still debated and are not necessarily relevant to a solution. In the 1970s they were encouraged by the West to borrow recycled oil money at variable rates of interest which were subsequently to rocket skywards. They soon became sucked into a vicious spiral – forced to pay ever-increasing interest payments out of collapsing commodity prices, an explosive situation aggravated by civil strife, corrupt or inexperienced governments and the consequences of famine. To add insult to injury, hardly any Western countries came remotely near their UN commitment to channel 0.7 per cent of GDP to developing nations as aid. The statistics of Africa almost beggar belief. While the West improved its living standards year in and year out, most countries in sub-Saharan Africa are worse off in real terms than when they got independence 30 years ago. For years, despite impoverishment, they were forced to pay more in interest to the West than they received in trade and other flows – a cure equivalent to treating haemophiliacs by demanding more blood.

In recent years there have been tentative signs of improvement. Africa's economy grew by 5.2 per cent in 1996 and the deterioration to 3.7 per cent last year was partly due to the exceptional drought in North Africa. Even so there is no chance at all of Africa being able to repay its debts. It is now vital that the yoke is lifted. This week's Group of Eight meeting in Birmingham – at which supporters of Jubilee 2000 (backed by the *Guardian*) plan to hold hands in a human chain around the building where the meeting is taking place – must agree an immediate solution. To be fair, the West has been trying to get its act together, but at an agonisingly slow pace and without universal commitment. The 1996 Highly Indebted Poor Countries initiative at least provides a framework. But its target of reducing debt repayments to 25 per cent of export earnings is far too modest (why not 10 to 15 per cent?) and the timescale of up to six years to satisfy the IMF is ludicrously onerous. (Compare that with the way the Maastricht criteria were fudged for candidate members of EMU.) There are other interesting initiatives, like the way Britain's Export Credits Guarantee Department organises sales of a developing country's debt in order to liberate funds for productive investment in the debtor country. But none of them will have an impact on the scale required.

What is needed, as Jubilee 2000 advocates, is a Big Bang of debt repayment comparable to the historic ones of recent history (like post-war Germany and America's forgiveness of British debt in the 1930s). Sure, there are big problems. Like where do you draw the line? What do you do about 'good' countries which

Eclipse of the sunrise

have worked their way out of trouble? And what do you do about undemocratic, despotic countries like Nigeria which have indigenous wealth of their own (oil) and who have squandered past wealth and might do the same again? The answer is that the underserving poor of Nigeria have as much right to be free of debt repayment as any other country but in future distributions must be targeted on life's essentials – water, health and education – and monitored so they aren't hijacked by corrupt politicians and administrators. It may be impractical to link debt write-offs to moves towards more democracy, but at least improved education ought to hasten the process.

Debt forgiveness should also be accompanied by increased international coordination to track down the astonishing sums of money that have been siphoned off from past aid by corrupt politicians, businessmen and administrators. Morgan Guaranty Trust estimates that no less than $198 billion disappeared from 18 developing countries during the 1980s, of which $31 billion was deposited in secret American bank accounts (and much of the rest, doubtless, in Swiss accounts).

Debt relief has humanitarian motives (though these should not be exaggerated since a lot of the debt has no possibility of being repaid). But it is also self-interested from the West's point of view. Debt relief would give a much needed stimulus to the stuttering recovery apparent even in the sub-Saharan region. Increased economic growth would be good for intra-African trade and also for the West, which would have enlarged export opportunities. The G8 nations have talked about debt reduction for years without producing a solution that matches the scale of the problem. Now is their chance to escape from their talking-shop image. And there is no more suitable place to start than Birmingham, which had a leading role in Britain's industrial revolution two centuries ago. Let it now be the place where Africa gets a helping hand. •

19 February 1998
Maggie O'Kane
The pitiful victims

There is a new weapon in the Western powers' line-up against the Iraqi dictator, Saddam Hussein. It is not as high-tech as the stealth bomber, it lacks the punch of the cruise missile and it can be seen only under a microscope. Travelling on the back of the female sand-fly, it strikes hardest in the spring.

On the second floor of al-Qadisiya hospital on the outskirts of Baghdad, the children's ward has on show some of the collateral damage from this new microscopic weapon. Kena Azar is six months old and wrapped up so only his head is peeping from a pink and cream blanket. The parasite moved first into

Eclipse of the sunrise

his bone marrow, to eat the cells that make his blood, and now it has taken over his liver and spleen. He is sleeping easily, for this parasite kills without pain.

The hospital, with its scruffy foam mattresses, battered metal beds and grubby sheets, does not have the pentostan medicine that Kena needs to help his six-month-old body fight. 'He has a 10 per cent chance of living. Before the sanctions and with the medicine, it would have been 90 per cent,' says the consultant, Dr Alia Sultan.

In the 1960s leishmaniasis, known as the 'black plague', was common in Iraq. Now it's back. A shortage of insecticides (banned under United Nations sanctions) and the collapse of the sanitation system with the absence of spare parts (because of the sanctions) have seen the sand-fly flourish again.

In the bed beside Kena lies Saleema Jura's second-born child, who is recovering from gastroenteritis, the most common infection in Iraqi children, caused by bad sanitation. Ms Jura, aged 30, calls the doctor over and begs him gently to help her eldest son, Ali, aged four, who is at home. She shows a piece of paper with the name of another unobtainable medicine. 'Please help me, if there is anything I can give to my baby. He was walking and talking and everything, then he got this infection and now he can't move his legs or speak any more.'

Dr Sultan explains that Ali has a viral infection of the brain that is untreatable in Iraq. 'He needs physiotherapy, speech therapy, things we don't have any more.'

As the doctor walks away Ms Jura turns suddenly and says, 'You can tell all those people abroad that Ali really was talking and playing. Then all of a sudden he got this and I have nothing to give him. That is what your people have done to my child.'

The economic-sanctions weapon, used for the past seven years in the belief that it will compel President Saddam to comply with UN resolutions on disarmament, has led to a sixfold increase in infant mortality, according to the UN Children's Fund (Unicef).

A study last year by the Harvard medical group put the number of Iraqi children dead or ill because of sanctions at half a million. In 10 out of 15 beds in this children's ward at al-Qadisiya hospital – just one of Baghdad's 12 hospitals – at least half are here because of sanctions.

There is despair in this hospital, absolute despair. Dr Ali Rasim, aged 32, the paediatrician on the ward, says, 'I have watched children dying here from renal failure because we didn't have sodium bicarbonate – that's baking soda.'

In the premature delivery suite, the incubators are patched with sky-blue supermarket bags, there are no bulbs in the incubators' overhead lights and a mother is holding an oxygen tube, as thick as a pencil, under the nose of her 3lb baby who has a head the size of an apple.

'There are no oxygen masks left for the babies, and these are the thinnest tubes we have,' says Dr Rasim, almost apologetically.

Britain and the United States continue to be the strongest supporters of economic sanctions and all that comes with them – now, the rebirth of the sand-fly and her black plague.

'I am a soldier without a weapon,' says Dr Rashid, the hospital's consultant paediatrician. •

20 February 1998
Robin Cook
Saddam is to blame

Kofi Annan arrives in Baghdad today. He carries with him all our hopes for peace. None of us wants to use force. We would gladly stand our military down if we could find a peaceful and workable agreement with Saddam Hussein. We are keeping the door to peace open as wide as possible for as long as we can.

Maggie O'Kane told the story in yesterday's *Guardian* of Kena Azar, a six-month-old Iraqi boy suffering from a plague borne on a sand-fly. She used his sad story to argue that the sanctions regime on Iraq should be torn down. But the sanctions regime does not prevent medicines or food from getting to the Iraqi people. Imports of food and medicine have never been banned. In fact, the reverse is true. Ever since sanctions were last imposed, Britain has led efforts to make sure that the impact on the Iraqi people was minimised, and that the impact on the regime was maximised. In 1991 we tabled a UN Resolution allowing Iraq to sell oil in return for humanitarian supplies. It was Saddam who refused to implement it. We tried again later that year with another Resolution. Again, the UN adopted it and Saddam ignored it.

In 1995 we tried again, passing oil-for-food Resolution 986. This allows Iraq to sell $2 billion of oil every six months, and spend the proceeds not just on food and medicines, but also on water and sanitation equipment, and on tasks like mine clearance in agricultural areas. These are the things that could make a real difference to the lives of children like Kena. They have not done so, because Saddam has consistently blocked the UN's attempts to help his people. The Iraqi government rejected Resolution 986 for over a year. For months afterwards they prevented its implementation. And when they did sell oil, and got the proceeds to help the Iraqi people, Saddam used the money to lower by an equivalent amount his government's own welfare spending. Each family's ration of baby milk was actually reduced – and so canned baby milk is now piled up in Iraq's markets.

The inescapable conclusion is that Saddam has no regard for the plight of his own people. He has consistently rejected all the UN's attempts to help, and instead prefers to use their suffering as another tool in his propaganda strategy. He spends vast sums on his weapons programmes. He has spent at least £1 billion on dozens of presidential palaces.

Eclipse of the sunrise

At the end of the Gulf War Saddam pledged to destroy his chemical and biological weapons, and to let UN inspectors verify this. For the past seven years he has systematically deceived and obstructed those inspectors, while continuing his efforts to rebuild an arsenal of weapons that could wipe out cities. Four out of five of their inspections have been blocked or delayed. Large quantities of the ingredients for chemical and biological weapons are still unaccounted for. If Saddam had fulfilled his pledges, then sanctions would have been lifted long ago. But his weapons programme matters far more to him than his people do.

Saddam Hussein's writ does not run in northern Iraq, and it is no accident that the people there are hugely better off. The contrast with the rest of the country could not be starker.

A Resolution drafted by Britain goes before the Security Council today, more than doubling the size of the oil-for-food programme from $2 to over $5 billion. It contains safeguards to make sure the extra money actually helps the Iraqi people. It could pay for the food and medicines that the Iraqi people need so badly. It could restore clean water and proper sanitation to hundreds of thousands of Iraqis, restore electricity to their homes and help their farmers increase their output. If Saddam accepts the Resolution, sad stories like that of Kena Azar can become part of Iraq's tragic history. If he does not, then the Iraqi people will know exactly who to blame.

Robin Cook is Foreign Secretary. •

....

22 August 1998
Martin Woollacott
Schoolboy vices

The slow shipwreck of the Clinton presidency began long ago during his first term. In domestic and foreign policy alike, a characteristic pattern emerged, combining a readiness to retreat under pressure with an excessively obedient attention to American public opinion. In spite of certain undeniable achievements, it has been a presidency of the easy way out, proceeding by a series of short-term solutions to the problems of the week, the day, and even the hour. But what makes a president look good on a Monday may make him look bad by the following Friday, and a fool, or worse than a fool, half a year later.

The events of the last week, the confession and the missile attacks, are related because both spring from this same pattern of behaviour. It is not so much that the bombings may have been ordered to divert attention from the Lewinsky mess, although they may have been. It is more that the double crisis of Clinton's life as a private person and his life as the chief executive of the United States arises from a habit of decision-making fixated on immediate advantage and on the

Eclipse of the sunrise

postponement of hard choices, a fixation that demoted all other considerations, including that of telling the truth. There ought to be grave reservations about the untrammelled nature of the power of the Special Prosecutor in the US. Clinton is right to argue that this new office is too powerful, too intrusive, and too open to partisan manipulation. Yet what has been discovered, has been discovered, and the most important truth about Clinton's behaviour since he was first charged with having an improper relationship with Monica Lewinsky is that he has displayed the same faults in this affair as he often has in matters of public policy. Prevarication, procrastination, and a failure to think things through – a schoolmaster's list of schoolboy vices, from which few are entirely free. But in a president they can have global consequences.

What America ought now to be considering, along with the rest of us, is the broad failure of foreign policy and international management that the state of the world now reveals. To load on the shoulders of Clinton alone, or on the American government alone, the responsibility for what has gone wrong in Russia, in Asia, in the Indian sub-continent, in the Balkans, or in the Middle East would be to exaggerate the extent to which humanity, even American humanity, is in control of its affairs. But a more consistent, more reflective, and tougher president than Clinton has been would undoubtedly have made a difference. For all his undoubted intelligence and contacts with academics and intellectuals, Clinton has been ruled by conventional and often shallow ideas in foreign policy. Even on these terms he has subverted his own purposes by his preoccupation with day-to-day popularity.

Clinton could have been the Western leader who spotted how cumulatively disastrous was the impact on Russia of the economic changes urged by the West. He could have been the leader who saw that there were more problems to the Asian economic miracle than that of trying to secure as large a piece of the trade action for America as possible. He might, if he had had more success in disarmament, have headed off India's and Pakistan's testing of nuclear weapons. He might, had he been ready to take more risks, including that of daring to think that the Kosovo Albanians had the same right of secession as the other units of former Yugoslavia, have been able to avoid a new war in the Balkans. He could also have been the president, which has been more often noted, who used America's once large capital of influence in the Middle East to push through a peace settlement between Israelis and the Palestinians, instead of letting Netanyahu's obstructionism prevail.

The bombings of the American missions in Nairobi and Dar es Salaam did not come out of nowhere. Terrorism is not a fixed, demonic force that always exists and always strives to do evil, which is how it so often figures in political rhetoric and how it figured in Clinton's explanation of the missile attacks. Men seeking change by violent means respond to the coherence and the success of the policies of the governments they oppose. They retreat, they change, they

Eclipse of the sunrise

accommodate themselves to such success, even to the point of embracing peaceful means. That, we hope, is the story of Northern Ireland. Equally, they respond to weakness, lack of coherence, the sense that there is no plan or goal. It is unprovable, but it seems unlikely that the African attacks would have taken place had there been the sort of new dispensation in the Middle East that seemed possible in the aftermath of the Gulf war. It may be that, even against a background of failure to deliver the promise of 1991, they would not have taken place had Clinton not seemed, in mid-1998, an irrevocably weakened president. What the president has now done could make things worse. Revenge is not policy. It is, in any case, a dish best eaten cold. Did the word go out from Martha's Vineyard to obliterate certain places in Khost and Khartoum because the United States genuinely believed this to be the best way to prevent new terrorist attempts? Or did it go out because those insidious little polls that guide the US government showed citizens would relish quick retaliation?

Crossing international frontiers to unilaterally inflict punishment should not be done lightly, especially at a time when America does not have the standing it once had. If it can be justified, as it has been in Iraq and might be again there or in former Yugoslavia, these are exceptions that prove the rule. The American attacks, assuming they were aimed at the right targets, will not remove the capacity for fresh outrages against American or other Western installations and people. They could signal the resumption of a war that had been in remission, involving a sequence of such outrages and American responses that will serve no rational purpose. Indeed, as in the past with Reagan, such a confrontation could take the place of genuinely flexible policy-making and further polarise the Middle East at both the governmental and popular levels. As American commentators were already pointing out before the news of the missile attacks, it matters less whether any particular show of strength by America is or is not a device to distract attention from the president's problems at home than that it will inevitably be seen as such whatever the reality. It is strange that Bill Clinton had only to confirm what nearly everybody in the world already believed to be true to transform the way in which he is perceived by those same people. His denials, unconvincing though they may have been, were like a gate holding back disquiet, anger, and condemnation. Yet his deceptions over the affair are not his main offence. Even had his relations with Monica Lewinsky remained, as they should have remained, a personal matter between the few people directly affected, he was already a leader who had disappointed. Or perhaps it would be fairer to say that he had already failed to be the leader who could transcend America's and the West's parochialism, who could go beyond easy formulas about peace, democracy, economic growth, and fight against, rather than go along with, the tendency to see policy as a commodity devised to gratify the public rather than an instrument to serve it. •

James Joyce, F. R. Leavis and the Director of Public Prosecutions (left to right)

Ulysses and the Little Horrors

Ulysses and the Little Horrors

....
15 May 1998
Alan Travis
How they tried to kill off *Ulysses*

An excerpt from the curious history, drawn from newly disclosed Public Record Office documents, of how publication in Paris in 1922 of the limited first edition of James Joyce's masterpiece Ulysses *rattled the British establishment.*

22 December 1922

Customs seize a copy of *Ulysses* at Croydon Airport and ask for a Home Office decision as to whether it is prohibited as being indecent.

29 December 1922

Sir Archibald Bodkin, Director of Public Prosecutions: 'As might be supposed I have not had the time, nor may I add the inclination to read through this book. I have however read pages 690 to 732. I am entirely unable to appreciate how those pages are relevant to the rest of the book or indeed what the book itself is about. I can discover no story. The pages above mentioned, written as they are as if composed by a more or less illiterate vulgar woman, form an entirely detached part of this production. In my opinion, there is more, and a great deal more, than mere vulgarity or coarseness, there is a great deal of unmitigated filth and obscenity. It is in the pages mentioned above that the glaring obscenity and filth appears. In my opinion the book is obscene and indecent, and on that ground the Customs authorities would be justified in refusing to part with it.'

17 July 1926

Request from Chief Constable of Cambridge saying Charles Porter of Cambridge booksellers Galloway and Porter, asks for permission to import a copy for Dr F. R. Leavis of Emmanuel College and whether copies may be supplied to students in connection with lectures at Cambridge University.

Ulysses and the Little Horrors

22 July 1926

SWH [Home Office official]: 'This is an amazing proposition. A lecturer at Cambridge who proposes to make this book a textbook for a mixed class of undergraduates must be a dangerous crank. Permission must of course be refused.'

Sir Archibald Bodkin, the Director of Public Prosecutions, adds, 'Mr Leavis must be a crank or worse.'

6 August 1926

Bodkin writes to the Vice-Chancellor: 'This is not the first occasion on which I have known of a book containing disgusting passages being favourably reviewed by "literary critics".' He says he is concerned to prevent any knowledge of this book *Ulysses* spreading amongst university students of either sex as knowledge of it may awake curiosity and may lead to possibly successful efforts to obtain it.

SWH of the Home Office likes the DPP's style: 'This is a model of the way to address Vice-Chancellors,' he notes.

[the same day]
The Vice-Chancellor has seen Leavis, who says he has not recommended his students to buy the book but he wants to refer to it in his lectures and asked Galloway and Porter to obtain a copy to illustrate them. DPP tells the Chief Constable to inform Galloway and Porter that the book is entirely prohibited and anybody found dealing in it shall be prosecuted.

'Should you learn that F. R. Leavis has referred to the book further, I shall be glad to know, as I should then probably consider it right to address a communication to Dr Leavis personally.'

The lectures do not go ahead.

8 August 1936

The ban crumbles and *Ulysses* is published in London. •

....

6 April 1998
Pat Kane
Wee girl power

It's the best noise I've ever heard at the end of a gig. Nine thousand voices and 18,000 feet, screaming and stamping – except they all belonged to eight-year-old girls. A strange tumult, very large but very light – like the last echo of a much grander roar.

Ulysses and the Little Horrors

I watched the massed lassies waving their thousands of light-sticks at the departing Spice Girls, and it felt like some gigantic feminist cult meeting, a youth rally for the Wannabe Party. This was, very tangibly, Wee Girl Power. But the power to do what?

A cynic would say: to consume the Spice Girls. The first things to hit the eye were the endorsements projected across the stage, and Pepsi, Impulse and Kodak songs were given pride of place in the middle of the set.

Even when the Girls are at their best – Scary doing boxercise, Posh slinking away in her off-the-shoulder numbers, Baby skipping around like a size-14 Lolita, Sporty hitting her migraine-inducing high notes, Ginger trying to stay in her dress – their Spice is a resolutely banal, workwomanlike thing, the songs as solid and dull as fleet cars. Yet when mere perspiration inspires sheer devotion like this, you have to ask what little girls understand about the Fab Five that adult males don't.

It's essentially this: boys are always rubbish, girls are always great – whether they're vamps or victors. This was a night of militant matriarchy, led by the decidedly woman-shaped Geri, who strode through the proceedings with an almost matronly authority.

The five Spice Boys – facelessly perfect young men – were rudely chucked off stage, commanded to venerate the girls on a catwalk, debagged by the Spice collective. They were even forced to sit, Christine Keeler-like, naked and spread-eagled on chairs (after the Spices had, of course, performed an entire ballad nude). The last song was 'Mama, I Love You', with childhood snapshots of the Spices beaming out across the hordes.

This gig was handled like a pier-end panto – except the dames wore Versace and the set was more cyber sci-fi than Brothers Grimm. Mel B (Scary) and Mel C (Sporty) did a *Puss in Boots* skit, where they pretended to run from the rest in order to perform a high-kicking version of 'Sisters are Doing It for Themselves'. Sporty leapt about in a Scotland football top, Girl Power slogans slammed out of the video screen.

Widow Twanky mainlining on Camille Paglia: you had to smile.

'I think this side of the hall is berrah than the rest!' screamed Scary Spice in her dulcet Yorkshire tones. 'Lemme 'ear yer Zigga-Ziggah!' Oh, we heard.

My eight-year-old dragged me out of the hall a few times – and on the way, close to the front, I saw two extreme sights: a hall full of ecstatic schoolkids, glitter-haired, united in sheer girliness, and a stage full of evidently exhausted hoofers, their banter misfiring and forced, working hard for the money. That's the story of pop – not girl power but fan power. As long as wee lassies want to hand-dance among themselves, the Spices will be around. •

Ulysses and the Little Horrors

A soccer fan gives his verdict after Richard Eyre presented his critical report on the Royal Opera House to the Culture Minister, Chris Smith

Ulysses and the Little Horrors

4 October 1997

Andrew Clements
Little horrors

When a piece of fiction is turned into opera it becomes a very different animal, with its own self-contained structure and dramatic imperatives. In those circumstances going back to the original text for insights can be dangerous. Yet in its reference to Henry James's novella, Deborah Warner's staging of *The Turn of the Screw* – the latest Royal Opera production in the Barbican Theatre – is a quite superb realisation of Britten's most perfectly balanced and yet most baffling stage work.

With a design by Jean Kalman and John Pye that strips the stage down to its bare walls and makes do with just a handful of props – a row of fir trees, a blackboard, a piano, a forest of suspended wooden planks – all coolly lit, Warner makes the two children, Miles and Flora, the very core of the drama.

In Britten's opera, Flora, the younger child, is invariably sung by a young adult soprano. Warner, however, has cast a 10-year-old, the astoundingly good Pippa Woodrow, and realigned the whole relationship between orphaned brother (the forthright Edward Burrowes) and sister. They behave just like children of that age, constantly active, skipping and cartwheeling about the stage, sulky then exuberant, and so emphasise the apparent normality of the household into which their new governess arrives. What then unfolds is all the more horrifying and inexplicable.

The traditional lines between good and bad, the corruption of innocence and growing sexual awareness, are intriguingly blurred. Warner demonstrates that this is an opera without moral absolutes. What has already happened to those children before the opera begins goes unexplained here, as it does in the book and in Myfanwy Piper's libretto. There may have been child abuse or there may not. The ghosts of Peter Quint and Miss Jessel that the governess sees may be real, or they may be the projection of her own fevered imagination. But they are both flesh and blood on stage, observing much of the action even when they are not heard – at one point Quint sweeps a vase of flowers from the piano with shocking effect.

There is no doubt either of the children's emotional dependency upon this dead couple as their surrogate (or even, perhaps, their real) parents. Miss Jessel (strongly, unaffectedly played by Vivian Tierney) cradles Flora in her arms just before the girl is hurried away by the housekeeper Mrs Grose (another of Jane Henschel's perfectly focused performances) and, in the final moments of the opera as the governess bends over the dead Miles, Quint comes forward and gives him a farewell kiss, a gesture without the slightest hint of sexual menace.

As Ian Bostridge's immaculate performance reveals, the most ravishing music in the opera is given to Quint. His vocal lines may seem to summon and seduce, but they also promise the children something no one else in the opera can provide. Bostridge's stage presence, languid and graceful in modern dress rather than the Victoriana of the rest of the cast, makes him a detached observer too.

The counterweight is supplied by Joan Rodgers as the governess, who gives an exquisitely sung and intricately drawn portrayal, by turns motherly and hysterical, and as much to blame as anyone for the final tragedy. In the pit, Colin Davis extracts every ounce of eloquence from the Royal Opera House Orchestra and the taut, spare lines of Britten's score to set the seal on what, by any standards, is a remarkable achievement. •

17 March 1998
Adrian Searle
Power to shock

Thin rain falling in Brussels, through a sky cluttered with rocks, yesterday's loaves and bowler-hatted men. On the balconies, the women sit in their coffins and watch the world go by. Behind the curtained windows, the trains are running on time in the fireplace. And in the café, conversation is

The shards of glass retain the shattered image of a green field:
The Key to the Fields by René Magritte

Ulysses and the Little Horrors

confounded by floating seashells, a jug, a sponge, a pretty blue bow and a lemon. The tuba's caught fire again and no one looks surprised. I order a bottle of wine and a plate of ham. The ham stares back at me with its one unblinking eye. Over in the corner a man is staring fixedly at the wall. It's René Magritte, sitting in the bar in the mid-1920s, having an epiphany over a glass of Belgian beer, undergoing, as he put it later, 'a prolonged contemplative experience . . . in an unpretentious Brussels brasserie: I was in a frame of mind such that the mouldings on a door seemed to me to be imbued with a mysterious quality of existence and for a long time I stayed in contact with their reality.'

Having gone through an apprenticeship of journeyman portraiture, belated Futurism and underwhelming abstractions, Magritte found his subject, and his way.

The world is indeed mysterious, and sometimes our apprehension of it takes on a strangeness and weight that are inexplicable. You don't need a surfeit of Belgian beer, or drugs, or anything else, for the world to unhinge itself before you. You don't have to be disturbed for the world to become disturbing, for the ordinary to leap up and bite you. You don't even have to be in Belgium. It can happen anywhere. But the strangeness of the world, the enigma of being, does not usually manifest itself in overtly aberrant visions. It is all already there, in the everyday, in the curtain's shadow, the passing clouds, sunlight on a brick wall, the objects on the table, in a glimpse of a white tablecloth on a table in an empty room. The surreal is always with us. Surrealism, like Freudianism, simply discovered what was already there, a world in waiting, a world of inexplicable disclosures.

Some artists, and their work, become ubiquitous. Like the *Mona Lisa*, like Van Gogh's ear, like a Picasso woman with her eye on her cheek, like the hole in a Henry Moore or a Dali melting watch, Magritte's work has become part of the furniture of the modern mind, however indifferent that mind might be to works of art. His work stands for the mystery of things, and gives form and names to the nameless. When people respond to Magritte as a kind of fantastical revelation, as psychic entertainment, they miss his true strength. It is when he gives form to what we felt all along, but didn't have a name for, or didn't truly recognise in ourselves and our experience, that his real strength and originality reveal themselves.

Almost everyone knows Magritte's work, even if they have never been in an art gallery, or couldn't tell you the artist's name. Magritte's impassive, imperturbable enigmas have become common currency. Magritte's juxtapositions, his artful displacements and contradictions, provide the model for innumerable ad campaigns, and his paintings – or jigged-about, cropped versions of them – have ended up on countless book covers and record sleeves, from the neurological ruminations of Oliver Sacks to the album covers of Led Zeppelin.

The reasons are not hard to fathom. Not only are Magritte's images arresting – the inflammable tuba, the huge green apple filling the living room, a castle-

Ulysses and the Little Horrors

capped rock afloat in the sky — but they are also immediately readable and deceptively accessible. Magritte's paintings provide us with both the comfort of naturalistic, conventional representations of people and things, and the shock, the frisson, of the unreal and the enigmatic. This is Magritte's charm, and the key to his popularity. His images are both accessible and strange: Magritte hands enigma to us, along with the one-eyed ham, on a plate.

This year marks the centenary of the artist's birth. A commemorative retrospective of his work opened last week in Brussels, where Magritte spent most of his working life. The show is compendious, covering every aspect of his work. Here are his early portraits and lurid abstractions. Here his commercial wallpaper designs, the posters for concerts, the sheet music illustrations and other commercial commissions he continued to undertake till quite late on in his career. Here are his letters, postcards, his illustrations for Lautréamont and de Sade, his Surrealist objects and his home movies. And here are 300 paintings and gouaches, covering the artist's entire career, up to his death in 1967. Here are the paintings and here are the crowds.

Magritte, in his home town, is immensely popular. The tourist office, the clothes shops in the Brussels arcades, the book stores and travel agents have gone Magritte for the occasion. But too much Surrealism is wearing. After the first couple of rooms of the retrospective, the surprise and shock of his work begin to come as no surprise at all. The haunting ceases to haunt.

A man walks beside me, stopping every so often before an image. He stands in front of a painting of an ordinary window that looks out on to an ordinary landscape. The windowpane has been smashed and the shards of glass that have fallen into the room retain the shattered image of a green field, the blue sky and a clump of trees. The man guffaws, moves on to the next painting and guffaws again. His harrumphing and self-satisfied smirk — his evident pleasure, even — are getting on my nerves. Is this all there is, I ask myself, this mild amusement at Magritte's conundrums and contradictions? What has happened to the strangeness, the weirdness of Magritte's world? It has become hard to look at Magritte with fresh eyes. Hard to be astonished, harder still to be unsettled. The aura, the mystery, pall with repetition. There is something too arch about many of his paintings, too mechanical and (with hindsight) too strained for them to be altogether arresting. Oddly, although most of Magritte's poetic, surreal images leave me unmoved, the idea of them spawns a world of further images in my brain. Recognition of the paintings themselves is only the starting point.

It is the idea of Magritte that remains, for me, compelling: the careful, edited naturalism of his depictions, in which the world is rendered with a matter-of-fact plainness, and in which the shocks are delivered with an unemotional calm. It is the calm with which he paints things that lingers and grows in the mind — not the feet that have metamorphosed into shoes, not the bottle transmogrifying

Ulysses and the Little Horrors

into a carrot, not the fact that a dress hanging in the cupboard has a woman's breasts or that men stroll in the sky.

Magritte remains important for his plays on representation, his game with things and their names. The paintings that mix words and images, things and the names of things, seem far more poetic than those in which spectacular apparitions are conjured before us. Magritte's continuing importance is in his game with the language of representation. A man walks away from us in an indeterminate space. Black, lumpen forms litter his way. They are labelled with the names of things — *horizon, cheval, nuage* — yet the lumps are not yet the things they are called on to represent. They remain formless, the possibility of a world of objects. The labelled lumps have been called on to take shape, yet fail to do so. It's a world on the edge of existence, either about to come into being or a world declining into formlessness. A world, as it were, on the tip of the artist's tongue. Magritte's articulations of the inarticulated are a kind of modern, lapsed sublime.

At his best, Magritte was superb, and superbly disturbing. But not, perhaps, in his most famous images, in the stereotypical Magritte that everyone knows. The popular Magritte is the lesser artist than Magritte at his most furtive and least spectacular. Something slick intermittently entered his work and diminished him. But his importance remains in a kind of atmosphere, of time suspended, interminable waiting, emptiness, a sort of grief at the world's indifference. •

....

15 May 1998
Harold Pinter
It's actually a state of war

Here are three images from Duncan Green's book *Silent Revolution* (Cassell/Latin American Bureau, £11.99):

1. A village in Bolivia:
'The tiny adobe house is crammed with gnarled Bolivian mining women in patched shawls and battered felt hats, whose calloused hands work breaking up rocks on the surface in search of scraps of tin ore. The paths between the miners' huts are strewn with plastic bags and human excrement, dried black in the sun.'

2. A Bolivian woman speaks:
'In the old days women used to stay at home because the men had work. Now we have to work. Many of our children have been abandoned. Their fathers have left and there's no love left in us when we get home late from work. We leave food for them. They play in the streets. There are always accidents and no doctors. I feel like a slave in my own country. We get up at 4 a.m. and at 11

at night we are still working. I have vomited blood for weeks at a time and still had to keep working.'

3. World Bank delegates at dinner:
'The dinner was catered by Ridgewells at $200 per person. Guests began with crab cakes, caviare, crème fraîche, smoked salmon and mini beef Wellingtons. The fish course was lobster with corn rounds, followed by citrus sorbet. The entrée was duck with lime sauce served with artichoke bottoms filled with baby carrots. A hearts of palm salad was offered, accompanied by sage cheese soufflés with a port-wine dressing. Dessert was a German chocolate turnip sauced with raspberry coulis, ice-cream bon-bons and flaming coffee royale.'

(I'm still waiting for the wine list.)

It's actually a state of war. The powerful against the rest. That may be a truism but it is none the less true. The strategy of the powerful is pretty straightforward.

What you do is make benevolent, grave and sympathetic noises while ensuring that countries have no education or health systems, no public resources and no money, so that people find themselves paralysed, at the end of their spiritual and physical tether, and consequently of no threat to your structures. You talk till the cows come home about 'democracy' and 'freedom', while your financial empires merrily rule the roost, indifferent and remorseless.

Where people resist, you call them terrorists. In the old days you called them communists, but the enemy was in fact always the poor and remains the poor now.

What are the spoils for the victor? Colossal interest payments and never-ending duck with lime sauce served with artichoke bottoms filled with baby carrots and masses of ice-cream bon-bons. •

3 January 1998
Simon Hattenstone
A tale of two Quentins

Eleven p.m., New York. A night of Quentins. Quentin Crisp, the oldest, campest cowboy in America, is taking me to the new Quentin Tarantino movie. It's a marriage made in heaven. Quentin Crisp loves violence, smacks his lips every time a character is blown away. Quentin Tarantino loves blowing people away.

We're celebrating Quentin C's eighty-ninth birthday, so it's appropriate that he's dressed to the nines – buckled cowboy hat, matching belt, a floral cravat to die for, a smidgeon of orange lipstick, dash of purple eyeliner, blue shirt ironed flat as a runway.

It's been a long time since Quentin Crisp was a British eccentric, the subject of

The Naked Civil Servant and the country's most famous homosexual. Seventeen years ago he caught a flight to New York, rented a new bedsit and, he says, discovered America was how they promised in the movies. He became a very happy old man.

I'm a little worried that Quentin (the elder) will not last the pace. He bustles his way to the front of the theatre, leaves me trailing and grabs a seat. The film opens with one of those audacious tracking shots that draws comparisons with Orson Welles. Tarantino will love that.

Three-quarters of the way through, I worry that the film isn't violent enough for Quentin C. But his eyes are as sharp and focused as a torch beam.

Bang! Bang! Splat! Bang! No worries. Tarantino eventually provides us with the trademark bullets to prop up the giddy emotional stuff. We both leave happy. 'That was lovely,' says Quentin. '*Lovely*. Ooooh, all that shooting.' He's smacking his lips again. And, sissy that I am, I'm aching for Jackie Brown's lost love and the drip-drip of happiness dribbling away. •

....

23 January 1998
Quentin Crisp
A tale by one Quentin

Your very own Mr Hattenstone invaded New York and, with his harem, came to take me to dinner and to a movie. He chose the Miracle Grill and I chose *Jackie Brown*. The former was a failure, the latter a success. His little friend said in a dreamy voice, 'I don't think I've ever eaten more disgusting food.' Mr Hattenstone did not apologise. We arrived at the movie house for the 11 o'clock performance. It was almost full, exclusively of young people who laughed in all the wrong places.

We remained silent. It took all our concentration to try to unravel the plot and indeed to understand the language, which was spoken with a black accent and sprinkled liberally with obscenities.

We could none of us follow the intricacies but were all greatly frightened. It is a very exciting film, full of menace and as complicated as a Chandler picture. Almost everyone got shot. The only thing that was clear was the shooting. The sex was short and kinky, the shooting short and straight. The chief victim of both was the new Miss Fonda. It concentrated on the mechanics of betrayal. I would say that *JB* was Mr Tarantino's best film since *Reservoir Dogs*, which I consider a masterpiece of cruelty and intrigue. I greatly prefer death to sex. I forgot to ask Mr Hattenstone where in this context his preferences lay.

I am so old that I can remember when Bette Davis was a nice girl, but she moved slowly forward until she was given the part of Regina in *The Little Foxes*, and that gave her the chance to say, 'Very well then, Guy, I'll be waiting for you to die.' What do we read from the bulging eyes and the mouth worn upside down? These features tell us that those were the words she had been waiting to say (probably to Jack Warner) since 1936. The time had now come when she too had entered the profession of being. She no longer acted, because the parts she played were aspects of herself. •

7 November 1997
Richard Williams
Fear in Provence

It's high summer on a farm near the Luberon hills. This is Peter Mayle country, or near enough – a land of legendary abundance. Sure enough, the first thing we see in *Will It Snow for Christmas?* is a group of children playing amid the hay bales, bathed in the light of all the summers of memory. Don't be fooled. It won't last. Swiftly undermining the mood of those opening seconds, Sandrine Veysset's film evolves into something much more interesting: an account of a mother's struggle to sustain the lives of her children in the face of their father's cruelty.

On this land, a fortyish woman is bringing up the seven children she's borne her lover. The father, who owns the property, lives with his wife and their several older children on another farm nearby. He visits his second family occasionally, to supervise the gathering of the produce – tomatoes, onions, beetroot, parsley, radishes – and to collect his ration of sex with the woman. Among her children, he generates fear and resentment.

The farm buildings could easily be seen as picturesque and the lives of their inhabitants as an idyll. But while the woman attends to her children's needs, making do in a house that lacks heating, a bathroom or an indoor lavatory, we gradually begin to see her stoicism and to understand that it is acquired rather than inherent. And now, as the seasons pass, the man's behaviour – his bullying, his fumbled pass at his own daughter – is starting to break it down.

It helps the film that neither Dominique Reymond nor Daniel Duval, who play the couple, has a familiar face. With, say, Depardieu and Deneuve in their places, our response would have been very different. Reymond and Duval are good-looking people, but not disruptively so. Each has a particular sort of strength. We can easily believe in the power of their original passion, and in the possibility of its survival in unorthodox circumstances. Both of them, after all, are benefiting. The woman long ago traded a full relationship for a life among her children. The man gets a secondary source of sex and an additional labour force, although it is characteristic of the movie's intelligence that the director never tries to persuade us that his existence is anything other than arduous. Kindness and its opposite are on show here, but it is clear that they are not subject to simple judgements. No one, surely, makes plans for a relation-

Ulysses and the Little Horrors

ship such as this. But it happens, and people sometimes find themselves making the best of it, for as long as they can.

Claude Berri's version of Pagnol's Provence seems very far away, as does the East Anglia of Peter Hall's *Akenfield*, for that matter. *Will It Snow for Christmas?* comes from a far more profound and complicated sensibility. The only comparison I can make is with Robert Bresson's *Au Hasard, Balthazar*, a similarly unvarnished study of rural life in *la France profonde*.

Unlike most French first-time directors, Veysset is no dedicated cinéaste. She is a 30-year-old English graduate from Avignon who cared little for the cinema before she took a job as a set-dresser on Leos Carax's *Les Amants du Pont-Neuf*. Carax kept her on as his chauffeur, and encouraged her to write something. The result turned into this film, winner of the César award for the best first film earlier this year.

It should be said straight away that *Will It Snow for Christmas?* bears absolutely no sign of Carax's influence. The reverse, in fact. Nothing in it seems staged. And Veysset completely avoids the sort of detailing so often used to disguise an absence of content. We are in Provence, but the actors don't have regional accents. It seems to be the 1970s, but there are no topical references. This director cares only for the souls of her characters, and their effect on each other.

The impression of directness is reinforced by a technical quality not much beyond that of a home movie. When the winter comes, there is nothing appealing about the bare trees or the rain. This world looks an uncomfortable place.

The film ends on Christmas night, with what might be seen as an attempt to impose drama and pathos on the story. But Veysset's honesty and rigour give her the licence to persuade us that this is how the story is resolved.

And then, finally, comes the director's dedication: *A ma mère*. So maybe this is her own story, after all. In which case, goodness knows what she'll do for an encore. For now, all that really matters is that here is a powerful and unflinching film, self-evidently the product of an independent mind. Don't miss it. •

17 November 1997

Jonathan Glancey
Who would live in a world like this?

When Tony Blair wanted to show Jacques Chirac, the French President, and Lionel Jospin, his Prime Minister, his vision of New Britain, he chose Canary Wharf Tower, that single-minded monument to Thatcherism. There are many things Canary Wharf can be accused of, but being Modern isn't one of them. Far from it.

Ulysses and the Little Horrors

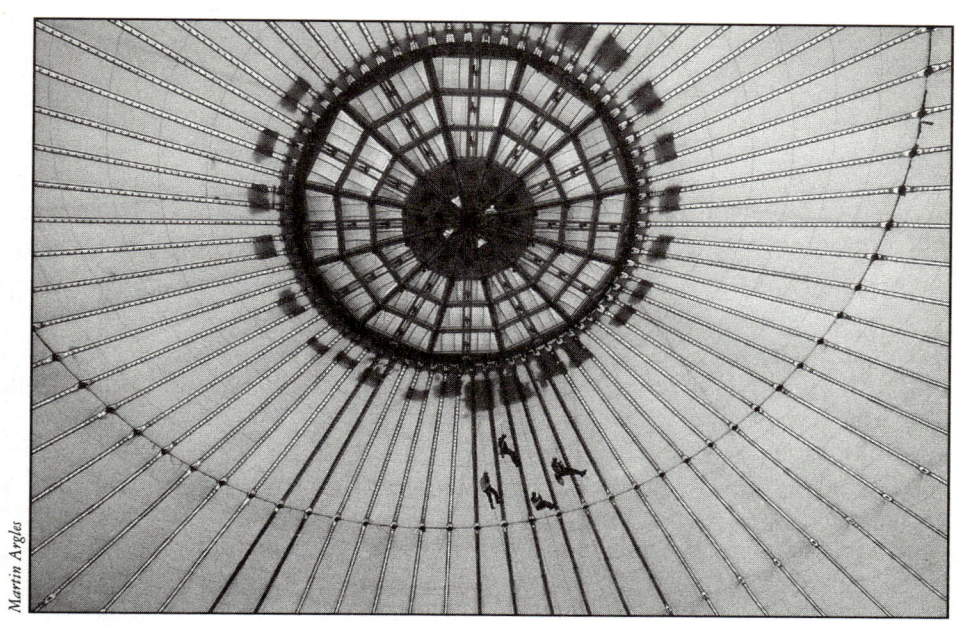

Abseiling from the Millennium Dome

In form and spirit, as well as in structure and purpose, Canary Wharf Tower is a late-flowering Chicago or Manhattan skyscraper, an artefact rooted in the late nineteenth century. It happens to be shiny and populated with neatly coiffed men and women sporting the same sort of lounge suits (or 'Gordon Browns') today's thrusting young Labour politicians prefer. It boasts a US-style shopping mall, a migraine-inducing choice of take-away coffees, US-style security guards and the soul of Mammon unmitigated and writ as large as architecture has ever been in these islands.

There is no doubt that what moves certain members of the Cabinet and their advisers, at least on the surface, is architecture that looks new and says 'New!' even though it has been brewing away slowly for several decades, through the days of Old Labour, One Nation Toryism, Thatcherism and New Labour itself. But Modern with a capital 'M' it ain't. And this needs spelling out. For all its chic accoutrements of the money-mad 1980s, it is no more and no less than eighteenth-century Lancashire cotton mill in the guise of a late-nineteenth-century Yankee skyscraper thrusting a stainless-steel finger up at London.

Old-fashioned, mid-Atlantic and a homage to Baroness Thatcher and her money men, Canary Wharf represents the transformation of Britain from a welfare state to a neo-Victorian free-market economy. In terms of architecture, it is an aggressively retrogressive step. Yet here we have a government with socialist and labour roots (it wishes to forget) embracing it. In its rush to be seen as fresh and forward-looking, the Government has the gloss of the Modern world without the substance. As has the Greenwich Dome. As has the appoint-

Ulysses and the Little Horrors

ment of the Thatcherite advertising agency, Saatchi's, to make us love the Dome.

This shouldn't be all that surprising. Tony Blair, Gordon Brown and Robin Cook, the heavyweight trio who wooed Chirac and Jospin at Canary Wharf Tower a fortnight ago, are, in their different ways, old-fashioned chaps who climbed to the top of the greasy pole in the wake of the Iron Lady. But to understand what is Modern as opposed to new is, for politicians, a way of seeing how the shape of the man-made world can make a stronger, fairer, healthier and wealthier society. Or it could be.

Herbert Morrison, Peter Mandelson's great-uncle, understood the notion of Modern, when as head of the old London County Council he drove through modernising reforms in housing, public transport, health-care and education that were a model for the rest of the world. The London Passenger Transport Board he made possible, for example, was not simply the finest of its type in the world, but a truly modernising agent. How? In terms of its brand-new architecture, engineering, public works and staff relations, it pioneered new territory, both with new tracks and trolley-bus wires radiating from the heart of the capital, and socially by offering workers good rates of pay, high standards of training, welfare and leisure.

The LCC and local authorities pioneered new forms of housing (the LCC estate at Arnold Circus, Shoreditch, was a truly radical statement of intent: magnanimous flats for the East End poor, who were to be housed in the latest, and beautifully built, Arts and Crafts architecture).

Throughout Britain, and up until the 1980s, local councils, education authorities, universities and other public or publicly minded bodies fused Modern architecture to Modern ideologies. There was the superb schools programme executed in Hertfordshire in the 1950s. There was a spate of radical university building in the 1960s. There were design programmes led by organisations as diverse as British Railways and the Design Council that worked hard not simply to create the shiny and new, but to modernise class-divided, low-wage Britain.

New Labour has inherited this Thatcherite penchant for fancy dress and has yet to separate in its mind the New from the Modern. The former is all about fashion; the latter about the health of the body wearing the latest clothes.

It is hard to believe, unless he was turning on a pump of Gallic charm, that President Chirac was impressed by Canary Wharf or saw in it the modernising spirit that New Labour says it believes in. He might have suggested that Blair come with him on a trip to, say, Lyons, to see how truly Modern urban planning and design can work to continually upgrade a big city, and how that planning is little to do with hobnobbing with fashionable designers, artists and couturiers, and everything to do with a modernising spirit that needs hard, patient graft to make it work.

Plans for the improvement of Lyons – the sort of city the Blairs and their peers would genuinely enjoy – have been continually revised since 1964. No jargon, no soundbites, no 'spin', just steady progress, a large shot of imagination

Ulysses and the Little Horrors

and another of 100 per cent proof civic spirit. Terrifying housing estates as well as city centre squares have been tackled with equal weight and equal flair. The standard of new architecture, public transport equipment and public art is consistently high. And, yes, the food is brilliant too. •

The way we live now

The way we live now

10 January 1998

Catherine Bennett
Who we are

Who we are. What we do. Where we live. These, Peter Mandelson has disclosed, are the themes which will make his Millennium Dome 'a powerful statement to the rest of the world about Britain's new-found pride and self-confidence'. Until recently, he was loath to elaborate, other than to promise wonders on 'an almost unimaginable scale'. He feared the anticipation might be too much for us – 'There's not much point working people up into a premature frenzy of excitement.'

But last week, in Disney World, Mandelson risked public delirium. Perhaps stung by the derisive journalists who accompanied him everywhere, perhaps feeling, as ambassador to Main Street, USA, that he should demonstrate some of Britain's bountiful new pride and self-confidence, he revealed that schemes for the inside of his Dome are far more advanced than had previously been alleged.

For instance, inside the Dome has been conceptualised as a 'millennium doughnut', with themed zones arranged around a 'vast, striking' hole. The three Ws – apparently representing Mr Mandelson's 'own vision' – will each be subdivided into three zones: 'Who We Are' into Mind, Body and Soul; 'What We Do' into Work, Rest and Play; and 'Where We Live' into Our Local Neighbourhood, Our Country and Our Planet.

For simplicity, the plan can hardly be faulted. Some, however, unconvinced by Mandelson's assurances that the Dome Experience will be positively drenched in spirituality, feel that What We Believe deserves more than a segment of doughnut. In his 'Ode to a Dome', Ben Okri pleads:

> May this Dome, in its throne, redeem our solemn woes,
> For we know not how the wind of judgement blows.

Admittedly, as visions go, Mandelson's seems remarkably prosaic. Did he not consider Why We Bother, or Where We Went Wrong?

Still, the modesty of the concept should make any further trips to exotic theme parks unnecessary. If the Dome purpose is to reflect our own lives and preoccupations back at us, virtually all the required fact-finding can be had for £32, the price of the new handbook, *Britain 1998*.

Though the guide is not, as some reviewers have observed, the bounciest of reads, it presents its figures in touchingly upbeat style – 'the general level of nutrition remains high' – and, under headings such as 'The Availability of

The way we live now

Certain Durable Goods', it contains more illuminating material on Who We Are, etc., than will ever be found up Splash Mountain.

On leisure, its findings suggest that the Dome's What We Do zone should be further simplified, down to the sub-themes: 'Watch Telly' and 'Get Pissed'. Television (we watch an average of 25 hours per week; 82 per cent have a video) demands dramatic recognition: one pictures a colossal set and sofa, on which millions of visitors can recline simultaneously. Each will be issued with a fag ('cigarette smoking is the greatest single cause of preventable illness and death in Britain'), a copy of the *Sun* ('popular newspapers appeal to people wanting news of a more upbeat character, presented more concisely') and a beer ('the cost of alcohol misuse in England and Wales is £2,700 million a year').

In the next zone, Football, and a huge, flag-draped, three-dimensional, interactive display illustrating its influence on national life: 'Legislation has made it an offence in England and Wales to throw objects at football matches, run on to the playing area or chant indecent or racist abuse.' In contrast, the arts can make do with minimal representation – a daily parade of novelists or poets? A grotto containing Melvyn Bragg? – for, as the handbook notes, culture has yet to become 'a part of everyday life'.

Who We Are: Body – here Mandelson should just remodel the hollow giant, through whose androgynous limbs he promises 'a fun-filled educational odyssey'.

It can only add to the merriment if the figure shows that we are becoming a nation of withered hypochondriacs who eat too much, shun exercise and reject greens.

A confined space will suffice for Who We Are: Mind, for as the authors of *Britain 1998* report, 'standards of literacy have not changed significantly since 1945'. Who We Are: Soul – Mandelson must resist episcopal pressure to make Christianity pre-eminent. Though still fairly popular for weddings (32 per cent), the Anglican Church now baptises under a quarter of New British infants, and is helpless in the face of cohabitation. Instead, our proud divorce rate, the highest in Europe, could perhaps be acknowledged with an attraction similar to Disney World's wedding pavilion: instead of a marriage, visiting couples will experience a very special and memorable separation.

Mandelson has rightly described Where We Live as the 'most complicated and ambitious' of his themes. How can the Dome convey the population density, the 22 million cars, trashed landscape, packed trains, stinking tubes, executive estates, heaving prisons, overflowing hospitals?

With a fairground trick? If the millennium Dome is to portray us as the 1998 handbook tells us we are – a nation of loud, passive, uncultured, greedy slobs – then perhaps all it need contain is a gigantic hall of mirrors. Non-distorting, of course. •

The way we live now

26 March 1998

Joanna Coles
Southern comfort eating

No one in America needs a survey like the one published last week by the Centres for Disease Control to tell them that the fattest people in the US live in the Bible Belt. Or as one headline put it, 'The Meek Shall Inherit the Girth'. It's apparent the moment you put your Reeboks outside any big city. Compared to New York, those in Georgia, Kentucky, Texas and New Orleans – last week officially identified as the city with the fattest people in the country – seem like another species. They're not even the same shape; they're spherical, as if each one has been inflated by a God armed with a bicycle pump.

And they're getting bigger by the day. Aged 50, the average woman is now half a stone heavier than her mother was and wears a size 14, which is equivalent to size 16–18 in Britain. As to why, the answer is obvious. Compared to Europeans, Americans eat all the time. And if a certain food claims to contain half the fat of its rivals, they eat twice as much. At the hairdresser's, in their cars, during college lectures, while waiting in hospital and at the cinema, where they arrive clutching monster buckets of popcorn, Dobermann-sized hot-dogs and quart – quart! – containers of Diet Pepsi.

It's as if they can't bear to be away from food. Several commercials now target office workers with products that can be nibbled discreetly out of view from disapproving colleagues, and Boost – a high-energy drink in a can – is specifically aimed for consumption at 4 p.m., as if this is an obvious punctuation mark, like lunch or dinner, in the regular day.

In Texas last month, I watched a woman pedalling furiously on an exercise bike while simultaneously munching a Power Bar which contained 2,000 calories. In New Hampshire, I stayed in a hotel which boasted a 24-hour café, 'Because Hunger Can Strike at Any Time!' Two years ago, when America was thinking of adopting a national motto, citizens were asked to send in suggestions and the slogan which came second read simply, 'America: More of Everything!' (No one can remember what came first and the idea was quickly abandoned.) The only exception to America's gluttony is New York, or, more precisely, Manhattan, where people view fatness not only as a character flaw but as a moral failing. As a friend of mine observed only last week while applying for a new job, it would probably help to put her erstwhile dalliances with anorexia and bulimia on her CV. 'Female bosses love it,' she said. 'It demonstrates total control in the face of natural cravings. It's like parties – the more delicious the canapé, the more important it is to refuse it publicly.' In *Bonfire of the Vanities*, Tom Wolfe coined the term 'social X-rays' for the rich skeletal women who

The way we live now

drift airlessly around the New York party circuit, and they were out in force on Monday for the city's Oscar night parties. I kicked off at 21 Club, the official Academy bash, where Carol Channing, Robert Loggia, Robert Vaughan and Susan Seidelman stood out for their normality in a frankly bizarre-looking crowd of ageing city socialites pretending we were having more fun than those at the real thing in LA. The difference between London parties and their Manhattan equivalents is the freak value of the older ladies who've had endless plastic surgery. Some of it's so bad it makes you squint just to look at it. One woman I spoke to had had so many lifts that the skin which God had intended to give her eyelids was now so far up her forehead it was tattooed with false eyebrows. As a result, she could no longer blink – a not uncommon phenomenon.

These days, you can tell a woman's real age by counting the rings on her neck. But plastic surgery doesn't make you look younger, it just makes you look weirder, as Jocelyn Wildenstein, an Upper East Side veteran of 59 separate nips, tucks and slices, shows. Acknowledging she now looks otherworldly, her defence is that she was trying to turn herself into a human panther.

At Elaine's, the Oscar party organised by *Entertainment Weekly*, the crowd was younger and hipper. Donald Trump, now divorced from Marla Maples, turned up with a model called Celina Midelfar, who looked like a younger version of both Marla and Ivana combined, while Dennis Hopper's wife and daughter managed the enviable feat of looking like twins. •

13 April 1998
Victor Keegan
Funny old ways of creating wealth

Naïve people who like to believe there is a connection between effort and reward have had a bad time of it recently. This is an age of fortuitous wealth creation on an unprecedented scale. Vast fortunes are being created, literally, overnight and the recipients soon convince themselves either that they have worked hard to make their good fortune possible or that it is merely 'paper money' and of no consequence. It is true that, if everyone tried to sell their gains at the same time, the market would collapse and everyone would lose. It is partly for that reason that it rarely happens.

The latest case of fortuitous wealth syndrome happened a few days ago in the US. Two American corporations (Citicorp and Travelers) announced they would join together in financial matrimony. As a result their joint value on the stock markets increased by $31 billion (£18.5 billion) in a single day – surely the most dramatic example of instant wealth creation in history.

The way we live now

This made a lot of people very happy. It has taken ICI the best part of the century to reach a market capitalisation of around $12 billion, yet Citicorp and Travelers can earn nearly three times as much from a single handshake.

They are not alone. Last week an *Observer* survey found that 30 top UK directors had increased their wealth last year (mainly through stock options) by a cool £100 million. They were probably on the golf course when Gordon Brown was appealing for wage restraint.

It would be reassuring if this had been the result of improved performance. But it wasn't. It was because share prices in general had rocketed up last year by 25 per cent, contrary to all expectations, including those of the City experts who had told the *Financial Times* annual survey at the end of 1996 that shares would fall in 1997.

In fact, they not only went up by a record amount (in cash terms) last year, but have also continued to rise strongly. Since the beginning of January the UK stock market has risen by another 18 per cent (nearly twice the average for a typical year). The share price rocket seems to have left the Earth's atmosphere.

A few years ago the value of the shares traded on the UK stock market was about a third of the value of the Tokyo stock market. Now London is worth more. (Think for a moment what would happen if a Japanese-style crash happened here.)

Paper wealth, albeit on a less dramatic scale, has also returned to the housing market. Gazumping is back in fashion and in parts of London we have returned to the situation of the late 1980s, when employees gained more in unearned income from the appreciation of their houses than they did in work. Millions of people who own houses or shares, or who are in equity-based pension funds, are wallowing in the fruits of their shrewdness. Others will be serious losers – like thwarted first-time buyers unable to afford even a studio and people who inevitably will buy at the top of the market only to nurse negative equity later; and those too poor even to contemplate buying shares or property.

Curiously, this surge in personal wealth has not been accompanied by an increase in giving to charity. Why should anyone want to give away their hard-won gains to the undeserving poor? And woe betide the government that tries to cut itself a slice of the action through an increase in income tax.

Happily for the *nouveaux riches* of the equity and share markets, the question of income redistribution is off the political agenda. This Government is about enablement, not crude redistribution. The dispossessed and unemployed will have opportunities to join the world of the employed – but there are no short cuts. They must get a job and save to get on the equity gravy train themselves.

Yet, as Robert Reich, the former US Labor Secretary, has observed, economic growth has not solved the problem of income inequality. Economists on the American right, such as Paul Craig Roberts, argue that income inequality is the natural consequence of a free society and that to say otherwise is to judge capitalism by the standards of communism.

The way we live now

An American philosopher (David Kelley) even argues that the disgraced junk bond advocate Michael Milken 'was a greater benefactor to mankind than Mother Teresa'. Why? Because he created wealth while she merely redistributed wealth donated by philanthropists. (Discuss . . .)

Until recently the economies of east Asia managed to combine growth with fairness in a way that the West was beginning to forget about. Years before the crash of communism, the Russians sent a fact-finding delegation to Tokyo to discover how such a highly capitalistic country as Japan could combine great economic success with much lower income differentials between rich and poor than the citadel of communism itself.

Now, alas, Japan has suffered an unprecedented decline in wealth, as measured by shares and property, which may lead to a contraction in the whole economy.

It remains to be seen whether recent, tentative signs of a reduction in inequality among poorer workers in Britain and the US lead to the whole question coming back on to the agenda. As La Rochefoucauld observed, plenty of people despise money but few know how to give it away. •

....

7 January 1998
Flora Luck
Cries in the dark: diary of an emergency social worker

4 a.m.

I am wiping cold water from my face with police station paper towels. I am spared the indignity of my make-up running, because I didn't have time to put any on when I was woken at 2.30 a.m. and asked to attend to make an assessment under Section 136 of the Mental Health Act. The client has objected to my presence, and proved it when she asked for a drink of water and then threw it in my face.

She has been found wandering the streets in a nightdress and thinks someone has been tapping her phone, a paranoia which has been made all the worse now she has been apprehended by the police and brought to the station for an interview. We agree to admit her to hospital for assessment. I accompany her with section papers, grabbing a cup of coffee on the ward to keep me awake while we all wait for the usual desperate reshuffle to free a bed.

The way we live now

5 a.m.

Back to bed for a few hours. I've been on duty for 12 hours, with another 24 to go. We work weekends and nights – when the enormous machinery of the Social Services Department is closed down – with a maximum of two people on duty. People ringing at 1 a.m. to change the time of an appointment seem to think social workers never sleep. They are often quite surprised to be told that the team deals with emergencies only.

9 a.m.

My first job of the day is to deal with the property of the woman sectioned this morning. Unfortunately, she has three cats and two dogs.

Under the National Assistance Act, these become our responsibility too, and they need to be fed. Accompanied by a neighbour, I let myself in to the house. The neighbour tells me that no one has been allowed in for years. It transpires that the animals have never been let out either. I tread on thick layers of faeces to put down food and water for the pets.

I worry about what will happen to them if their owner can't return home. We deal only with the situations we are presented with, knowing little of the history and rarely hearing the outcome.

In the meantime, my colleague has taken a telephone call from a family who are demanding their children be taken 'into care'. We have no detailed knowledge of the family, so a knee-jerk reaction from us might upset months of work by the daytime teams, who are probably trying to keep them together. The father forces our hand by putting the six- and eight-year-old children outside in the street. He claims they are 'out of control'. When I turn up with the police, the children are sitting on the edge of the kerb with a bin-bag full of clothes. A heated discussion ensues between myself and the father, during which I struggle to maintain the Children's Act principles of working in partnership with parents. The father tells me in no uncertain terms that the kids are now my problem, not his. Eventually, we establish that there is an aunt living nearby and she agrees to take the children in until the situation can be properly assessed on Monday. Calls like this are common during weekends, when families have no break from each other and, ironically, most of the support services are closed.

4.30 p.m.

With luck, I might get a break soon before the police start calling for me to attend interviews with juveniles: girls who have been shoplifting on Saturday afternoons and boys who joy-ride on Saturday nights. Back home, though, the phone rings immediately with my next call. A family have arrived by coach from London, fleeing domestic violence. The mother used to come on holiday

The way we live now

here as a child and has decided, on impulse, to return to make a new start. She has three kids and no money. All the refuges are full and the B&Bs are packed with holidaymakers. The problem with working in any seaside town is that at a time of trauma, people will often make an escape there; their memories of childhood holidays make it seem an idyllic place. The reality is different. If they get rehoused at all, it will be on one of the enormous out-of-town estates. As I take the family to the emergency hostel I drive along the seafront, so that the kids can see the beach. They squeal with excitement. Through tired and cynical eyes, I look at the sea, and wonder when they'll get to see it again. •

3 July 1998
Mark Irving
'To tell the truth, we're desperate'

Thank God for the car. 'The first thing I did when moving to Queen's Park was to do a test run and time how long it would take me to drive from 192 to my house,' explains Alexandra Shulman, editor of *Vogue* (192 is a restaurant in Notting Hill, dear reader). 'Four minutes!' she exclaims with relief. 'I'm just addicted to the Portobello Road, you know, but there are no restaurants in my area of any real note – OK, there's the ethnic sort, I know, and there's the Organic Café, but it's not very, well, chic,' she mutters. 'In time, I suspect only a Café Rouge will come in, not a decent restaurant. To tell the truth, we're desperate.'

The 'we' refers to that influential gaggle of fashion *edittore e scrittore* who have migrated north from Notting Hill and Holland Park in a search for the one thing so dear to their hearts: a large family house. Once they recognised that property prices in Ladbroke Grove, with its strange mix of gang-land frisson and trustafarian chic, had reached lunatic heights and that they couldn't afford Maida Vale, it was not long before they came to view the grim lands north of the Harrow Road in a more rosy light.

Ask one of the Prada-bag-clutching types who live there what they like about Queen's Park and the response tends to be ever so slightly gushing. 'About half our office seems to have moved here. It's very residential and light and open,' says Shulman, who bought a five-bedroom house north of the park four years ago, 'and there's that simply wonderful park – so perfect for the children. In fact, it slightly amazes me that people live there who don't have kids!' Incredible, really.

Queen's Park, sandwiched between Kilburn, Kensal Rise and West Hampstead, is characterised by deceptively large Edwardian houses of three to

The way we live now

four bedrooms with small on-street façades and long gardens. Far from being an urban jungle – the most fearsome animal you're likely to come across is a corpulent squirrel fed to bursting by the neighbourhood's well-bred, flaxen-haired tots – the half-square-mile zone gives off the pleasant tang of leather car seats and expensive perfume. Walk among its leafy avenues, and all sense of the humming city disappears; peer through the well-maintained bay windows and you spy one spotless white-linen sitting room after another.

Lesley Dilcock, a freelance fashion director at *Marie Claire*, moved to Montrose Avenue a few years ago. She says her late husband, the photographer Trevor Key, 'wouldn't have believed how trendy it's become'. 'We knocked the ceiling out over the extension at the rear of the house so it looks like a loft now.' There's an irony here: how the very same people who happily project a metropolitan, hard-edged urban chic in their magazines play Terry and June when at home.

But then, who said they should practise what they sell? This said, it's interesting how certain key stories have developed about life in Queen's Park: there's the apocryphal one of the memo which went around the *Vogue* office banning people from off-loading samples of fashionable clothes and accessories at the local fabled Helen's Car Boot Sale, bringing irresistible images of sandal-clad catfights among the Farhi knitwear in the schoolyard.

'Actually, this just isn't true,' says a television producer who lives just on the edge of Queen's Park. 'I tried Helen's a few times but it was mostly rubbish. It just shows how the place is crying out for interesting shops. There's this sizeable group of people with money to spend and yet it's not being catered for.' It seems that all is not well in Arcadia.

On the hill above, Sally Mackereth, of Wells Mackereth Architects, looks down from her third-floor mansion-block apartment in West Hampstead to the sleeping streets of Queen's Park below. 'There's been a strange displacement of people moving north from west London. Now that Notting Hill is full of the idiot City rich crowd, the *Elle Deco*-scene types have found their parquet floors and traditional French doors in Queen's Park,' she says. 'I know there's the Organic Café –' situated in Lonsdale Road, it (justly) makes much of its healthy, chemical-free cuisine – 'but it's very Clapham. All scrubbed pine tables and a cobbled mews,' she adds. 'I really wouldn't want to live in Queen's Park at all. You see, from where I am, you can see the Trellick Tower, the Tube line and even that white marble temple in Neasden. You're much more conscious of an urban relationship between everything.'

But as the fashion émigrés in Queen's Park have shown, being truly modern is not the easiest thing to live up to. •

The way we live now

14 February 1998
Roy Greenslade
Icon still pushes up sales

Icons do not die. They are worshipped for eternity in the temples of the media by an adoring public. So it is with Diana, Princess of Wales, the woman loved to death by newspapers and now transformed into their patron saint.

Her face still sells, staring out from the newsstands and smiling from the magazine shelves, more enigmatic than ever but just as potent for circulation-chasing editors.

Broadsheets have unashamedly joined tabloids in the rush to satisfy the people's craving for a daily diet of Diana. Stories, pictures, investigations, promotions and all manner of diverse souvenirs enhancing the legend of Diana are guaranteed to do well.

The Times's serialisation of Thomas Sancton and Scott MacLeod's book *Death of a Princess* has added about 2 per cent to the paper's sales. The *Mirror*'s interview with Mohamed Al Fayed this week, now on its third day, has been avidly followed by other papers and news media. The *Daily Mail*'s magazine on the life of Diana by the reporter who knew her best, Richard Kay, has boosted its Saturday sale by more than 400,000 for three successive weeks. The *Mail* is also offering readers a 'fabulous' Diana video and Diana rose bushes. The *News of the World* recently saw its sale rise by 330,000 when it published a 24-page magazine investigation into Diana's death by John Stalker. *Hello!* magazine's recent Diana issue sold 15 per cent better than normal issues.

Other attempts to cash in on her name have bordered on the tasteless. Among them have been stories headlined 'So did Diana really love Charles until the day she died?' (*Mail*); 'Di Ecstasy tablets being sold in London' (*Evening Standard*); and '5 million calls to Di grave hotline' (*Mirror*).

It has made little difference. Short of saying something very rude about the Princess some six months after her death, the public don't mind what they get, as long as they get it. They appear to have adopted the role of the paparazzi they affected to loathe. They chase her image through every page, seeking out every reworked detail of her life, unconcerned at the ethics, such as the possible effect on her sons and the rest of her family. She is in death, as she was in life, public property.

Yet she is also a somewhat different woman in the eyes of those beholders. The split that existed in life between her and the royal family, a split which was then dividing the nation and engendering anti-royal views, appears to have vanished. In life, she lost her royal status. In death, she is royalty once again. For the irony is that the beneficiaries of the new Diana cult are the royal family. Virulent attacks on the attitudes of the Windsors during her divorce

The way we live now

and immediately after her death have dissipated. Royalty is, dare I say it, chic once more.

To an extent, this has taken some newspapers by surprise. When the Queen Mother went into hospital for a hip operation a couple of weeks ago, the red-top tabloids did not make as much of it as their middle-market cousins, the *Mail* and *Express*. But they quickly caught up. Prince Charles's tours are being covered with an enthusiasm not seen since the earliest days of his marriage, due in part to his advisers' good work, but also because papers detect that the heir to the throne fills the vacuum better than they first imagined. Their correspondents, who virtually ignored the Prince of Wales once he parted from Diana, are happily travelling the world with him again. Even the *Independent*, for so long sceptical about the need for palace coverage, came up with a royal scoop of sorts this week. It devoted more than two pages a day to 'intimate and historic photographs from the private family albums of the Duke of Windsor'. Not quite Diana. But it's only a matter of time. •

6 April 1998

Roy Greenslade
Diana: now the press gets off its knees

Is the backlash against Diana here at last? A breach opened last week in the relentless press hagiography of Diana with trenchant criticism in three newspapers. Faced with the possibility of a national orgy of nauseating, self-indulgent lamentation to mark the anniversary of her death, journalists dared to criticise the sickly sweet iconisation of the Princess.

Sun columnist Richard Littlejohn questioned the demand for a two-minute silence on 31 August, calling it 'the latest insanity to emerge from the Lady Di industry'. The *Daily Mail*'s Lynda Lee-Potter agreed: 'If realistic common sense prevails over hysteria, the idea will be quashed from the outset.' Littlejohn pointed to the danger of repeating the 'menacing mass hysteria' on the day of Diana's funeral when the population was dragooned into mourning by 'mob rule'. He argued that an official silence was, for people like him who thought Diana 'a flawed, privileged young woman who filled in time between exotic holidays and shopping for clothes by putting in a bit of work for various high-profile charities', a disproportionate tribute.

Brian Sewell, in the London *Evening Standard*, was just a little kinder about Diana's charitable work. Through it she 'earned the people's love', he wrote, implying that it had left him cold. After sarcastically excusing the necessary hypocrisy following her death, he bewailed the fact 'the sane man' is 'helpless

The way we live now

before the still-prevailing tide of sentiment that beatified Diana'. For him she was a cross between 'a promiscuous playgirl and a harridan'. In a piece headlined 'Diana, medallion woman', he also took side-swipes at Elton John ('yowlings of a nincompoop at the piano') and Dodi Fayed ('a shopkeeper's son, an Islamic Casanova').

So how did readers react to these assaults on the memory of the Queen of Hearts? The *Sun* received 'several' phone calls but most were in support of Littlejohn. The *Evening Standard* got no calls at all, evidently disappointing, and surprising, the iconoclastic Sewell.

Before we rush to judgement, imagining that the cult of Diana is on the wane, I think we have to see this as part of the pattern of hypocrisy which informs this whole subject. Apart from the division between those who go on applauding her and those who are entirely uninterested, there are many people who maintain both positions, being both critical and adulatory at the same time.

While nodding at Littlejohn, they go on lapping up the endless material on offer. The *Daily Mail*'s Diana part-work, which reached its penultimate stage on Saturday, is still attracting many thousands of extra buyers. A fortnight ago the *Sun*'s eight-page pullout featuring poems written by members of the public about Diana was hugely successful in attracting sales for the book *Poems for a Princess*. 'We had thousands of orders,' said a spokeswoman.

Other Diana offers in various newspapers, for stamps, rose bushes and videos, have gone down well. Diana stories of any kind continue to turn up every other day on one front page or another. Her pictures continue to stare at us from newsstands.

Nor is this only a tabloid obsession. Broadsheets have found ways to keep Diana's name and face on their pages. University students taking media and cultural studies courses are getting used to lectures and seminars about the 'meaning' of Diana. Dianology has even become fashionable among the left. Last week I attended a debate organised by the leftist magazine *Red Pepper* entitled 'Diana and the people: the spectacle and the realities'. People across the world are fascinated by the subject. Last weekend I was in Norway, talking to 300 journalists about the way Diana's death has affected press regulation. I shall be speaking about it again next month, in Japan, at the World Congress of Editors.

It is understandable that journalists, and everyone interested in the relationship between the media and its audience, should investigate the Diana phenomenon and its impact on society. But we may be doing so at the moment when a sort of backlash is about to occur. If the cynicism of Littlejohn, Lee-Potter and Sewell takes hold, then people may begin to ask themselves deeper questions about their extraordinary reaction to the death of a wayward princess.

Perhaps we shouldn't see this as hypocrisy, but as a form of denial. People who flocked in their hundreds of thousands to pile up flowers at Kensington Palace and to attend the funeral believe they were exercising their free will.

The way we live now

They cannot countenance the idea that they were caught up by the hysteria or that they might have been manipulated. But the tame acceptance of Littlejohn's polemic suggests that they were. Of course, that begs two profound questions: who manipulated whom, and how was it achieved? •

....

7 April 1998
Leader
The big bad wolf: Murdoch has his price

Rupert Murdoch is the big bad wolf of British national life. He is reviled by both left and right for debasing our language and our popular culture. Feminists loathe his Page 3 girls, monarchists resent his war against the Windsors. Europhiles hate his campaign against Brussels, sports fans begrudge paying extra dosh to see the big games they used to watch for free. Murdochisation has become a synonym for decline, deterioration and – in that dread phrase – dumbing down. The ICM survey we publish today shows that the Australian tycoon is just as remote from the affections of the British people as ever. Two of his defining business practices are opposed by overwhelming majorities: more than 80 per cent of us dislike the transfer of major sporting events from terrestrial TV to cable and satellite, while 58 per cent would support

The way we live now

a law to halt predatory pricing – the selling of newspapers below cost in order to drive rival titles out of business.

But, like the big bad wolf in the story, Mr Murdoch occasionally tries to hide his fangs. Yesterday at an EU conference on audio-visual communications in Birmingham, he sought to play grandma to allay the fears of the Little Red Riding Hood public. He insisted it was pure 'myth' to suggest that News International owned too much of the European media. Two daily and two Sunday newspapers in Europe's third or fourth largest economy – Britain – was 'hardly a monopoly', he said. Even combined, *The Times*, *Sunday Times*, the *Sun* and the *News of the World* amounted to only 20 per cent of British newspaper circulation – and that market share was the fruit of genuine hard graft and business savvy. As for his evil designs on broadcasting, Mr Murdoch pointed out that BSkyB accounts for just 5 per cent of all television viewing in Britain. Keen to soothe his audience of politicians and media bigs, he used the language of pluralism to cast his vast global empire as a humble media cornershop, a 'relatively small part of an ever-widening rainbow of outlets for the dissemination of diverse views'.

No one should be fooled by Mr Murdoch's grandma act. For all the who-could-be-scared-of-little-ol'-me? rhetoric, yesterday's speech revealed the familiar predatory instincts: it was an undisguised attack on public service broadcasting in general and the BBC in particular. Mr Murdoch laid into the Beeb's 24-hour news channel – which he admitted had 'seriously undermined' his own Sky News – for using public money to produce a service available only to the cabled few.

Branding the BBC 'the biggest media owner in Britain', artificially propped up by the 'compulsory poll tax' of the licence fee, he claimed it was only whingeing and special pleading that had enabled state broadcasters to retain their monopoly over rights to air key events – from the Olympics to the World Cup, from Wimbledon to Test cricket. The implication was clear: Rupert Murdoch wants old European cronyism to give way to the brisk free-market forces of the Australian and American New World. That way he can set his sights on the crown jewels of world broadcasting, now in the hands of public service networks such as the BBC. Grandma, my, what big teeth you have. The BBC Director-General, John Birt, was right to shoot back in Birmingham with a warning that pay-per-view would eventually create a 'knowledge underclass', denied access to key events in the national culture through lack of cash. In the mixed-media economy, public broadcasters are an essential counterweight to their commercial colleagues. It's no surprise if the big bad wolf wants to gobble them up, but we – and our government – should do all we can to stop him. If Tony Blair believes otherwise, and keeps on cosying up to Mr Murdoch, we offer five little words of advice: remember Little Red Riding Hood. ●

The way we live now

18 December 1997

David McKie
That old-time, dumbed-down para-religion

This time next week there will be people seen in the churches who aren't usually seen in churches. They will have come for the Christmas story. They will turn up for Midnight Mass in the last hour of Christmas Eve: some reverent, some even tearful, some mildly drunk. They will not want to miss out.

This is an age forsaking religion; or, to put it another way, taking up irreligion – though the two are not quite the same. In a lecture to the Citizenship Foundation in London last week, Roger Jowell and Alison Park of Social and Community Planning Research examined the question of whether today's young generation is – as some analyses, notably from Demos, have suggested – radically different from any before it. They were sceptical. Of three instances they examined, one, the young's libertarianism, or, as some would say, their permissiveness, did suggest new dimensions: in their attitudes to sexual morality, the 18–24-year-olds, compared with those over 55, could almost belong, said Jowell and Park, to a different planet. On a second test, their political indifference proved to be consistent with much past evidence that young people have always tended not to be bothered with politics, having more important things to think about: sex, for instance. Marriage, a mortgage, and a family traditionally alter that.

The third of their tests was religion. The young, said Jowell and Park, were overwhelmingly less religious than their elders. A mere quarter of over-55s, according to their research, did not regard themselves as belonging to any religion. That rose to around half among those between 25 and 55, and to two-thirds in the 18–24 age group.

But again the young merely magnified a trend apparent everywhere. In 1983, 31 per cent of respondents professed no religion; that has now risen to 43 per cent. The oldest groups in society still tend to think of these things far more than the youngest – perhaps because they are nearer to death – yet even they are defecting.

But we shouldn't assume that those who are not religious can be classed as anti-religious. As religion declines, so we see the growth of what might be called para-religion. Paramedics resemble medics, but not in some of the senses that matter most. Para-religion resembles religion, but with even more crucial exemptions. You can see the rise of para-religion in music: the astonishing success of music which would once have been thought antique or alien, propelling

The way we live now

composers from Abbess Hildegard of Bingen to Gorecki and Part and John Tavener into the Classic FM charts. It's the hope of inducing a feeling of reverence (though preferably not for too long) that explains the appeal of Pachelbel's *Canon* and Albinoni's *Adagio* and the Samuel Barber *Adagio* – which now in this context scores double, the composer having refurbished it as a setting of the *Agnus Dei*. You can see it even more powerfully in the surge of grief and commitment which followed the death of Princess Diana, with some of the kerbside interviews couched specifically in terms more often associated with gods than mere mortals, and evocations of saints (or saints-to-be like Mother Teresa, whose death came so close to Diana's) and even the Virgin Mary.

But of course this isn't religion. It's religion with the awkward, unwelcome, non-negotiable bits left out. It's the balm without the demands and the obligations and even the fear. And in this it resembles much else in an age which constantly says: don't make things too difficult. Concert promoters, I saw it reported this week, are turning against the symphony, which audiences find too long and demanding. Schedule Strauss's *Four Last Songs*, one promoter was quoted as saying, and you sell every seat. Strauss's *Four Last Songs* have to do with death, which is big in para-religion as well as religion; they conjure up beauty and awe; and they're over in 20 minutes. See also, *inter alia*, the steady erosion of real cricket by para-cricket; or in places, it has to be said, of real journalism by para-journalism.

The mood of the para-religious is overwhelmingly wistful. They (well, all right then, in this case, we) may have entered a church to admire the fifteenth-century reredos (mentioned by Pevsner, commended by dear old Betjeman); but once there, how we wish that involvement with places like this could have been part of our culture! The poet of para-religion is Philip Larkin, not a religious man but infected by a kind of religiousness with nowhere to go. I shall shun the more famous poems and cite a lesser one.

> What are days for?
> Days are where we live.
> They come, they wake us,
> Time and time over.
> They are to be happy in:
> Where can we live but days?
>
> Ah, solving that question
> Brings the priest and the doctor
> In their long coats
> Running over the fields.

Gervase Phinn, with children (see page 172)

Voices from elsewhere

Voices from elsewhere

11 March 1998
Joseph Harker
Notes & Queries

This column – much imitated by other newspapers – is where *Guardian* readers seek to answer questions posed the previous week by other readers.

Why can't we all just love each other?

Evolution has endowed us, along with our close relatives the gorillas and chimpanzees, with two relevant primal urges. We live in social groups prepared to defend a territory and we form hierarchies within those groups. The groups were originally extended families (indeed the protection of a specific set of genes provided their evolutionary justification), but have grown to the size of countries.

Most wars arise from violations of territory instigated by strong leaders, although civil wars happen when a country splits into two groups due to struggles within its hierarchy. When our perceived social groups do not correspond to our countries, the result is anything from simmering discontent (e.g. black people in the United States) to all-out war (e.g. the former Yugoslavia).

What we call love must have originated as a force to hold our groups together by ensuring the co-operative, mutually supportive behaviour that characterises our intra-group interactions. To this day, while we may extend hospitality to individual foreigners, we remain suspicious of them *en masse*. Fortunately our primal urges can be overridden by our intelligence. It is not a coincidence that the best of us preach universal brotherhood, that is tolerance of those outside our group, and equality, meaning the overthrow of hierarchies. These are themes that reappear from Christ to Jefferson (excluding black people) to Lenin (excluding capitalists but including, in theory, women). Nor is it a coincidence that those who advocate firm leadership, a strong military, racial purity, immigration controls and a form of capitalism that creates huge disparities in wealth are called Conservatives, for they seek to conserve our urges no matter what our intelligence may say about them. Loving each other thus involves muzzling Conservatives and improving education so that we can see the whole of humanity as our social group.

Graham Andrews
Oregon, USA

Voices from elsewhere

14 January 1998
Erwin James
Diary of a prison inmate

Two days before my first Christmas in prison, shortly after the cell door opened for 'slop out' and breakfast, I learned that the man in the cell immediately above mine had hanged himself the previous night. I vaguely remembered hearing noises from up above earlier in the morning – footsteps, keys, voices. So that's what it was: a man had died.

As I queued for breakfast, the talk was of what had happened. Some spoke animatedly, some spoke in hushed tones, someone tried to joke about it. But I had nothing to say; I felt as if I'd taken a blow in a sensitive area and did not know whether to laugh or cry.

As I walked along the gantry back to my cell, an image of how the man had died while I slept not 10 feet below appeared vividly in my mind. I didn't know the man and had never seen him, as we took our daily half-hour exercise by landings. But I'd learned a little about him in the breakfast queue. Freshly sentenced and in a local London prison, I was spending 23 hours a day locked in a cell – as had been the man above me. I was at the beginning of a long prison sentence and was in the local prison waiting to be allocated to a long-term dispersal prison – as was he. I was anxious, frightened, lonely, unprepared – so was he. The only difference between us, it seemed, was that I was coping.

That incident happened almost 13 years ago and, luckily, I am still coping. Along the way, however, there have been many more who have not been so lucky. A man makes many acquaintances during a long prison sentence, but he learns to receive impassively the news that someone known to him personally has died in prison by his own hand. After shedding a tear later, when the cell door is closed, he will be thankful that he is still coping.

If pressed, I could name at least a dozen such acquaintances, but especially I remember Chris in Wakefield, Eddie and Barry in Long Lartin, Ray in Stocken, and Fred and Michael in Nottingham. As the years passed, I'd stopped shedding secret tears. I thought I had become hardened to self-inflicted death in prison – until Michael.

Michael died last year. He was in a cell seven doors down from mine. One Sunday afternoon, at around 2.30, he was found hanging from the bars of his cell window. Several days later, the prison authorities allowed his two sisters and his mother to go into the cell where he had died. They pressed their hands and their faces against the wall underneath the window and called out his name in anguish. The other prisoners had been left unlocked, and as the women wept many stood by their doors in respectful silence. In an unprecedented gesture of compassion, the prison governor allowed Michael's family to leave wreaths by his

Voices from elsewhere

cell door. This was like a revelation – an official acknowledgement of Michael's humanity. The usual procedure had always been for the dead man's cell to be cleaned and reoccupied the next day, even the same day. But Michael's wreaths were left outside the sealed cell door for over a week, accompanied by a lighted candle.

In the prison chapel the following Sunday morning, the chaplain read out a letter from one of Michael's sisters in which she thanked his 'mates' for their courtesy during the family visit to his cell. She was glad that 'at least he had some good mates in there'. I could not hold back my tears as I listened to her words.

The sense of my own humanity had been dulled over many years of living in an environment where human dignity is routinely forsaken and where a suicide merits less as a topic of discussion than who's managed to smuggle in a 'parcel' [drugs]. Barely noticing, I'd sunk deeper and deeper into a mire of cynicism. But Michael's death and the authorities' humane response pulled me back.

I hope that the call by the Chief Inspector of Prisons for the Prison Service to carry out an urgent review of suicide-awareness strategies delivers a similar message to the outside world. The news that those in prison are six times more likely to commit suicide than those on the outside, and the fact that last year's shameful figure of 83 prison suicides in England and Wales is an all-time record, should bring an end to the era of complacency.

It is right that those who seriously offend against society should suffer the deprivation of their liberty. But surely not the deprivation of their humanity? •

3 February 1998
Linda Grant
Youth isn't so cool

Just as the lights were going down in the Odeon Leicester Square on Friday night, I said, 'Who's the hunk factor in this apart from Leonardo DiCaprio?' No one knew. Not Billy Zane, obviously. It turned out there wasn't one. We had to sit through three and a half hours staring at the 10ft features of a baby-faced 23-year-old whose puppy fat still filled his cheeks. The kid is barely out of zit cream. Where, we wanted to know, was Alan Rickman, smouldering erotically in a pea jacket? Or Sean Connery in captain's cap, head-butting the iceberg for its presumption? Or Liam Neeson in steerage, heavy in his boots in the Irish dancing? Or Sam Shepard as transatlantic gentleman card sharp from Missouri, making his own luck? In *Schindler's List* you got Liam Neeson and Ralph Fiennes. That's what I call a picture. The next day, the Turkish dry-cleaner told me she wasn't going to bother to see *Titanic*. 'What's in it for us?' she demanded. 'My daughter here, she's going next week. But she likes Leonardo

Voices from elsewhere

DiCaprio, don't you?' The girl sighed meaningfully and rolled her eyes. 'Ye-es,' she breathed. 'You see? He's for teenagers. This is a teenage film.' I agreed. In *Titanic* you see how completely the world has been taken over by adolescents and adolescent values. Here's a blockbuster movie for all the family – enjoyable tosh with great special effects – with absolutely no sex appeal for any woman over the age of 35 and in which no one over the age of 20 has any morality or goodness or courage apart from the unsinkable Molly Brown, here transformed into Young Love's accomplice.

For a good two bum-numbing hours the plot hinges around the escapades of a couple of naughty adolescents trying to evade the authority of the grown-ups in order to have sex, which eventually takes place, as most of it does at that age, in the back seat of a car. Meanwhile, the ship plunges on towards its terrible destiny and the teeny-weeny, self-important world of the adolescents is overtaken by events, and indeed reality.

Does this remind you of anything? Ring any bells? Any resonance here? All last week political commentators with lines and the odd grey hair, giving every appearance of being adults, were asking each other whether the approaching war with Iraq was being got up as a smokescreen to shift attention away from what really mattered: the US President's sex life. It seemed to occur to no one that it might be the other way round: that the 'Me, me, look at me' cries of the young women who may or may not have gone down on Bill Clinton were distracting us from potential military action against a mad dictator with an arsenal of chemical weapons. Whether you are for or against war with Saddam Hussein, you have to concede that if there is a burning issue of the moment it isn't the shape of the President's penis. That metaphor about rearranging the deck-chairs on the *Titanic* has never seemed so freshly minted.

Madeleine Albright is touring the Middle East to drum up support for air strikes and here we all are, fixated and focused on Clinton's extramarital affairs with women just about young enough to be his daughters. Like Clinton himself, we are mesmerised by the teenagers. With a grown-up wife beside him in the White House – and smart enough to get him off the hook – he still prefers the fleeting company of bimbos. I know I shouldn't call them that – Monica Lewinsky was a White House intern, after all – but if you spend your time giving blowjobs to older men instead of memorising the US Constitution and its many amendments, that's the label you are going to get stuck with.

The sexual power of young women is a force which seems capable of pulling the whole world off kilter. Adolescence has many, many attractions – you need spend almost nothing on moisturiser (just as well, as the pocket money doesn't stretch to it); you can stay up all night energised by a tab of E and a bag of chips and still look ravishing in the morning; and you can endure the discomfort of a tree-top camp for days on end while you stop a bypass. But in the virtues of adolescence lie its faults. Its condition is to see things in black and white, never to be plagued by uncertainty, or submit to expediency and compromise,

Voices from elsewhere

and never, ever to have to worry about mortgages, pension plans, household contents and building insurance or whether or not remembering where you put your keys is an early warning sign of senile dementia.

The downside to this ruthless confidence in the self-evident correctness of whatever moral high ground you have chosen is that it can fall easily into fundamentalist error, such as the date-rape frenzy which took over American campuses a few years ago in which teenage students single-handedly attempted to abolish the uncertainty of the sexual encounter by the institution of a written code of behaviour. The Iranian revolution was carried out by the teenage zealots of the Revolutionary Guards, zipping around on motorbikes spray-painting the arms of anyone wearing a T-shirt. Who winds up in cults? Teenagers.

Teenage radicalism is a product of the mistaken belief that yours is the first generation that ever lived to discern that the world teems with injustice. When Swampy's mum looks at him, does she also see Kevin the Teenager and his ancestral cry – handed down through the genetic pathways and emerging with the first pubic hair – of 'It's not fair' and 'I didn't ask to be born'? I'm sorry, teenagers, you are not the centre of the universe. I do not care about your doomed love affairs, whether they take place fictionally on board the *Titanic*, in a cupboard in the White House, or under the concealing darkness of the local bus shelter. I know you think your life will be ruined if you are made to come home no later than midnight by your cruel and oppressive parents, but you don't know what ruined means until you've seen a chemical weapon in action.

Last week Peter Mandelson asked an eight-year-old to hold forth on his views about the contents of the Dome. Hey, why not ask him to run America's foreign policy too? Put him in charge of the whole shooting match; let those Sony Play Station reflexes zap the baddies. Put Baby Spice in charge of United Nations weapons inspection. Give Kate Moss the presidency of the European Union. If youth is so cool, let them try running a few countries and see if the rubbish gets taken out, the beds get made and there's something to eat in the cupboard. •

....

8 April 1998
Alan Randall
Diary of a hospital chief executive

It was probably the worst moment of my mother's life. The fall was predictable but nevertheless devastating. She and all the staff in the rest home knew immediately that it was a nasty fracture of the leg. At 85, it meant not just pain and intense discomfort but also the prospect of a further loss of the remaining traces of independence and dignity.

Voices from elsewhere

Her needs when she arrived at the hospital were obvious – pain relief, a comfortable bed and loads of love and reassurance. Instead she received six hours of further pain and agony on a trolley, hurried care from hard-pressed nurses and doctors and, eventually, a temporary transfer to the only available bed in the hospital on an Ear, Nose and Throat ward.

As a relative, the feelings of anger and helplessness were intense. Somebody had to be blamed. But who? It was not the fault of the staff on duty: they were doing all they could to cope with patients in A&E. Surely the blame rests with the hospital's managers. How could they allow a large, modern general hospital to reach the point where there were no beds immediately available for a frail, elderly patient in need of help? But as a chief executive of a similar hospital 100 miles away, I knew that other people's mothers were receiving similar treatment – or lack of it – in my hospital.

Most hospitals are now running without a comfortable margin of empty beds to cope with the surges in demand. When the surges occur, patients suffer the consequences. They wait hours on trolleys in A&E while efforts are made to free up beds. They are discharged home or transferred to other hospitals. Less urgent patients, gearing themselves up for a long-awaited operation, are told it has been postponed.

These practices are now routine in many hospitals. The danger is that they come to be so commonplace that they are thought of as inevitable. They are not and should not occur in a wealthy, civilised country. The root cause of the problem stems from the laudable aim of trying to deliver greater efficiency.

In the early years of NHS efficiency targets, managers moaned that they could not meet the national targets of 1 per cent, 2 per cent or 3 per cent extra efficiency. But the targets were met and indeed often even exceeded. Restrictive practices were rooted out. Programmes of market-testing of hotel services, of changes to shift and working practices, of energy savings and of site rationalisation all helped to deliver more patient care at no extra cost. Then came changes to clinical practice, including a push to encourage more day surgery and ambulatory care.

The NHS became, if not the envy of the world's health ministers, then certainly of the finance ministers. The Treasury was delighted and the setting of annual efficiency targets became an unquestioned feature of an NHS manager's life. In the tough world of the NHS marketplace, the bottom line was so important it became a sign of weakness to question one's own ability to deliver further year-on-year efficiency gains. So, with the easy hits of the early years already ticked off, attention turned to delivering apparent efficiency at the expense of quality. The most popular target became bed occupancy. If one could treat more patients with fewer beds, efficiency targets could still be hit.

Hospitals now commonly run their wards at a planned bed occupancy of 95 per cent. The airline industry's practice of overbooking flights has been taken up by the NHS. Purely from an efficiency point of view, this is sensible. The difference, however, is obvious. The price paid by passengers of an over-booked flight is not too great – a few extra hours' waiting, compensated for by free flight vouchers. For the NHS patient, the consequence is extra suffering at a time of greatest need.

The time has come to call a halt to the universal and annual demand for year-on-year efficiency gains. The recent government White Paper, 'The New NHS', signalled a welcome emphasis on quality to match the emphasis on financial performance. The shift of emphasis is long overdue. It is surely not setting too ambitious a goal to expect that there should be a hospital bed available when required. My mother deserved it and so does everyone else.

Alan Randall is chief executive of Worthing and Southlands Hospitals NHS Trust. •

14 April 1998
Elaine Williams
The master storyteller

Children who live in remote uplands areas like the Yorkshire Dales can be disarmingly blunt. Gervase Phinn, an Ofsted inspector and the principal education adviser for North Yorkshire, finds himself constantly put on the spot. On one school visit to a tiny primary up the dale he had asked young pupils to read from Beatrix Potter's *Peter Rabbit*. John, 'a serious little boy of about seven or eight', had begun to falter in his reading. Phinn tried to engage the boy and move him on. 'What a terrible thing it would be if poor Peter Rabbit should be caught,' he suggested. The boy grew angry and turned on him: 'We shoot 'em. They can eat their way through a rape crop in a week, can rabbits.' A girl of 10 with 'round cheeks and closely cropped red hair' concurred. 'We gas ours,' she added.

On another visit he had asked a daydreaming child what he was thinking. The boy answered, 'I was just thinking, Mr Phinn, that when I'm 21 you'll be dead.' On *The Other Side of the Dale*, Gervase Phinn's first novel, published this week, is an autobiographical account of his first year as school inspector for English and drama to North Yorkshire. And it is full of such stunning one-liners. Michael Joseph, the publisher, which also publishes James Herriott, is hoping that Phinn will capture hearts and minds for working life in Yorkshire's rural schools as Herriott has done for veterinary practice.

Gervase Phinn is aware that he is likely to be criticised for a sanitised, romantic portrayal – here are well-run schools in country places with quaint pupils and committed staff who at worst are endearingly eccentric. But he's ready for the brickbats. These schools really do exist and this book celebrates

Voices from elsewhere

the achievement of teachers, which he believes to be considerable. 'I make no apologies,' he says. 'I think this redresses the balance.'

He is a born raconteur, a published storyteller, poet and editor of anthologies, who has been collecting children's poems, sayings and doings for years. With a mop of black hair, a piercing gaze and pale skin, his Irish descent is obvious. He shares with Seamus Heaney a love for 'the crack of language' and revels in the broad guttural dialect of Yorkshire. When once asked by a government official how teachers were adapting to the latest set of changes to the national curriculum, he said he thought they were 'fair riggwelted'. That, as one small boy explained to him on a school inspection, is when the 'yow' is 'heavy pregnant, so heavy you see, she falls over on her back and just can't move. She's helpless. Sticks her legs in t'air and just can't shift.'

As a performer whose wit and timing are worthy of a stand-up comic, he is heavily booked as an after-dinner speaker, most recently as a guest at the Secondary Heads Association Conference and this year's North of England Education Conference, where he spoke at a table alongside Sir Herman Ouseley, chairman of the Commission for Racial Equality. Whether he is addressing parents about their children's reading, or the great and the good, his performances are always uproarious, as he shares his penchant for the ludicrous and the absurd about school life and the zany ways that children view the world. But there's no sniping here. Phinn believes that children are innately creative, deserve the best and that schools mostly give of their best.

As a passionate protagonist of children it is perhaps no accident that he was discovered by Esther Rantzen. He is a regular speaker for both Cafod and Childline and it was after a Childline dinner which she attended that he was invited on to her show. He read children's poetry, talked about children and their teachers and made such a hit that he was invited on a second time.

He can remember reducing a cameraman to tears. 'I collect poems and there's this wonderful poem by a boy, James, aged 11,' he says. 'His teacher had asked his class to write about something they'd lost and he wrote about his baby sister who'd died in hospital the day before:

> Her fingers were like tiny sticks,
> And her nails like little seashells,
> And her hair like white feathers.
> And now she's gone and my mum can't stop crying,
> And my dad stares at nothing.

'It's a beautiful poem and I read it and this bloke just started weeping. But then children do express themselves powerfully and good teachers bring that out.'

The Other Side of the Dale, by Gervase Phinn (Michael Joseph, £15.99). •

Voices from elsewhere

2 June 1998

Helen Parnham
My hell from bullying

'Sticks and stones may break my bones but names will never hurt me.' Whoever first said that couldn't have been more wrong. Physical wounds can heal, emotional ones will always scar.

It was about two years ago when I discovered this. I was enjoying my first year at secondary school in the same form as a few friends. I did better in the annual exams than one of my so-called 'friends' and they started making snide remarks. As others caught on, I became isolated.

The comments came day in, day out. Before long, I found I was on my own all day and both my self-esteem and my self-confidence were rapidly going downhill. Although I didn't show it, every comment used to eat away inside me. Because I didn't want anyone to know how I felt, I put up a barrier. I think everyone else thought I was just a snob, but underneath I was hurting.

A favourite remark was 'Billy no mates', which they all found incredibly funny. Said on its own like that, it doesn't mean anything but when you are so low, it really hurts, especially several times a day.

At the Christmas concert my clarinet solo caused problems and soon I hated being able to play an instrument. I had attended the music centre in town once a week but I stopped. I didn't go out or take an interest in anything and I had started to hate myself and the things I was good at or enjoyed because people had used them to get to me. I believed that because I didn't have any friends I wasn't worth liking. Because I had also received comments on my appearance I hated looking into mirrors.

The day after my grandma's funeral in the January I had my first panic attack, only then I didn't know what it was. As I sat in morning assembly, I started to feel dizzy and my eyesight went blurred. My heartbeat got faster and when the panic reached its strongest, I thought I was going to be sick. I was allowed out and in the toilets I felt scared. I had no idea what was happening to me. Over the next month or so I began to feel tired and took quite a few days off. I started getting pains in my abdomen and doctors diagnosed appendicitis. After the operation I was told the diagnosis was wrong. I now know the pains could have been caused by stress.

After I had got over the operation, I went back to school. That day was horrible and so was the next. It was the last time I spent a whole day in school. For weeks after that I never really left the house.

I was so low my mum always carried the paracetamol and any other tablets with her so that I couldn't take an overdose. It wasn't that I wanted to die, I just thought I didn't do any good while I was alive and I couldn't see things changing. I believed that if I was dead, no one would miss me because all I seemed to do was annoy people and have arguments.

I had a home tutor for a couple of months and attempts were made to get me back into school, but even walking past made me panic.

My parents decided they would teach me at home. At first it was a huge relief, but when I started trying to work I became angrier at myself because I found that everything I had been able to do easily before I could no longer manage. Even so, I was a lot happier.

I had time to be by myself and gain back the confidence I had lost. In fact, my mum said that for the first time in over a year she had seen me smile. That was around January 1997 and now I am happier than I have been for a long time. On a self-confidence scale of one to 10 I am now about seven.

I think writing this will be beneficial because, until a few months ago, I had never really told anyone and I hope this will help get rid of the 'niggle' I have inside.

I can't forget. All this has happened to me and the people who started it have been able to carry on. But with help from my therapists I'm getting back to a regular way of life. I know the only way to get rid of the anxiety I have is to go to face it, and that is what I am now doing. Also, with the work I'm doing at home, I hope to go to college.

The most important thing, though, is that I'm starting to like myself again. I have been laughed at and picked on but, if anything, it has made me stronger and more determined to make something of myself, while they will always be the same, shallow people. The only way for me now is up. By working at home, I may not be able to achieve the highest of qualifications but at least I'm happy.

Helen Parnham was 14 when she wrote this for Guardian *Education.* •

6 January 1998
Linda Grant
Girls on top form

For most of last year I was a confiding ear to the hysterical mother of a 12-year-old boy. 'I was hysterical,' she told me on Sunday night, 'I concede that.' In September 1996 her son started at the local comprehensive in a south-east town. It was not a flagship school but it got good results in the league tables, especially compared to many inner-city ones. Its A-level grades were excellent. So why was it that within half a term Sean turned from pleasant, thoughtful primary school pupil to Monster Boy? Sean grew up in a household where foreign holidays, restaurant meals, hardback books, films and theatre were

Voices from elsewhere

taken for granted. He assumed that he would one day have the same standard of living himself.

Two months in the comprehensive severed any links that existed in his mind between effort and attainment. 'You only live once so why not have fun?' was the philosophy of his new mates and now it was his creed too. The teachers described him as rude and naughty. His academic performance was harder to assess. There were no exams and homework was infrequently assigned. At the end of the summer term he got his first report, which was mostly Cs and Ds. The teachers thought he could do better but he'd put in no effort. But by that time his mother – terrified by a vision, eight years into the future, of a bored, disaffected, unemployable 20-year-old still hanging around the house, scrounging money and smoking dope all day – swallowed her Labour principles and, gagging, put him into a private school.

To get in, Sean had to sit an entrance exam. It turned out to be the turning point in his acceptance that he was going to be moved whether he liked it or not. His mother gave him some sample papers. 'Let's do another,' he cried excitedly. He burned with the challenge. Good at sport, he saw preparing for the exam as training for a big race or match. He passed easily. The new school sets tests in the middle and the end of each term. He got three As before he broke up before Christmas.

His results in almost every subject are better than his coursework. There's another boy who gets As in almost everything. Sean was beside himself when he beat Mr Clever Clogs in a history test. Monster Boy has vanished. His new head described him as a pleasure to have in the school.

To his mother, he's a pleasure to have in the house. He's 13 and aiming for London University, 'because London is where the best clubs are. What grades will I need to get in?' Why did he fail so badly in the comprehensive? It was well placed in the league tables, after all. But when his mother investigated further, she found out that it was girls who were getting the good GCSEs. The school, and Sean's situation, is a microcosm of the whole of Britain, in which girls officially now outperform boys in every subject.

Why? At this stage there are just suggestions. Because of the toxic effects of lad culture, which teaches boys to despise activities such as reading, sitting still and paying attention, as unmasculine? Because of an instinctive sense that boys have from an early age that society has barely any use for them in the dominant service sector? Because girls are no longer held back by society's low expectations of them? Yet at university the difference between boys and girls disappears. Partly because the low-achievers have dropped out along the way, but maybe too because universities by their nature are competitive environments in which assertion – even aggression – attention-seeking and elitism are encouraged and nowhere more markedly than the Oxbridge tutorial system, which continues to produce the people who land the top jobs. One of the changes to educational qualifications has been the introduction of coursework to GCSEs, an innovation which may favour girls over boys.

The Freethinkers' Guide to the Educational Universe, a selection of quotations on education by Professor Ronald Meighan, contains the thought: 'Nobody grew taller by being measured.' Sean, however, did. Asked why he was doing better at his new school, he told me, 'First, because I know my mum's paying a lot of money for my education now and I don't want to waste it. Second, because you have to be clever to get into this school so that tells you that you've got potential.' This statement drips with heresies; it's virtually an invitation to the reintroduction of selection, for a start. But for the speaker, unfamiliar with ideology, it's true. Sean has more unpalatable messages. I asked him why he did better in exams than coursework. 'With exams it's more glorified when you get a good mark,' he replied. 'Teachers try to create competition with merit charts, but you can't get people to compete for an artificial thing like that. Sometimes, at my old school, they'd say, "You'll get a Mars bar if you do well", but you can buy a Mars bar yourself. They're not going to say: "Whoever gets the best mark gets £50."' Describing the boy in his class who always gets As, Sean says, 'He's a geek. He looks like a prat and he's a bit smug, but he's just that way. He's always going to get all As and no one is bad to him. If he was in my old school he'd get beaten up because the person couldn't get as good a mark as him.' Sean thinks this is because the private school sets the boy as the standard for everyone to achieve. In the comprehensive, this type of competitiveness was discouraged.

Judging by Sean's SATS results and the marks on his private school entrance exam, if he'd been born 20 years earlier, he would have passed the 11-plus and gone to grammar school. But in the comprehensive, he instantly identified with the low-achieving boys in his class, because they were the ones with the coolest clothes and music; they were the ones who were smoking cigarettes and rolling joints on the school playing fields at break. He turned his competitiveness in another direction, towards who had the best trainers, who had gone all the way with a girl first. Why couldn't he identify with the clever boys? 'Because they were geeks,' he says. The only way you could compete with them was academically and how could you know if you were beating them when you only ever got a grade once a year, in your annual report? I don't think that a lack of competitive system in comprehensives is the single cause of boys' educational failure. It is one factor which has its roots in a male culture which exists unchanging while everything else has been transformed all around it – the structures of the economy, the new role that women are playing in society and their demands for a better life which are not dependent on a sole male breadwinner, the shift towards communication-based work, a call for emotional literacy.

But if you look at the areas in which boys succeed, you find that they are very, very good at playing computer games, those zap-the-baddies exercises in

Voices from elsewhere

high-speed wrist skills in which everything is reduced to the urge to pass from one level to another, to some final unseen reward.

'Do girls have Play Stations?' I asked Sean. 'No,' he said, flatly.

When the education ministry examines ways of challenging the male culture of the playground it will have to look very carefully at the Play Station, and instead of condemning it as a pernicious form of American dumbing down, ask why boys are willing to devote so many hours to sitting attentively in front of its screen, motivated, willing themselves to succeed, beating girls, who are barely in the race.

What makes boys winners then? And how do we then devise an educational system in which both sexes come out on top? •

....

8 June 1998
John Ryle
Casualties of two conflicts

Last week a friend of mine, Steven, died. He was 36. I flew back to England from Africa — on a night flight from the war zone to the viral battlefield — in time to see him on his way out, one more casualty in the 15-year struggle that has spread to all continents, the struggle against an epidemic that, like war, fells men and women in their youth, leaving sorrowing mothers, fathers, friends and lovers in its train.

Grief drives a pin through the folds of memory: at Steven's funeral, in a dreary crematorium in south London, I found myself taking a mental roll call of the victims of two conflicts, the war in Sudan and the health crisis created by AIDS.

The AIDS epidemic and the Sudanese civil war started, as it happens, at the same time. At an age when you don't expect your friends to die, I was caught up in both. Having been an anthropological researcher among the Dinka of southern Sudan before the war, I became an aid worker in 1988, in the early days of the relief effort. Over the next few years, as I went back and forth from the killing fields of Sudan to London and New York, I found death visiting the metropolis too, and saw the ranks of old lovers and friends thinned by the plague.

Philip Lloyd-Bostock, an academic and novelist, was the first person I knew with AIDS. He died in 1985. A year or two later, Robert Maker, my former research assistant in Sudan, a sweet-tempered teacher who joined the southern rebel army, was killed in action by Sudan government troops. Zakaria Manyang, another teacher I worked with before the war, died in the Bahr-al-Ghazal famine of 1987–9. Benjamin Bol, a former government minister, was killed by his own comrades-in-arms.

Voices from elsewhere

Of course, there is AIDS in Sudan too. But in the midst of war and hunger, it goes almost unnoticed: just another in a bundle of afflictions.

Meanwhile, back home, the death toll has continued to rise: Tim Swales, Eduardo Guimaraes and Ramadan Muchoki went the way of Philip Lloyd-Bostock. In my address book crosses marked their names. And slowly the book became a garden of remembrance.

All just names – except to their families and friends. But in the chapel where Steven's body slid into the flames there were many people with lists like this in their heads. Death spreads like a chain letter; funerals fan the embers of old grief. The dead rise up like revenants in the minds of mourners. And that, as every pulpit homily reminds us, is where they live on, in the recollections of those who survive them.

I have been reading *The Farewell Symphony*, Edmund White's sprawling AIDS elegy. Towards the end, a sense of emptiness descends, as the reader realises that all the characters save the narrator are dead. The narrator, it transpires, is the lone performer in the piece by Haydn from which the novel takes its name, a symphony where the instrumentalists leave the stage one by one till only a single violin is left playing. *The Farewell Symphony* is a *roman-à-clef*; it belies the elegant metaphor of its title, becoming a memorial for those who figure in it, White's closest friends, most of them gay and childless, touching them with the immortality of art.

For Steven, a man without enemies, there is no book, but his name will come to mind at funeral after funeral, while those who knew him are alive.

In Sudan they do it differently. If you are a Dinka, or if you are from any of the Nilotic peoples of the Sudan, it is impossible to die without offspring. Nilotes practise ghost marriage. Even in the carnage of war someone who dies unmarried, adult or child, will have descendants raised in their name. Another friend of mine, Joseph Malual – happily still living – explains the Dinka system of ghost marriage in a haunting book on death edited by Rosemary Dinnage, *The Ruffian on the Stair*.

The Dinka, he explains, are patrilineal and polygamous. If you die before your time, your brother, or some other kinsman, will marry for you. The children of such a marriage will figure in your lineage, not his. Women who die childless may become classificatory males. Children will be raised in their name too – and they themselves will figure in the patriline as men. For the Dinka and other Nilotic peoples, physical death is an everyday event. The war has seen to that. But social death is a contradiction in terms. The language of kinship inscribes the names of the dead in the memory of the tribe. This is a kind of immortality too. ●

John Hodder

Bishop Trevor Huddleston

Final calls

Final calls

21 April 1998
Desmond Tutu
Bishop Trevor Huddleston: courageous warrior of Africa

I must have been eight or nine when I first saw Trevor Huddleston, though I did not know then it was he. My mother was a cook at a hostel for blind black women. Those were the days when South Africa's policies were only slightly less vicious than they became under the apartheid laws. If you were black, you counted for little in the land of your birth. As a black woman, you were even more disadvantaged, treated as a perpetual minor in the eyes of the law. My mother was not well educated. In the eyes of the world, this lovely person was a nonentity. I was standing with her on the hostel veranda when this tall white man, in a flowing black cassock, swept past. He doffed his hat to my mother in greeting. I was quite taken aback; a white man raising his hat to a black woman! Such things did not happen in real life. I learned much later that the man was Father Trevor Huddleston.

That gesture left an indelible impression. Perhaps it helped deep down to make me realise we were precious to God and to this white man; perhaps it helped me not to become anti-white, despite the harsh treatment we received at the hands of most white people.

Subsequently, I went to a high school in Johannesburg. The fathers of the Community of the Resurrection, of which Father Trevor was a member, ran a hostel for young blacks in Sophiatown, where I stayed. I made my first really good sacramental confession to him. His office would, one moment, have several of what he called his 'creatures' playing marbles on the floor, the next it would be his meeting place with, say, Yehudi Menuhin, who came to play in Christ the King Church.

I used to sit on Trevor's lap, as did others of his protégés, among whom are Archbishop Walter Makhulu, of central Africa, and the jazz trumpeter Hugh Masekela. Archbishop Trevor got Hugh his first trumpet as a gift from the great Louis Armstrong. When I contracted tuberculosis and spent 22 months in hospital, Father Trevor visited me nearly every week. How special he made me feel, this eloquent critic of the evil of racism.

If there was one person who pricked the world's conscience about apartheid, it was Trevor Huddleston. With the Anti-Apartheid Movement, he made sure the issue remained on the world's agenda as a moral issue. Our spectacular victory in 1994 owes a very great deal to the untiring efforts of 'the Jerry' — the nickname he was given in Sophiatown.

He often said he hoped apartheid would die before he did. That happened.

Final calls

What a tremendous man he was. God certainly knew what he was doing when he created Trevor.

Ernest Urban Huddleston, clergyman and anti-apartheid campaigner, born 15 June 1913; died 20 April 1998. •

13 June 1998
Alastair Campbell
Ellie Merritt: a graduation in grief

As the hospital priest tried to comfort Ellie Merritt's mother, Lindsay Nicholson, a nurse commented that this was cruelty almost beyond invention. Almost six years ago, in another hospital, another priest had been comforting Lindsay after her husband, John Merritt, died.

John Merritt was the finest reporter I ever knew. He fought a two and a half year battle against leukaemia, the same supposedly non-hereditary illness that had taken his mother when he was 13. He was finally killed by a haemorrhage.

This week Ellie Merritt, John and Lindsay's nine-year-old daughter, died in the same way. Her battle against leukaemia did not last as long as her father's, but it was just as painful, the wait for a matching bone-marrow transplant just as fruitless. In the end, the haemorrhage was just as fatal.

How do you record a nine-year-old's life? Her best friend was called Lara. She went to St Gilda's and St Peter's School in north London, whose children wrote to her daily while she was in hospital. She once had a pony called Poppy. She liked painting her toenails different lurid colours. Sporty was her favourite Spice Girl. She and her godmother, Terry Tavner, were founder members of the 'Bad Girl's Club', invented by Terry because she was worried Ellie Merritt was too good.

But she had real character and a powerful kind of wisdom, the product no doubt of her early graduation in grief. Shortly before her death, she told her mother that she was mapping out a book about her illness, and that she had already decided the chapter headings. She could, and did, describe exactly what she saw and felt as she tossed a single rose into John's grave on the day of his funeral.

She loved talking about her father. She could remember doodles he had drawn, little messages he left around the house for her. She wanted to know about the stories he wrote, the injustices he exposed, the executives he monstered, the crazy things he did.

For those who knew John, and above all for Lindsay, it has been wretched to

Final calls

watch Ellie go the same way. She looked like him. She had the same thick red hair that thinned and then disappeared. She had the same slow and elegant walk; the same light blue eyes; the same wicked humour; the same courage too.

Almost 20,000 people responded to an appeal in February for a matching bone-marrow donor for Ellie. None was found, but it may mean someone else's life will be saved. Her mother, Lindsay, and sister, Hope, survive her.

Ellie Merritt, born 3 December 1988; died 11 June 1998
To offer a blood sample for tissue analysis, call the Anthony Nolan Bone Marrow Trust on 0990 111 533. ●

....

16 May 1998
William Kennedy
Frank Sinatra: the song was you, pal

The remarkable thing about Sinatra recordings: you can listen to them not only for ever, but also at great length without overdosing, once you have been infected. I say this not only on my own behalf but on behalf of the entire set in which I move, and which I have helped infect to the point that Frank is now a common denominator among this group of seriously disparate ages and types.

In the 1950s, there came *In the Wee Small Hours*, which conditioned your life, especially with a young woman with lush blonde hair who used to put the record on and pray to Frank for a lover. All that perfumed hair, and it came undone. That certainly was a good year, but it remained for another album, *Swing Easy*, to teach you how to play a record 12 times in one night, which was merely a warm-up for 1983, when you listened to 'New York, New York' for the first time seriously and then played it 60 times until 5 a.m., also calling your friends in New York and Aspen and permitting them to stop sleeping and get out of bed and listen along.

The true thing about this phenomenon is that you do not have to have Frank on video, or in a movie or TV show. You really don't need those presences. All you need is the music the man has made and that has been with you all your life.

The finale of all this is that six years later Frank turned up in our home town, Albany, as the opening act for the brand new Knickerbocker Arena, with 17,000 seats. Would Albany turn out for him in any numbers? Word had gone out, as it always does with these myth-making events, that Frank wasn't well, that

Final calls

Liza Minnelli was standing by to go on if he crumpled. What's more, Ava had just died and so maybe this was not one of those very good years.

And yet here he came, six years older than when I'd last seen him, looking smaller, his seventy-fifth year just barely under way. He's wearing his single-breasted tux with an orange pocket handkerchief, his hair totally silver. Then he opens his mouth. 'Come fly with me,' he sings, and a cheer goes up from the 17,000 who have packed the place to hear and see this legendary character.

A lifetime of staying young at centre-stage: how can anybody be so good for so long? You listen and know that this is not Frank in his best voice ever but it doesn't matter. It's his sound, his cadence, his tunes, him, and it's as good as it can be and that's still very, very good. He moseys to the improvised bar on stage with the Jack Daniel's and the ice bucket and he sits on the bar stool and says, 'I think it's about time to have a drink. I don't drink a lot, but I don't drink a little either.' And then he opens his mouth again: 'It's quarter to three,' and the crowd roars.

And then he segues into 'New York, New York' and the spotlights circle the crowd, and Frank is making love to all here. He opens his arms, points to everybody. 'It's up to you, New York, New York.' Then it's over and the spots cross on him, and the ageing bobby-soxers, having come full circle from 48 years gone, reach up to shake his hand, and he fades down the stairs and out, and you follow him with your eyes because he is carrying the sound of your youth, the songs of your middle age. And then you think, the song is you, pal, the song is you.

Francis Albert Sinatra, singer and actor, born 12 December 1915; died 15 May 1998. •

4 April 1998
David Robinson
Stephen Archibald: brief lives on mean streets

Stephen Archibald, who has died aged 38, gave the cinema one of its most unforgettable faces. He played the protagonist, Jamie, in all three parts of Bill Douglas's autobiographical trilogy – *My Childhood* (1972), *My Ain Folk* (1973) and *My Way Home* (1977) – in the years when he matured, along with the character, from 12 to 17. The films recall Douglas's own deprived youth in Newcraighall, a poor mining community on the outskirts of Edinburgh, as an illegitimate child, constantly shunted from one uncaring relative to another.

Archibald's background was not so different from Douglas's. He was born and brought up a few miles away, in another depressed outcrop of Edinburgh,

Final calls

the Craigmillar Estate. Craigmillar had begun as an idealistic 1930s rehousing project, but the collapse of local industries from the 1950s reduced it to one of Western Europe's most deprived places. He was one of five brothers and two sisters. Three generations of the family – Stephen, his father and his own son – have never known regular employment. In these districts, as the trilogy exposes, frustration and anger pass from generation to generation.

Douglas discovered Archibald in 1971 or 1972, when he was in Edinburgh preparing *My Childhood*. Two 12-year-old truants accosted him at a bus stop, demanding 'a drag on your fag, mister'. He courteously refused, but the pair chatted on, with the elder, Hughie Restorick, doing more of the talking than his taciturn friend, Stephen.

Douglas recalled, 'I kept answering their questions – and then I suddenly realised there they were; I needn't go any further. And I said to them, "Would you like to be in a film?" "What's the story about?" And I said, "Oh, never mind the story." "How much do we get?" And I said, just off the top of my head, "Well, £4."' The boys leapt at it, even though Stephen, out of natural reflex, gave Douglas a false address, which made it hard to find him again.

Their headmaster was full of foreboding – he had, he said, much brighter, better-looking and certainly less troublesome boys. But Douglas insisted. Their attendance on the set was officially restricted to two days a week, but the boys' enthusiasm, combined with their taste for truancy, overcame that problem. 'So engrossed were they that I had difficulty making them go home at the day's end,' said Douglas. 'Seeing the children visibly improving themselves, I chose to break the law. As luck would have it, it wasn't until the final day of shooting that the headmaster sent the law in my direction.'

The following year, Archibald and Hughie (as Jamie's elder brother, Tommy) worked with Douglas again on *My Ain Folk*. In *My Way Home*, Stephen – at 17 already married, even though he was still a shade too young and small for his role as national serviceman – appeared again, this time without Hughie.

'Stephen was very like me,' Douglas recalled. 'His quietness was the quietness and introspection I once had, and I think I still have a bit.' He hardly had to explain what he needed from his actor. 'I'd look into his eye, and I could see that he knew exactly what I was talking about. I'd just glance at him and say, "Oh, you know what I mean." It was as if he was my left arm.'

Even allowing for Douglas's skill with non-professional actors, Stephen Archibald showed an extraordinary instinct, and over the five years' work developed a useful professional awareness. Years after seeing the films, people still recall individual moments, invariably Stephen's, and particularly the sparse hints of tenderness, as when Jamie closes his ailing granny's hand around a warmed tea-mug.

A Bill Douglas shoot was a purgatorial experience for everyone, but most of all for the director, simultaneously tormented by reawakened childhood traumas and the tyranny of his own artistic vision. When filming, the normally shy,

Final calls

Security at Linda McCartney's memorial service on 8 June 1998

Final calls

charming Douglas was transformed. Yet, with all his tantrums, furniture-smashing and suicide threats, he seems never to have taken it out on his small *alter ego*. 'Whether I liked it or not, I had a responsibility to him. I couldn't play with his life; I had to be aware of the effect, once it was no longer a novelty, that this experience would have on him. Of course, the inevitable had happened and he wanted to act for the rest of his life.'

In *My Way Home*, the final part of the trilogy, Jamie, now a national serviceman, is posted to Egypt. A fellow airman – English, middle-class and intellectual – offers him friendship, encouragement and an introduction to the world of books and art that will transform his life. In Douglas's case, it really happened like that: the friend, Peter Jewell, gave him practical and moral support for the rest of his life, and, after his death, established the Bill Douglas Centre for Cinema Studies at Exeter University.

Young Stephen Archibald had no such luck. The chances to act did not come, and by the time Douglas finally devised a role for him in his only feature film, *Comrades*, Stephen was in jail. Job-training schemes brought no results; his marriage collapsed, although he maintained a relationship with his son.

He was not without friends, and 100 people turned up for his funeral last week, for, deprived as it is, Craigmillar retains a sense of community. In 1962, Helen Crummy, who played a schoolteacher in *My Childhood*, got together with other mothers on the estate to form the Craigmillar Festival Society, with the aim of letting people express themselves creatively.

Stephen was intermittently in touch with the society, though he was not to be one of its successes. Mrs Crummy first met him about the time he first worked with Douglas and remembers him with warmth. 'Poor Stephen was the most damaged child I ever saw,' she said. 'I think I never saw him smile. Even as a child, he often looked like a little, depressed old man. The filming with Bill was the best part of his life.'

A Craigmillar local councillor, David Brown, kept in touch with Stephen, even though he recognised that unemployment, the failure of self-esteem, and addictions endemic to despair were to prove too much. Latterly, Stephen looked far older than his years. His fellow actor Hughie Restorick died some years before him.

Bill Douglas died in 1991; on his gravestone is written, 'We only have to love one another to know what we must do.' Thanks to his inspired collaboration, these kids, who were given so little, seemingly only born to fail, have left their legacy. The Bill Douglas trilogy is one of the treasures of British – specifically Scottish – cinema; Stephen's yearning, anxious eyes and sullen mouth, and Hughie's brighter, cheekier look stand for the face of deprived childhood in developed societies of the late twentieth century.

Stephen Archibald, unemployed, briefly a child actor, born 5 May 1959; died 24 March 1998. •

Final calls

8 June 1998

James Ivory
Geoffrey Kendal: Everyman's Shakespeare

Geoffrey Kendal, who has died aged 88, was born Geoffrey Bragg in the Cumbrian town of Kendal, but is known best as the Shakespeare Wallah, a name combining his two lifelong and closely linked passions: the plays of Shakespeare and India. Another passion, to be sure, was his family, made up of three remarkable actresses who became his principal players and with whom he moved over the subcontinent and beyond: Laura Liddell, his wife, and Jennifer and Felicity, his daughters.

Together they made up the Shakespeareana Company, adding other actors as they went along, both English and Indian (including Shashi Kapoor, who later married the elder daughter, Jennifer). Ask any educated Indian over the age of 40 where he or she first heard Shakespeare's lines and the answer is almost always the same – from one of the makeshift stages on which the troupe appeared in the 1940s and 1950s up, down and across India.

The first English people I ever knew were the Kendals; they became my first English friends. This was in Bombay in the early 1960s, and I met them because they were Shashi Kapoor's family. Ismail Merchant and I described their adventures in *Shakespeare Wallah*, our second film, though that melancholy story was not the Kendals' story, as Geoffrey and Laura were quick to point out. Their adventures in India, beginning at the time of independence, had been a romantic dream come true for them.

Making *Shakespeare Wallah* was sometimes distasteful for the older Kendals. It was too close to their own experience for comfort, yet far enough away to seem to them at times a kind of lie. The premise of the film appeared to the Kendals to be the negation of everything they had worked for for so long. They looked upon the Indian part of their career as a triumph, and expected the film to be an affirmation of this (to them) wonderful life of actors on tour.

But the premise of *Shakespeare Wallah* was based on the failure of the Buckingham Players, as they were called in the film, to hold their audiences against the tides of modernisation sweeping over India (and also threatening the English language). The Kendals knew this was happening to them too – or would soon happen. So they felt uncomfortable, were hard put sometimes even to bring out their dialogue, which seemed to give utterance to thoughts which were at variance with everything they believed. It did not help that the stuff of their lives was being used in order to create a drama symbolic of a moment in history, or that they stood as an embodiment of all things English – then in the process of being cast aside.

Final calls

The Kendals were also my introduction to the world of the English stage in all its crotchety splendour. Geoffrey Kendal – a wandering player-king, irascible and mercurial – was the strolling embodiment, with his family, of this great tradition. They carried the English stage to the far corners of the empire – some very far and dusty corners indeed.

I was too wet behind the ears then to connect Geoffrey Kendal to any sort of tradition or to see how that might serve me in the future. He knew we did not speak the same language and he let me know how he despised the cinema – that the cinema was his enemy, as he wrote later, causing theatres to be empty and tours to be cancelled.

Kendal sometimes spoke to me in a way no one else ever had. Indeed, I'm not sure he would be happy to know I'm writing this obituary. He gave way to terrible rages on the set of *Shakespeare Wallah*, but his daughters said it was all just acting and to pay no attention. One night we worked until after midnight, and when he was finally released and was being driven home, he sat back in the seat and said icily to me as I stood at his window apologising that, naturally, he would never see me again. I believed him and ran after the car for a few paces until his daughter Jennifer pulled me back, laughing and saying, 'It's just a bluff, you fool. Can't you see?'

Another time he chased the stills photographer all around the set, threatening to smash his camera, because he had dared to take a picture of him while he was cat-napping. But his tirades prepared me for much worse ones in the years to come from other English actors, far away from India.

Later he mellowed towards *Shakespeare Wallah*, finding it ironic, he said, 'that, in the whirligig of time, it was the despised cinema that told the world of my existence and to a certain extent of my fight'.

His fight – always begging, borrowing, stealing – had been to be true to his first love, the theatre. He wrote, 'The theatre is female, and like all females, she will not be trifled with. She must be grasped with both hands and given one's whole self, body and soul, if she is to be a proper mate. She must not be dallied with or neglected or flirted with, or she will bite, and that bite will never heal.'

To this day I cannot watch a performance of *Othello* or *Twelfth Night* or *Antony and Cleopatra* and not see Geoffrey and Laura Kendal and hear their voices, which after nearly four decades are as distinct as the first time I heard them on our *Shakespeare Wallah* stages in Simla, Kasauli and Alwar – so much so that the modern interpreters of the Kendals' great parts seem, to my ear, to be doing something wrong.

> Come, come, and sit you down; you shall not budge;
> You go not till I set you up a glass
> Where you may see the inmost part of you.

Geoffrey Kendal, actor, born 7 September 1909; died 14 May 1998. •

Final calls

10 February 1998
Hugo Young
Enoch Powell: purveyor of tosh to the British

Enoch Powell made you listen. He had the gift of menace and surprise in greater portion than any speaker I ever heard. With the exception of Iain Macleod, all his contemporaries and successors in the Tory Party made listening a trial. These days, listening has been replaced by watching, doctoring, sussing out. There is no such thing as a public orator. There are soundbite operatives and sofa-sophisticates, neither of which functions requires a classical education or a concern for English grammar. Powell deployed verbs, literate allusions, the ever-imminent possibility of shock. Enoch Powell also made you think. He didn't recoil from original argument, or lack the courage to press it to the limit. He had a better mind than almost all his peer group. Considered simply as an instrument, a ratiocinating artefact, it was hard to beat. He was steeped in history, a fount of scholarship. Nobody was better at conferring iron logic on a mental process that began in the mists of prejudice: which is the way, after all, most politicians — most people — build their attitudes. As a stimulant to prejudice, for and against, Powell became uniquely reliable.

In both these capacities, orator and thinker, he was rare in politics. Nobody else could set the juices racing all round the House. Intellectually, and one might even say morally, he stood above the mass of men and women who take on the workaday task of running the country. He uttered from great heights of superiority. There's a place for such a vessel of independence, which is not to be judged wanting because of its failure to serve in Cabinet for more than a single year, 1962–63. Politicians with pretensions half as high as Powell's would regard his wilderness record with despair, and the man himself often reflected on it with mordancy. But office isn't what politics is all about. And the absence of office isn't the reason for casting a baleful eye on the titanic life that was so effusively memorialised in yesterday's papers.

Having failed with office, Powell opted for the role of prophet. The question a prophet must face is not whether he spoke mesmerically or argued with a clarity that improved on Delphi, but whether he was more often right than wrong. Did he wisely foretell the future? Was his case persuasive? Did he see what others missed? All political careers, Powell once said, end in failure. Here, at least, he knew what he was talking about.

He was a good prophet, I think, on only one count. As a political economist, he argued for the importance of money before monetarism was ever heard of. His political incorrectness in analysing some of the key causes of inflation,

Final calls

from the mid-1960s onwards, is impressive to recall. Even proto-Keynesians are obliged to acknowledge that what was once unmentionable in polite society has become commonplace. In the British political world, Powell was its first, rather courageous, begetter.

On every other continuous public question – I exempt some forays into individual cases, such as the Hola Camp scandal – what is impressive about Powell is not that he was shocking but that he was wrong. He was a bad prophet and, as such, a worse politician.

On immigration, which made him famous, his speculations were not merely incendiary but startlingly mistaken. The non-white numbers never reached the heights he forecast, and, even though they became higher than when he spoke, never had the destructive social consequences he prophesied. He said blood would flow. There has been very little blood. He said Britain could not become multiracial. Though things are far from perfect, both white Britain and black Britain have proved him malignly in error. Powell's whole immigration line was not just an unfortunate forensic solecism, as his friends were saying yesterday. It revealed existential misjudgement about the nature of Britain and the British.

On international affairs, a similar fallacy pervaded him. Britain Alone seemed to be his pitch. That's the only explanation for the statesman manqué who could find no ally fit to be received into the British embrace.

Worst of all was the European Community, over which Powell broke with the Tory Party, and which he spent 30 years defaming as the destroyer of the British nation-state. Once upon a time, he was a pro-European, who in the middle 1960s contributed to a zealous federalist tract. But he soon gave that up. The trenchant rhetoric masked a mind, it seemed, in febrile search of anything that sustained the narrowest, whitest, purest, most English form of Britishness.

His legacy is a coterie of cultists who worship the very mention of his name. They're not unimportant, being prominent in the clique that now wants to destroy the Tory Party as we've known it. They long for the world he described; dabble incoherently in the romance of Britishness; define that term with self-referential insularity; hark forever backwards not ahead; maintain an attitude to the world whose unreality does perfect justice to the man they blindly revere. Reading them yesterday, one better understood how important to the romance of a certain kind of politics is the incorrigible failure of the hero in question to persuade more than a tiny fraction of the people that his diagnoses reflect the truth.

What persuaded the Prime Minister to describe this singularly unsuccessful politician as one of the 'great figures of twentieth-century politics' is hard to understand. Are there no limits to the rightward inclusiveness of New Labour? Yes, Powell had a brilliant mind. Yes, he applied his great intellect to the largest problems of the age. Yes, he could hold an audience in magnetic thrall. But the great intellect's triumph, ironically, was of style over substance. On the

Final calls

substance, he spent three decades talking about a nation that does not, and should not, exist.

John Enoch Powell, politician, born 16 June 1912; died 8 February 1998. •

....

17 February 1998
Veronica Horwell
Martha Gellhorn: a witness to our world at war

The streetcars of her hometown of St Louis, Missouri, shaped the life of Martha Gellhorn, who has died aged 89. Her suffragette mother and doctor father had raised her to confidence and campaigning, and, as a child, she had freedoms her peers did not: she roamed the city alone on those cars, looking in on lives unlike her own. 'One bends one's twig and it stays bent,' she drawled long after.

She was briefly collegiate at Bryn Mawr. She was a cub reporter surviving on a diet of doughnuts. Then at 21, in 1930, her life began with a steerage-class passage to Europe, $75 and a suitcase. She went to Paris to become a foreign or, better still, a roving correspondent. Just like that.

Even for a girl who looked, as she once remarked, like the cartoon character Betty Boop – all batted eyelashes – and had limitless insouciance, it did not happen quite like that. Gellhorn sold any old writing she could and got a 'very high-class education – standing room at ground level to watch history as it happened'.

Her learning process involved European poverty and politics and an affair, later a short marriage, with the radical journalist Bertrand de Jouvenal, who, as a youth, had been the lover of a middle-aged Colette. She innocently took a room in a bawdy-house and knowingly bought absurd Parisian couture cheap at the end of the season. She was also introduced to her first Nazis, 'scrubbed and parrot-brained'. They didn't teach a girl any of that at Bryn Mawr.

The process also covered returning to – and crossing – America, walking in on an oil boom and on the great Russian film director Sergei Eisenstein, who was failing to film in Mexico, and writing her first novel. It took her on to the payroll of the Federal Relief Agency, for which she filed reports on the lives of the forgotten poor, which read like epic captions for Depression photographers; she was sacked for inspiring local revolutions. It allowed her the naivety to cadge room and board from H. G. Wells in London, where she wrote a vivid eyewitness account of a Southern lynching she later admitted that she had never seen; and to accept the offer of President Roosevelt and his wife, Eleanor – her

Final calls

mother's campaigning friend – to stay in the White House, which was pretty homey then. She put up there in Abraham Lincoln's bedroom and was fed regular meals during an awkward patch when her furious moral righteousness made her otherwise unemployable. There she finished *The Trouble I've Seen*, fiction based on her underclass investigations. It was published in 1936, with her portrait, blonde and elegant, on its dust jacket: this was a titillating combination and a success. She was immediately celebrated, but fled the hoopla by holidaying in Florida.

At a Key West bar called Sloppy Joe's, she ran into Ernest Hemingway, bulky in his 'odiferous Basque shorts'. Two big celebs in a small town. His books had been her models. She said so. He had seen her face on *Troubles*. All afternoon and evening, they drank Papa Dobles, two and a half jiggers of white Bacardi rum, juice of two fresh limes, swirled in a rusty electric blender. It sounds like a Hollywood 'meet-cute' – she walked into the bar in a black dress and high heels, with her terrific mother in tow. The Bacall and Bogart versions were merely remakes. She seems to have thought she had found the partner her nerve deserved. Hemingway was hooked.

He was also married and off to cover the Spanish Civil War. She decided to join the fight and him (perhaps not in that order), this time with a rucksack and $50, a letter of introduction from *Collier's* magazine, and a notion that the 'correct response to a war against fascism was simply to be present on the right side'. She thought that war correspondents reported the battlefield, and was surprised, but willing, when one suggested that a description of ordinary life in besieged Madrid was worth sending home.

Collier's printed the piece, put her name on their masthead, and there she was, a war correspondent and Hemingway's lover – and under his patronage, eating his tinned supplies and sharing his mattress on the road, yet still stubbornly independent. Her reports from Spain were more candid than his. The ration portion of dried salted cod weighed as heavily as the shells. She did not have to pretend to be an authority.

One editor at *Collier's* appreciated and trusted her copy and, for eight years after that, she could go where she wanted and write what she saw. 'I had the chance to see the life of my time, which was war.' The British unprepared for total war; the Czechoslovak army walking home after the German land-grab; the Finns democratic but frozen, fighting the Russians; the Chinese, in hunger and filth, out-enduring the Japanese invaders. Her base was a house outside Havana, which she had made over for Hemingway and herself. They married and settled in. They worked on fiction. But Gellhorn wanted to be in on the war at last breaking out in Europe, and a crazy Caribbean sea-hunt for U-boats (with a resulting, unpublished, extremely funny piece) was not enough. She was drinking daiquiris in a bar on the Mexican border when the newspaper boy hawked her the edition reporting Pearl Harbor.

Hemingway was having a fine time with his sporting Cuban buddies chasing

Final calls

phantom Nazi subs. He had already done global conflict. Gellhorn failed to persuade him to engage with the world at war a second time around. The marriage fractured. She reached London and followed the action in Europe and North Africa as closely as she could with, or usually without, official permission, and with directions from friends in useful places. She advanced recklessly up through Italy with the Allies. Hemingway's telegram to her there read: 'Are you a war correspondent or my wife in bed?'

This time, he eventually came after her. Their rivalry was not friendly any more. She seems to have been Hemingway's personal bullshit-detector, especially when she coldly watched him holding court in a London hospital after a drunken accident. Gellhorn stowed away on a D-Day hospital ship and went ashore at Normandy. Hemingway crossed the Channel as officially as possible, but did not land.

In a hotel in free Paris, Gellhorn was advised by her old buddy the photographer Robert Capa to demand a divorce. She did, then loosely attached herself to the 82nd Airborne through the bitter 1944–5 winter of the Battle of the Bulge, and also to its leader, the heroic General James Gavin. She was present when the chaotic mass of the Russian army swarmed up to the other Allies. She was in newly liberated Dachau, at the apex of her anger, when peace was declared.

What the inmates told her there – that it had been useless to protest or weep about what happened to them – was the antithesis of all she had believed in; she mistrusted Germany ever after. Her St Louis ancestry included both immigrant Germans and Jews.

About all of these places and people she wrote simply. An American prose style of Shaker plainness was laboured at by many of her contemporaries. To Gellhorn, it seems to have come naturally. She spoke that way. She believed real reporters did not take notes, but knew instinctively what remained forever important – trivia, the tone of the times. This might include a GI toasting himself a frontline cheese sandwich from K rations, or a Dutch slave labourer, recently freed, buying tulips in the ruins of a German city. It seldom included any utterance, or even mention, of a politician. 'All politicians are bores and liars and fakes. I talk to people,' she said. To read her dispatches (collected as *The Face of War* and *The View from the Ground*) is to be granted instant access to where she was, whenever it was.

The business in peace was to settle down. As a woman divorced on the grounds of abandonment, Gellhorn made some random gestures to pacification. These included acquiring a decrepit property in London, returning to Washington – only to find herself in solo outrage against McCarthyism – trying fiction and playwriting, and adopting a 15-month-old Italian orphan, Sandy. She brought him up, supporting their life together in cheap places like Mexico by journalism and writing potboilers for women's magazines – novellas differing from her own taste in their happy endings. And from her own life too, for General Gavin had married a nice young girl.

Final calls

Gellhorn's next love, David Gurewitsch (a protégé of Mrs Roosevelt) could barely cope with her. She was courted by Tom Matthews, a recently retired editor of *Time* magazine, with a Mount Rushmore profile and a sound mind, and they married. But he wanted an urbane life in Britain and she missed the excitement, and even more the whole-soul engagement, of the fight against fascism. 'I am a loner. I am not a team player,' she said once – she could certainly be unsociable, abrupt and grand – and, 'The ideal is to live five blocks away from a man who makes you laugh and is wrapped up in his work.' The marriage petered out after nine years.

And so, by the 1960s, she was wandering again, observing more of the 50-plus countries of her travels. She knew a lot about how people respond to place, especially when they respond by misbehaving: in that honestly funny book *Travels with Myself and Another*, she confessed how she misbehaved herself, how she was revolted by stench in west Africa and daunted by dengue fever going upriver by canoe. She repeatedly fell in love with countries, affairs which led her to hang curtains in impossible shacks. Her long-lasting final devotion was to a cottage on the Welsh borders, which had demanding vegetables in the garden.

Her association with *Collier's* had lapsed with her editor's death in the 1940s. Thereafter, she had often to give herself assignments, and pay her own expenses, to satisfy her curiosity. For one long period, she had a writer's block; for another, there was an editorial block against her copy – she was no longer a sexy novelty nor yet venerable, and the robustness of her New Deal attitude was out of fashion. Nevertheless, with help – which she remembered as rather minimal – from the *Guardian*, she reached Vietnam in 1966 to report on the war (of which she was ashamed) that confirmed America as a colonial power.

Her long perspective eventually became valued again, when she returned to Madrid at the time of Franco's death, or to Castro's Cuba, where she saw, in the splendour of the full-grown trees now filling the garden of her old home, 'the years of my life made real'. At 80, she took off to inquire into the US invasion of Panama, supple of spine and mind, stroppy as ever. Granta took her up as a sibyl; its editors and writers longed to have lived as she had done.

Gellhorn stayed flexible, except, notably, in her attitude to Israeli-Palestinian relations; she saw Israel always as the defiant David of its founding battles. She planned to go snorkelling with Paul Theroux well into her eighties. When surgery on her eyes went awry, she had the doctor professionally cursed by a Malagasy medicine man.

She dined with the BBC's John Simpson on his way to Bosnia. She saw off the East–West nuclear confrontation she most feared. She became part of the century's image bank. And to the end, this fierce pacifist reported drinking pitchers of red wine, or iced Scotch, with the children and the grandchildren of fighters she had known.

Martha Gellhorn, journalist, born 8 November 1908; died 15 February 1998. •

Final calls

2 December 1997

Linda Grant
Kathy Acker: a defiant, dangerous precedent

Kathy Acker, radical novelist, feminist punk, explorer of body politics, is dead at the age of 53. She died of breast cancer, having categorically assured readers of the *Guardian* in a long article at the beginning of this year that she was cured, the cancer had gone from her body, chased away by faith healers and shamans after her rejection of conventional medicine, in part based on her inability to pay for it as a patient without medical insurance in the United States.

'As I walked out of the surgeon's office, I realised that if I remained in the hands of mainstream medicine I would soon be dead, rather than diseased meat,' she wrote. She's as dead now as those who took the conventional route and failed, went with the chemotherapy and radiotherapy and all the invasive treatment of the reviled male medical establishment.

Acker, pierced and tattooed and shaven-headed, was a fan of self-mutilation which she named body art. Hence, at the first appearance of cancer she voluntarily underwent a double mastectomy and, after further tumours in her lymph nodes were diagnosed, took what she described as a leap of faith: that she could be healed and that she could heal herself. She learned to see disease as a body not in harmony with itself, as areas of blockage which are memories of old traumas, and that healing is about forgiveness of oneself. But it wasn't enough. None of it saved her, and she died, according to her obituary, in defiance of reason, still refusing to believe that the mystics and other utterly cool, beyond the edge, outside the mainstream characters she had put her faith in could no more give her life than the bad guys in white coats.

We do not know if Acker's case was curable by conventional means if she had had the money and the readiness to continue with it. She was diagnosed as having a 60 per cent chance of non-recurrence, and chemotherapy would only have added another 10 per cent. Acker, a radical to the last, chose her own path and if she needed to practise self-deceit towards the end as a way of saving face, who is to deny a dying woman the comfort of her illusions? Mainstream medicine seemed, in her own words, to deprive her of hope and the will to take control over her own life.

Hope became faith and will became willingness – to try anything at all other than confront death. But what of other women with breast cancer who read her assertion last February that she was cured? How many of them wondered whether they should stop going to the hospital, give up the nausea, the hair loss, the pills,

Final calls

striking out into territory that Acker had marked out for them, for everyone knew she was a pioneer? Instead of men with degrees, there were the purveyors of ancient Oriental wisdom or herbalists or acupuncturists or any of the swarm of alternative practitioners who have discovered that labelling anything 'natural' can be marketed as wholesome goodness. Forget about the fact that poison ivy is natural. An earthquake is natural. And typhoons. And volcanoes. And every other natural disaster known to blight humanity, killing crops and causing famines.

To Acker, modern medicine was big business, it was the establishment she had fought against all her life, what in the 1960s was designated the pharmaceutical-industrial complex to distinguish it from the military-industrial complex. They were twin evils, one killing innocent Vietnamese peasants, the other force-feeding women artificial hormones in the form of oral contraception. The feminist assault on conventional medicine in the United States, which grew out of the anti-war movement, began with the campaign against the Pill and against childbirth flat on one's back, drugged or unconscious.

Since then, parts of its progressive impetus have moved away from a desire to improve women's experience of conventional medicine – and indeed enter it as practitioners – and circled back in history until we find ourselves in a swamp of medieval unreason. A hundred years ago feminists fought against men telling

The actor Michael Elphic (extreme left), the broadcaster Ned Sherrin (left), the playwright and columnist Keith Waterhouse (centre), the actor Peter O'Toole (right) and Phillipa Clare, a friend (extreme right) at the London Cremation of the columnist and carouser Jeffrey Bernard on 11 September 1997.

Final calls

them that women could not be granted the responsibility of suffrage because their brains were too irrational to cope with public affairs. And now, at the last gasp of the twentieth century, women have constructed a whole anti-materialist philosophy out of witches, miracles, shamans, astrology and faith healers. Like Christabel Pankhurst who abandoned feminism to chase after the mystic Madame Blavatsky, second-wave feminism has fallen victim to nonsense.

Conventional medicine has, as it happens, made big advances in the past 10 years. Specific treatments include the removal of the lymph nodes which reduces the chance of cancer recurring in the breast or adjacent tissues, and the use of the drug Tamoxifen and chemotherapy which are associated with a 25 per cent increase in survival rates. The evidence of their successes is all around us. Many of us know women who have been diagnosed with breast cancer and are alive and well years later.

But the most significant success in reducing deaths from breast cancer operates neither in the high glamour world of the drug companies nor in the fetid tents of ancient mystics. It is carried out routinely, even mundanely every day, largely by middle-aged women in cardigans. It is breast screening, by which means cancer can be detected early enough to be successfully treated.

If we are ever to eradicate breast cancer it is likely to be through a host of activities, including investigating the effects of diet and environmental factors. The tragedy of Kathy Acker's early death should warn us against two things: the first is to move towards any kind of American model of health-care, the second is to confuse art with life. Acker placed her trust in metaphors – that diseases were traumas that could be cured by forgiveness, for example. Beneath the microscope, they were something else altogether.

Kathy Acker, writer and performance artist, born April 1944; died 29 November 1997. •

3 November 1997

W. Stephen Gilbert
Sydney Newman: golden age of the TV play

For ten brief but glorious years, Sydney Newman, who has died aged 80, was the most important impresario in Britain. The period that is now conventionally referred to as the 'golden age' of television drama, was presided over by this feisty Canadian who blagged his way into the industry and dared to challenge fusty conventions. His death marks not just the end of an era but the laying to rest of a whole philosophy of popular art.

Final calls

Newman was born in Toronto, the son of a Russian Jew who ran a shoe store. He developed an early passion for visual arts and, leaving school at 13, became a graphic designer, with a special knack for movie posters. But, as he put it at the first *Guardian* lecture in 1988, he 'couldn't make a living painting' and found his way into film.

The old prophet of documentary, John Grierson, was then head of the National Film Board of Canada and, after Newman had worked on some 350 movies in the Board's cutting rooms, he gave the young man a chance to prove himself as a producer of wartime propaganda.

After the war, Grierson got him an attachment to NBC in New York, where he closely observed the new wave of play-writing for television. He returned home much affected and, in 1952, gained through Grierson a foothold at CBC, the national broadcaster in Canada, where he rose quickly through the outside broadcast department until he ran it. 'Knowing nothing about drama,' he nevertheless persuaded CBC to let him move over and run the drama department, where he immediately put into practice the lessons he had learned in New York.

At CBC, Newman encouraged new writing and formed a stable of young directors such as Alvin Rakoff, William 'Ted' Kotcheff, Silvio Narizzano and Charles Jarrott. It was one of his productions, *Flight into Danger*, by the Newman discovery Arthur Hailey, which brought him to London.

The play was bought for screening on ITV and Howard Thomas, managing director of the London franchise-holder, ABC, invited him to produce a new Saturday night series of thrillers for the network. It was 1958.

Newman had barely opened his new office when the company's drama supervisor, Dennis Vance, was 'kicked upstairs' and Thomas offered the post to his new protégé. Newman took the offer with the proviso that he could personally produce a new Sunday night slot of straight plays and bring over his Canadian team to direct them. 'I decided that I would do original plays about the United Kingdom today,' he recalled 30 years later; and so, in 1959, Newman's *Armchair Theatre* was born, and changed the face of British television.

Newman was always more interested in journalists than literary types, and he cast his net wide for writers. He invented a key new post, that of the story editor, whose function was to go out into the hedgerows and find individuals with stories to tell. The first story editor was a book critic, Peter Luke, who once vividly described his boss as 'a cross between Genghis Khan and a pussycat'. It was Luke who found a Liverpudlian actor called Alun Owen and drew from him a play that set the standard in the first season of *Armchair Theatre*. The rough-hewn vitality of *No Trams to Lime Street* was hugely popular, which went some way to pacifying the American boss of ABPC, the owners of ABC, who 'didn't understand a goddamn word of it. My chauffeur's English. He didn't understand it either.'

Luke turned up another actor who was ready to write and, while Newman himself found the work hard to fathom, he fully backed his story editor's

Final calls

judgement. The play, *A Night Out*, by Harold Pinter, had the largest audience of the week.

The appetite for teledrama that Newman whetted was astonishing. The Pinter play was not the only time that *Armchair Theatre* had the week's best figures and a rating of 21 million, unthinkable for one-off drama today, was not uncommon. Moreover, the output was vast. In 1959, Newman personally produced 48 individual plays, each transmitted live. Anyone today who generates more than two productions in a year is thought to be a dangerous empire-builder.

It was inevitable that the BBC, where change was in the air under the leadership of Hugh Greene, would respond to *Armchair Theatre*'s success. Director of Television Kenneth Adam was duly dispatched to meet Newman in a pub, where he offered him the overlordship of all BBC television drama. Taking a salary dip, Newman took the job.

And he took BBC drama by the scruff. His division of the department into plays, serials and series has more or less remained the way BBC drama functions. He gave the green light, often more in hope than expectation, to such landmark projects as *The Forsyte Saga*, *Doctor Who* and *Adam Adamant*. His biggest gamble was to set up the *Wednesday Play* under the inventive producer James MacTaggart, whose name and achievements are honoured in the annual lecture given in his name at the Edinburgh Festival. 'Pick a good man and, boy, you're away' was Newman's attitude. In this remark resides his great gift as an administrator, the self-confidence to trust.

From 1964, the *Wednesday Play*, as much as any programme, defined the BBC's stance in an age of great change. Writers as diverse as John Osborne, Christopher Logue, J. B. Priestley, John Betjeman, N. F. Simpson and Raymond Williams contributed to it, but the new voices it introduced and/or developed make a roll call of remarkable quality: Dennis Potter, John Hopkins, David Mercer, Jeremy Sandford, David Rudkin, Jim Allen, Tony Parker, Nell Dunn, Colin Welland.

When the BBC contract ended in 1968, Newman decided to accept an offer to produce features for ABPC. The deal turned sour and he left after 18 months with nothing achieved. 'A futile waste,' he said. He returned to Canada, playing out his time in executive posts that asked too little of him.

Newman's favourite quote, from Thurber, was also the source of his favourite play's title: 'Let us not look back in anger, nor forward in fear, but around in awareness.' British television let Newman go when it needed him most. His legacy is almost played out because his every misgiving about television trends has come to pass. His wife, Elizabeth, died in 1981; he leaves three daughters.

Sydney Newman, television executive, born 1 April 1917; died 30 October 1997. •

Final calls

10 January 1998

Meirion Bowen
Sir Michael Tippett: shaping the harmonies of our time

For a long time, Sir Michael Tippett, who has died aged 93, languished under the shadow of Benjamin Britten. Britten, eight years his junior, was a musical prodigy, lauded in his teens, widely appreciated after the success of his opera *Peter Grimes* in 1945, and remaining prolific and popular up to his death in 1976. By contrast, Tippett, a late developer, was a slow, deliberate composer who won acceptance gradually. International fame came only in his late sixties. What distinguished the rest of his career was a prolonged Indian summer, for Tippett continued to write major new pieces until he was almost 90, breaking new ground, moreover, with each one.

Blessed with seemingly unremitting physical, creative and intellectual vitality, he became an almost legendary figure on the musical scene. His oratorio, *A Child of Our Time* (1939–41) – a moving assertion of humanitarianism in an epoch of catastrophe – acquired eventually the status of an icon.

Throughout his long life, Tippett ran against the grain of received British opinion. He early concluded that music and the arts were fundamentally international and rejected (as did Britten) the then prevalent mode of nationalist folk-music-based composition championed by Vaughan Williams. Tippett was a pluralist: a humanist who eschewed dogma; a socialist and pacifist; a Jungian who felt art was basically collective and archetypal; a visionary with a capacity to blend the most disparate ingredients – Beethoven, pre-classical counterpoint, jazz and gamelan music – within a single work, be it his exuberant First Piano Sonata (1936) or his bittersweet Triple Concerto (1979). Thus his largest-scale compositions – notably, the five operas and three major choral works – were all attempts at creative synthesis at different points in his career. Prefiguring these summary pieces, or developing out of them, were Tippett's four symphonies, five string quartets, five piano sonatas, concertos, songs and numerous shorter instrumental and choral works. Taken as a whole, however, this oeuvre had a consistent and distinctively modern stamp.

Tippett wrote little that could be called 'experimental'. His friend and mentor, T. S. Eliot said that for him, as a poet, 'the words come last'; likewise, with Tippett, the notes came last, following upon a lengthy period of gestation and structural planning. His sense of the line and shape of a piece was such that in his maturity he invariably wrote from beginning to end in sequence, sending each completed section to his publishers, confident that there would be no need for significant revisions. Tippett's quirky, maverick musical

Final calls

Sir Michael Tippett

personality sometimes distracted attention from his assured craftsmanship.

His early encounter with jazz and blues, above all, convinced him that music retained a universal expressive potential, albeit tinged with irony. In his Third (and longest) Symphony (1972), Tippett polarised Beethoven and the blues: the work quotes the Ninth Symphony within a sequence of searing vocal blues, sketching a journey from innocence to experience in a world of concentration camps and atom bombs.

Tippett was born in London and grew up in Suffolk. His intellectuality was nurtured in early childhood by his highly articulate, well-read (and equally long-lived) parents. From his lawyer father, Tippett inherited a fascination with languages. As a child, he quickly became fluent in French and taught himself Italian and German as a student. From his mother – a nurse, active Labour Party member and a suffragette (for which she was imprisoned) – he derived notions of collective social responsibility, humane values and ultimately pacifism.

He was sent to board at Fettes School, Edinburgh, where he led a successful crusade against bullying, then to Stamford Grammar School. Holidaying in

Final calls

Germany in the 1920s, he observed the 'progressive' methods of schools for destitute children; decades later, this experience was reawakened when he came to write his opera *New Year*, in whose plot the problems of orphaned, uprooted young people are in the foreground.

His parents found incomprehensible his determination to become a composer, prompted by a concert he attended in Leicester conducted by Malcolm Sargent. Having persuaded them to support him at the Royal College of Music, however, Tippett came to London in the summer of 1923. But he lacked the fluency and versatility of his fellow students and his teachers, who included Sargent and Adrian Boult, often despaired.

During the Depression, Tippett worked among the unemployed in the north of England, galvanising a mixture of out-of-work miners and their families, students and friends for performances of *The Beggar's Opera* and a specially composed ballad opera, *Robin Hood*.

The climax of Tippett's extra-musical commitment – which had included brief membership of the Communist Party – came in July 1943, when he served a three-month sentence at Wormwood Scrubbs for failing to comply with the conditions of service as a conscientious objector. This, in his mother's view, was his finest hour. Over the years, Tippett became one of foremost leaders of the British pacifist movement – president of the Peace Pledge Union and a CND supporter. His identification with human rights causes in general was ultimately crystallised in the rhetorical cry of the Present, 'One humanity, one justice,' at the end of *New Year*.

As a student, Tippett accepted his homosexual leanings without qualm. By this time, his family life had disintegrated. Thereafter, Tippett yearned for the warmth he observed within the families of working-class friends. With his charm, charisma and good looks, Tippett attracted many female admirers. Two became very close friends: Evelyn Maude, an older married woman and a regular source of wise counsel (in prison, allowed to write letters to only one person, Tippett chose her); and Francesca Allinson, a choral conductor, folk-song researcher and puppeteer, with whom he considered starting a family. The latter's suicide in 1944 prompted one of Tippett's most poignant compositions, the song-cycle *The Heart's Assurance*.

Few of Tippett's close relationships survived his ruthless creative obsession: one of the longest-lasting, with painter Karl Hawker, ended with a contrived separation and the latter's suicide.

Tippett's personal turmoil coincided with the rise of Nazism in central Europe and Stalinism in the Soviet Union. Tippett identified strongly with those made scapegoats by intolerance and self-righteousness. That was the inspiration underlying his oratorio *A Child of Our Time*, which had begun as an opera about the Easter Uprising in Ireland, but gelled as a protest against the 1938 Kristallnacht in Nazi Germany. Tippett asked Eliot – whom he had recently met – to write the text; but Eliot, having looked at Tippett's draft libretto, advised him to

Final calls

construct his own text in full, as the poet's literary flights might conflict with the composer's musical concepts. After that, Tippett always fashioned his own libretti.

At its première in 1944, *A Child of Our Time* was understood primarily as a response to the Nazi persecution of the Jews. But its message – summed up in the final ensemble in characteristically Jungian language: 'I would know my shadow and my light/So shall I at last be whole' – suits all situations where intolerance has thrown up victims and outcasts. *A Child of Our Time* was the first work of Tippett's to be heard outside the UK; now it is constantly performed worldwide.

The oratorio's success in the mid-1940s helped Tippett's reputation to prosper. Meanwhile, he was attracting attention by making Morley College – whose musical director he had become in 1941 – the most lively concert-giving organisation in wartime London.

After the war, Tippett's priority was his first opera, *The Midsummer Marriage*, which absorbed his energies completely for six years (1946–52). Gradually relinquishing his Morley College duties, he finally resigned in 1951. When, unexpectedly (for he had no commission to write it), the opera was premièred at Covent Garden in 1955, audiences and critics, though baffled by the libretto, were bowled over by the score's unfettered lyrical ardour and radiance. In 1963 the BBC broadcast *The Midsummer Marriage* with a cast that included the young Janet Baker as Sosostris. A new production at Covent Garden followed in 1966 with Colin Davis as conductor, leading eventually to a best-selling recording. There have since been more than a dozen productions at home and abroad, all of which have attracted varying mixtures of praise, scepticism and scorn.

The main gibes against Tippett's operas have always been directed at the libretti – quirky, magpie-ish mixtures of references and quotations (emulating *The Waste Land*) – despite the composer's insistence that they were meant not to be read as 'literature' but as 'gestures for music'.

The path to the international fame Tippett enjoyed in his late years was fraught with difficulties. It was a brilliant production by Sam Wanamaker at the 1962 Coventry Festival of Tippett's second opera, the epic-style *King Priam*, that began to turn the tide in his favour. In the mid-1960s, Tippett inherited the Bath Festival from Yehudi Menuhin, saved it from bankruptcy and widened its scope and audience appeal. Honours began to flow in: a CBE in 1959 and a knighthood in 1966; he was made a Companion of Honour in 1979 and received the Order of Merit in 1984. He valued most of all the Gold Medal of the Royal Philharmonic Society (1975) and awards such as that of the Association of British Orchestras (1966), which, he felt, came from 'my colleagues in the profession'.

Tippett's first visit to the US in 1965 as composer-in-residence at the Aspen Festival, Colorado, was a major turning point. He fell in love with the landscapes of the Far West and identified with the polyglot culture of the cities. America

Final calls

also took to Tippett in a big way. American commissions followed; the Fourth Symphony (1977) and *Byzantium* (1989) were premièred by Georg Solti and the Chicago Symphony.

Tippett's 'discovery' of what he called 'a Newfoundland of the spirit' in America also permeated his music from the mid-1960s onwards. Immediately, his third opera, *The Knot Garden* (1970), uncovered a new toughness and irony in his music, its harmonic character bluesy, its orchestration coloured by electric guitar sonorities. The scores and libretti of *The Ice Break* (1977) and *New Year* went even further. All three operas are explicitly about people of today, grappling with contemporary problems and leaving at the end to begin new lives.

Tippett was a mixture of seer and dreamer. Both are encountered in the two great choral compositions of his maturity, *The Vision of St Augustine* (1966) and *The Mask of Time* (1983). The former brings to the fore Tippett's fascination with concepts of time – above all, with the possibility that art is concerned with experiences in a virtual time-continuum, detached from everyday clock-time. Setting Latin texts from Augustine's *Confessions*, Tippett produced a typically unclassifiable work whose three movements unfold with complete organic freedom and inward momentum.

The Mask of Time was even more ambitious, a musician's answer to the scientific account of the development of civilisation in Jacob Bronowski's celebrated BBC film series *The Ascent of Man* (1973). An awesome conception, its 10 movements, lasting altogether 95 minutes, depict, in broad chronological leaps, the evolution of the universe and mankind's constant defiance of destructive forces, ending with a wordless song of survival and hope.

Observing often – notably in his first volume of essays, *Moving into Aquarius* (1959) – that the artist is relatively powerless in a society that invests the greater part of its resources in technology, Tippett drew strength from a sense of belonging to a tradition, age-old and ever-present, which is (he wrote, memorably) 'to create images from the depths of the imagination ... in an age of mediocrity and shattered dreams, images of abounding, generous, exuberant beauty.'

Michael Kemp Tippett, composer, born 2 January 1905; died 8 January 1998. ●

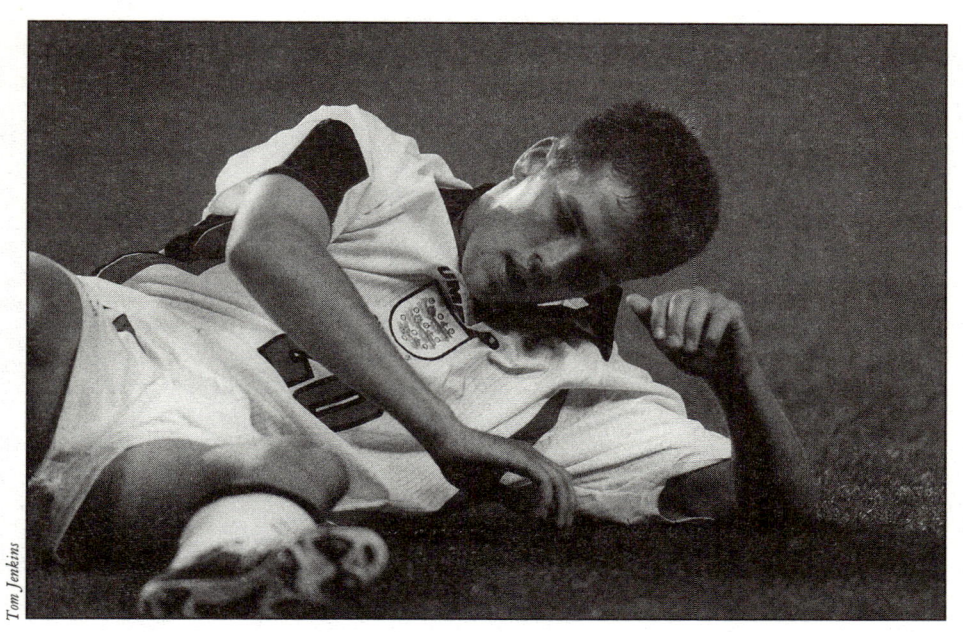

Michael Owen, the 18-year-old goalscoring virtuoso, takes a tumble during one of England's matches in the World Cup

A cracking few days

A cracking few days

12 February 1998

Paul Hayward
First-class honours for Owen

Parents are always saying how quickly kids grow up these days. It took Michael Owen less than five minutes last night to confirm himself a footballer of international renown. If the policemen all looked young, Owen looked a great deal older than his 18 years and 59 days.

His future will be speculated over endlessly, his past dug up by a media eager to trace his every move dating back to the womb. Somebody had better pull the wagons round England's youngest international this century. On last night's evidence there will be plenty of time for chat shows and biographies. Here is a youngster moving too fast for the ink to dry.

A resounding roar greeted his first touch of the ball. It was an eager dash along the right flank which produced a swerving cross in to Teddy Sheringham which he narrowly failed to meet. It was instant confirmation that Owen's graduation had excited the national imagination. Andy Cole's thigh strain must have twinged a little more painfully. On the bench Alan Shearer might have wondered how many years his reign as England's pre-eminent striker will last.

The Michael Owen story is moving far faster than the events around him. The result — a 2–0 defeat — was a disappointment, but his debut a thumping success. After the game he did his bit for the cameras and walked off, all businesslike, clutching a bottle of champagne for Man of the Match. It should have been Chile's Marcelo Salas really, but what the hell. Chauvinism is forgivable when the beneficiary is so young.

Owen started the season at Liverpool behind Karlheinz Riedle and Robbie Fowler in the Anfield hierarchy. His aim was merely to play 12 games. Already he is keeping Riedle on the bench and Fowler out of the England squad. There is still some road-testing to be done before the World Cup in June but Glenn Hoddle would be a brave man to leave such a talent on some Cheshire golf course.

Above all, Owen has the pace, boldness and control to run at defenders with the ball at his feet. Even Shearer can't do that, and the international striker he most resembles is the Brazilian Ronaldo, who terrifies opponents by running directly at them and changing direction off either foot. The fizz of anticipation that greeted Owen's every touch last night was an instinctive recognition that here is a player with those rare and special powers.

In the tunnel he exchanged soothing words with Sheringham (13 years his senior) and on the pitch shook hands with the great Sir Tom Finney. Opposite him was the muscular but skilful Chilean centre back Javier Margas, who would have scared most teenagers off the park. In fact many 18-year-olds would rather have been in a video arcade or warming the sofa with a remote control, with life's great challenges many years ahead.

Instead Owen was making history. There will not be a better lump of symmetry all year than Owen making his debut almost 40 years to the day after Duncan Edwards, the previous record-holder at 18 years and 183 days, died of his wounds from the Munich air disaster. Around Owen were some of the Manchester United youngsters who have retraced the footprints of the Busby Babes.

It would be easy to assume the honeyed praise for Owen is one more act of premature star creation. If Owen fails, a pox on all our houses for misreading such promising signals. But there is such an affecting aura about him, and such a dramatic suddenness about his ambitious bursts of speed, that the chances are we are witnessing the investiture of an English forward to extend the distinguished lineage of Jimmy Greaves, Bobby Charlton, Gary Lineker and Shearer himself.

He has little of Shearer's body-bumping physicality but has the same implacable demeanour and determination to excel. It took Owen 33 club games to get into the starting England line-up and five minutes last night before he was shooting powerfully on goal from a pull-back by Dion Dublin. He was forever looking to penetrate the space behind defenders. He was one of the few England players not to stand too statically on a night the team looked disjointed and imbalanced by Hoddle's widespread experimentation.

It was no reflection on Owen that the crowd chanted for Shearer when their team was a goal down. Three minutes later, in the penalty area, Owen halted deliciously before chipping a short cross on to Paul Ince's head from which England almost scored.

For Michael Owen, surely, there is room on the plane to France. •

22 June 1998
Mike Selvey
The cutting edge?

The bizarre realisation that the design for the new space-age media centre at Lord's has been based on nothing less than Wallace's piano-keyboard grin was not the most appropriate yesterday. This was no laughing place as England, teetering drunkenly from a sublime morning to a ridiculous afternoon, lost the second Test by 10 wickets, giving South Africa a one-match advantage in the series.

It was a case not so much of the wrong trousers (that was Mike Atherton here four years ago) as both legs in one hole. All it will need is for the footballers to foul up against Romania and for Tim Henman to exit Wimbledon in the

A cracking few days

first round to complete a cracking few days for English sport at the cutting edge.

It was ineptitude of a quality in which England appear to be brand leaders, even at a time when they appear to have their strongest squad for years. Having been bowled out by Allan Donald and Shaun Pollock in prime bowling conditions on Saturday – both could have shut their eyes and imagined they were running in at Kingsmead, such was the heat and stifling humidity – England, following on 250 behind, were 105 for two overnight, with Nasser Hussain unbeaten on 52.

They lost the nightwatchman Dean Headley early on but then flourished gloriously as Hussain and Alec Stewart took the attack to the bowlers with a fourth-wicket stand of 116, savaging the second new ball in the process. Shortly after lunch Hussain, to his unbridled joy, reached his first century at Lord's in any cricket and his seventh in Tests, and went on to reach 105, while Stewart made 56.

There it all but ended. The batsmen collapsed in the afternoon heat like guardsmen at the Trooping of the Colour. In the space of a dozen overs, 222 for three had become 233 for nine, the damage done not by Donald or Pollock but by the second-string spear-carriers Lance Klusener and Jacques Kallis, who swung the ball around disconcertingly at times.

Kallis, on the ground that became so familiar to him during his summer with Middlesex last year, took four for 24, the best figures of his Test career. County cricket is too often denigrated by those abroad, but it does not prevent them from using it as a finishing school. Kallis is merely the latest example of letting the enemy inspect your territory before the battle.

This may have been the longest day but, had it not been for a jaunty last-wicket partnership of 31 between Angus Fraser and Robert Croft, the match would not have extended beyond the tea interval.

As it was, the prospect of chasing all of 15 to win proved none too daunting for Gary Kirsten and Daryll Cullinan (opening instead of Adam Bacher, who hurt his right shoulder in the field).

Fraser's first over was dispatched for 10, including two boundaries to Kirsten, and a no-ball from Cork followed by Cullinan's clip to the midwicket fence saw them home at the start of the following over.

It was further evidence that England and these few acres of St John's Wood are not natural bedfellows. Afterwards Jonty Rhodes, awarded the Man of the Match award by Bob Willis for his century and superb fielding, was asked by David Gower to comment on the 'power of Lord's'.

To a born-again Christian, this was the longest half-volley of the week. Team England could do worse than reinstate the Rev Wingfield-Digby immediately.

There had been no indication of impending havoc during an exhilarating morning session which saw Donald and Pollock seen off and Paul Adams attacked

A cracking few days

with willingness. Fifty-nine runs came from 14 overs with the new ball, Hussain rampaging from 73 to 100 with the aid of six boundaries and a three.

It was Stewart's dismissal which sparked the slide. Driving at Kallis, he appeared to have edged to the wicketkeeper, although his demeanour and the long pause to watch the replay screen before he actually entered the Long Room conveyed the impression that he had not made contact.

Two overs later Graham Thorpe was given out lbw without scoring – a poor decision this by George Sharp, the ball pitching outside leg stump, although the umpire had excelled himself earlier in the over by turning down an appeal for a catch behind when the ball clipped the off stump without dislodging a bail.

Hussain followed likewise, delaying his departure a fraction too long for comfort, even though this decision by Darrell Hair looked fair enough. Mark Ramprakash was then immediately yorked by Klusener, although goodness only knows the state of his mind; on Saturday, amid the carnage, he had played out of his socks for an hour and a half, only to be adjudged by Hair to have been caught behind even though the ball came off his elbow. Ramprakash dawdled at the crease and then spoke to Hair on his way back to the pavilion. It was not to compliment him on the quality of his decision. •

....

23 June 1998
David Lacey
Petrescu shatters England

Suddenly England look vulnerable. Last night's defeat by Romania in the Municipal Stadium here has not in itself dealt a mortal blow to the chances of Glenn Hoddle's team reaching the knock-out stage of the World Cup but the manner of it posed serious questions about their ability to progress further.

From an English point of view the plot was cruel. Having lost the injured Paul Ince before half-time, they fell behind to a goal from Coventry City's Viorel Moldovan immediately after. Then Michael Owen, having replaced the labouring Teddy Sheringham, responded to his cue by bringing the scores level seven minutes from the end amid goalmouth confusion caused by Alan Shearer's hard-driven low cross.

A draw had been widely predicted – indeed, the last four meetings between England and Romania had been drawn – and a point each would have left both teams reasonably satisfied. But as the match moved into stoppage time a pass from Dorinel Munteanu sent in Dan Petrescu from the left. Graeme Le Saux, his Chelsea team-mate, came across to make a challenge more clumsy than effective and Petrescu managed to slip the winning goal through Seaman's legs

A cracking few days

as the England goalkeeper fell backwards. In a sadistic final twist, there was still time for Owen to hit a post.

England do not make a habit of losing World Cup matches to goals from Coventry strikers and Chelsea wing backs. Whether they get as far as meeting Arsenal, in the shape of Holland's Dennis Bergkamp and Marc Overmars, will depend on how well and quickly the lessons of this defeat are assimilated.

Hoddle has persevered with playing three at the back and qualified with distinction. Holding Italy in a goalless game in Rome seemed the ultimate vindication of the England coach's move away from 4–4–2. Now inevitably doubt will arise about his formation, especially given the increasing number of times last night Romania found space down the flanks.

While one could not argue with Hoddle's assertion that 'two sloppy goals were given away', Adrian Ilie's pass early in the second half would surely have produced another had Gheorghe Hagi, having raced past Gary Neville, not been let down by a poor first touch. Before half-time Ilie had also hit the England bar.

Until Romania scored there was a bounce in England's step. Buoyant after their opening 2–0 victory against Tunisia a week before, they dominated the first 45 minutes, with Darren Anderton looking much more like the Anderton of Euro 96.

Ince's departure with what looked like a damaged ankle was a blow that took a while to sink in and may take a while to clear up. Hoddle says he is doubtful for Friday. The initial effect was to bring on David Beckham, whose original omission had caused such controversy. For a time Beckham and Anderton promised to form an effective partnership, but once Romania had taken the lead there was a flabbiness about England's Ince-less midfield.

Hoddle argued afterwards that the result was down to defensive error rather than a poor overall performance. But questions will be posed in the next day or so about the continued presence of Sheringham in the side, given the speed of Owen's response to a crisis, and the fitness of Tony Adams, who went into the game amid rumour of a foot injury which was not dispersed by Romania's opening goal.

Little of that was apparent in the opening stages, when England created several chances. In the twenty-fifth minute, however, Ilie lobbed the advancing Seaman and 20,000 English hearts stopped as the ball sailed towards the net before rebounding from the bar.

England lost Ince round about that time. Then within two minutes of the second half they lost a goal. There seemed little immediate danger as Romania took a throw-in on the right, but Hagi drifted inside Le Saux with Campbell hesitating. Before Campbell could act, Hagi had lobbed the ball over a sluggish Adams, who turned to see Moldovan striding through to beat Seaman from close range.

The rest was all about elation and relief followed by deflation and disbelief.

A cracking few days

Now it is not so much a matter of football coming home as England trusting that their stay abroad will not be embarrassingly short-lived.

Valderrama may have something to say about that. •

An alleged England soccer hooligan is arrested

27 *June 1998*
David Lacey
The lions find their roar

If England can hang on to their bounding confidence of last night, Argentina may be in for a healthy surprise when the teams meet in the second round in St Etienne on Tuesday. Glenn Hoddle's side sent Colombia home with the sort of victory here which left the supporters believing that anything is possible.

England needed only to draw to qualify for the knock-out stage as runners-up in Group G to Romania, their conquerors in Toulouse last Monday night. In fact the minimum security of a point never entered their heads.

Hoddle wanted a performance to convince the growing band of doubters that England were not merely buying another four days in the World Cup before their inevitable overthrow by Argentina, widely believed to be the only side capable of stopping Brazil. His players could not have responded in a more rousing fashion.

A cracking few days

With David Beckham revelling in the extra freedom he always gets when he moves from right wing to midfield, England simply scattered Colombia's intricate passing game to the four winds. Two goals in the space of nine minutes during the first half, from Darren Anderton and Beckham, virtually guaranteed England's place in the last 16 and several more would have followed but for an outstanding display of goalkeeping by Farid Mondragon.

All the while Tunisia were beating the Romanians 1–0 at St Denis, England could look forward to playing Croatia in Bordeaux instead of meeting Argentina in the World Cup for the fourth time, but that prospect disappeared with Romania's equaliser. It is 12 years since the quarter-finals in Mexico City and the Hand of God. Perhaps the Hand of Hod will redress the balance.

Certainly England, in approaching their encounter with Ariel Ortega, Gabriel Batistuta and the rest of an Argentina team who so far have shown little of the cynicism of their predecessors, will be undaunted by the fact that they have drawn the shortest of straws. Before last night they had not beaten South American opposition for eight years. It is not a bad moment to reacquire the habit.

That said, it would do no harm to keep last night's success in perspective. Despite the enduring influence of the 36-year-old Carlos Valderrama, Colombia offered poorer opposition than Tunisia had presented to England in Marseilles. Mondragon's saves spared their defence the full consequences of a chronic weakness on crosses and their attack barely functioned within 30 yards of goal.

At the same time England achieved their most positive performance since they arrived in France. The combination of Beckham and Anderton gave them an early superiority on the right which was never yielded. Paul Scholes, subdued by canny Romanian defending in Toulouse, was again the player he had been in Marseilles.

As expected, Hoddle replaced Teddy Sheringham with Michael Owen on a wave of popular demand. Owen looked impressive when he took on defenders for pace and his runs contributed to the steady dismantling of Colombia's defence. Alan Shearer joined the lengthening queue to bulk up England's lead but, like everybody else in the second half, found Mondragon unbeatable.

Beckham has shown that, given the time and space, he can dictate the pattern and tempo of a match from the middle of the pitch. His partnership with Anderton, given a premature birth in Toulouse after Paul Ince had been forced off with an ankle injury, flourished last night.

Argentina will give the pair a harder examination than Colombia's pedestrian midfield but at least the Beckham–Anderton axis is no longer a matter of theory. With Ince and Scholes fore and aft and the partnership of Owen and Shearer surely due to be repeated, England have the means to score against the Argentinians. Keeping them out will be another matter.

Last night England went ahead after 21 minutes. Owen pressured the defence into error and then found Anderton in space and in range. This was the Anderton

A cracking few days

of old, snapping up the chance with a superbly struck, rising shot which beat Mondragon at the near post and ended up in the roof of the net.

On the half-hour England increased their lead with a goal which was pure Beckham. Ince had been brought down by Harold Lozano some 25 yards from goal and for Beckham the range and angle were ideal. Mondragon had no hope of reaching a shot which swung past him in a wide arc, taking a thin deflection on the way, and into the left-hand corner of the net.

Colombia replaced their two strikers for the second half, added the skills of Victor Aristizabal to their midfield and virtually gave up defending to search for goals. From then on England created scoring chances at will.

But for Mondragon Scholes alone would have scored three times, with two shots and a header, in the opening three minutes after half-time. The Colombia goalkeeper completed his evening by keeping out a free kick from Shearer before saving Tony Adams's attempt to score from the rebound feet-first.

Steve McManaman, Robert Lee and finally David Batty came off the bench to remind the World Cup of what Hoddle might have in reserve. Not that England have reserved a place in the last eight yet. But they will have given Argentina a little more to think about. •

1 July 1998
Richard Williams
Batty bites the roulette bullet

David Batty juggled the ball as he approached the penalty spot, like a man wanting to show the world an insouciance he didn't feel. You wanted to tell him to stop and go back. You wanted Glenn Hoddle to give the ball to someone who scores goals for a living. And then the worst happened, for Batty and for England.

The words of Christian Karembeu, spoken during Euro 96, came back, with a new resonance. 'It is not football,' the French midfield player said, after watching his friend Clarence Seedorf make a crucial miss for Holland in their semi-final. 'It is Russian roulette. It is loading a bullet into the chamber of the gun and asking everyone to pull the trigger. Someone will get the bullet, you know that. And it will reduce them to nothing, finish them. Fair? Fairness is not even an issue.'

One thing was for sure. Batty was not going to cry. But the hard man of the premiership will be changed, in one way or another, by those few seconds in the Stade Geoffroy Guichard last night. At least he has Paul Ince for company.

Michael Owen cried, which was reassuring, given the preternatural coolness the young striker had shown when delivering the night its most exalted moment with the goal that gave England a 2–1 lead.

A cracking few days

Given the night, given the context, given the meaning, given the sheer white-knuckle intensity of the occasion, when was the last time such a goal was scored in an England shirt? Not in Owen's short lifetime, anyway. Gazza's goal against Scotland in Euro 96 had a marvellous dizzy panache, but Owen's was a strike of true world class, against opponents as tough as the world can offer.

Argentina's defenders had conceded no goal during the tournament until Owen got among them. In the tenth minute, taking Paul Scholes's flick and racing into the area, he fell under Roberto Ayala's challenge and was awarded a penalty, which Alan Shearer put in to level the score.

Owen had put down his marker. Five minutes later he made his name. The run past José Chamot, keeping his feet this time, and the jinking dismissal of Ayala were followed by a shot of such exquisite technique that it made the blood run cold. What gives an 18-year-old the self-possession, playing for a place in the quarter-finals of the World Cup, to get his foot around the ball and guide it across the goalkeeper while running at full speed?

Sport, like music, is one of those fields of human endeavour which show us that some people's brains are just wired up differently. Gazza, in his chaotic way, was one of them. Owen, with his combination of a whippet's pace and a sniper's eye, is another.

And then, half an hour later, Argentina were level again. This was what we had come to see. This was a proper grown-up match between serious teams. This was the big occasion, redeeming a rather flat second phase of the tournament. What this World Cup needed was a real cracker of a battle between two heavyweights, and England and Argentina were providing it. This is a fixture requiring no gimmicks of hucksterism to boost the box-office takings. Yet the words of Gabriel Batistuta to an Italian journalist on the eve of the match suggested a proper human perspective on the historic conflicts between the two countries. Batistuta was 12 years old at the time of the Falklands War. The Argentinian people were victims of propaganda, he recalled: 'It was the same with Saddam and the Iraqi people in the Gulf War. They told us about great victories, and suddenly we got the lists of the dead.'

The journalist pressed him. Did the Falklands really belong to Argentina? 'They're still English. But no one really won. One way of putting it behind us will be to exchange shirts at the end of the game.' It wasn't just English newspapers, he said, that used a game of football to revive the memory of the conflict. 'Some Argentinian journalists try to play the same game. It isn't right. But people in sport have different values. Whether they're veterans like Shearer and me, or youngsters like Owen and Ortega, we all absorb certain values and we can use sport to display them. Sport can express peace and real values, not false ones.'

The national anthems received noisy receptions, but once the match got under way, the other stuff was where it belonged, in history. A penalty to each side inside the first 10 minutes — neither, as it happened, for violent play — drove

A cracking few days

Tony Adams, captain of Arsenal, hoists high the FA Carling Premiership trophy, having beaten Everton 4–0

all other thoughts out of the crowd's mind. But at that stage a recourse to the shoot-out seemed unthinkable.

Of course one should blame David Beckham rather than Kim Milton Neilsen for the fact that England were forced to play all but a minute of the second half with 10 men. Beckham was stupid to flick his foot at Diego Simeone after the Argentinian captain had flattened him. But if Neilsen had wagged his finger and let it go, no one would have noticed. Was Beckham's sin really any worse

A cracking few days

than that of Batistuta, who hacked at Beckham and Ince but escaped punishment?

With Hoddle on his feet reorganising the side, the resistance was magnificent. The players' willingness to shoulder the extra burden was typified by Shearer, who could often be found in the right wing back's position. Tracking his own marker, Nelson Vivas, deep into the England half, he was on the spot to make a crucial interception almost on the goal line when Vivas closed in on Claudio Lopez's clever cross. And when Daniel Passarella took off Batistuta and Lopez, the England defenders must have felt that, whatever the outcome, they had won an important point.

To no avail, in the end. If Batty is capable of taking consolation today, he may find it in the fact that England's performance did credit to everyone involved, far exceeding the expectations of most neutrals. But that, of course, will only make it worse. •

....

4 July 1998
Frank Keating
Tim's turn but no final twist

There were no end of turning points — there always are in tennis, a myriad of shots or passages, points or incidents that you solemnly asterisk in a notebook presuming them to be the vital swing, the crucial roundabout.

Was the pivotal moment when the two Dukes, Kent and Gloucester, stiffly tiptoed away from the royal box for a second cup of tea as soon as Sampras had closed down the first set? Certainly, as soon as they had gone, Henman broke the champion's service twice in succession.

Or was the turning point at 0–1 and 30-love at the beginning of the third set when a quite blistering service from Henman broke Sampras's racquet as if it were a dry piece of firewood for kindling? The American tossed the bent and wonky thing into the crowd, but Sampras's equally wonky grin told that a rueful champion's earlier confident assurance was looking more than slightly misplaced.

Or was the crucial moment four games later in the third set when, at 3–3, 30–40, Henman in mid-court bent low to get almost miraculously his forehand racquet on a raging starburst of a drive from Sampras which stopped the furiously flying fuzz in its tracks and caressingly dinked it back over the net gloriously to wrong-foot the American and thwart the service break? It was a dazzling moment — but, alas, also one of dying defiance, because Henman's glory was almost spent. For this occasion anyway.

One moment which suggested it would be no walkover, however, had come far earlier when, quite out of character, Sampras began to seethe and fanny about distractedly, fretting over a series of bum line calls.

A cracking few days

The composed champion of tennis and manners was suddenly seeming less so. He weathered that, just as he was to ultimately overcome the challenge. You could tell he himself knew the overwhelming turning point came when he took the third set 7–5 and essayed that split-second dervish dance of delight after a 40-minute switchback slog.

That probably was the crucial moment. Sampras obviously thought so and, you fancied, Henman knew it as well. The centre-court crowd had taken some time, like Henman, to raise their game. They did well enough in those two middle sets. But in the fourth they knew the outcome.

Oddly, they had taken a long time to warm to the fact. At Wimbledon, as the royal box has done all down the century with a rigid precision, afternoon tea comes first. As soon as the marathon last set in the preceding match finished – the heavyweights Ivanisevic and Krajicek slugging it out blow for blow for 28 games – the stadium half emptied and went to get a cuppa. Thus was the first set played in an almost eerie silence. There were few partisan cheers and the flags of the Union and St George were kept under wraps. The opening exchanges, as the old tennis writers used to say, 'went strictly to service'.

But in the always crucial seventh game Henman, over-desperate to stay in it at 30–40, pallidly served a double-fault to let Sampras at him. The champion duly leapt for the Englishman's throat and lost only one point in swiftly closing down the set.

It looked as if those flags would stay in their carrier bags for the duration. But, gloriously for a while, Henman's gallantry rose to make a compelling match with his sometimes flashing strokeplay and a memorable occasion.

With Henman's talent and age, yesterday's semi-final was more of a beginning to relish than an ending, as one would have felt with any other Briton reaching a semi-final – even before the Open era Roger Taylor was never really a Wimbledon finalist.

The last one, of course, was Fred Perry, all of 62 years ago. Fred turned pro after that victory – and the only other finalist, Bunny Austin, made it two years later but that was definitely his last. Though if, as Henman said yesterday, this was the 'biggest match of my life', for sure he has many similar ahead of him.

More than a few times in resplendent passages yesterday, Henman matched a maestro for athleticism, control and timing in the outer reaches of this intense serve and volley game. The jingoistic cries – 'Tim! Tim!' – were raining down from all corners of the old stadium in those middle sets and the throng began to buzz with the real possibility of an upset.

There was not one and there was never really going to be. Well, not quite. But here's to next year. And the decade after that for, come to think of it, Henman will be playing 'games of his life' far longer than Tony Blair will be Prime Minister. •

The Guardian Year '98

A cracking few days

11 August 1998
David Hopps
Victorious England break the mould

For once nobody can misrepresent England's cricketers as little better than a national joke. For once nobody can superficially pronounce that Test cricket in England has already entered its death throes. For once, and it is quite a turn-up to be able to declare it, the England cricket team can declare themselves to be winners.

Twelve years since an England win in a major series: that grating statistic had gathered strength all summer. Well, today it is little more than 12 hours ago, and for a team who have finally freed themselves from the inadequacies of the past, most of those will have been spent in a state of considerable intoxication.

'A little disdain is not amiss; a little scorn is alluring.' So wrote William Congreve in *The Way of the World* nearly 300 years ago. That has been the way of the world for English cricket for too long; briefly encouraging, often inept, a delightful invitation to ridicule. In its way, so very English.

That perception has been weakened, if not yet reversed, because England, with their deplorable record on tour, must go to Australia this winter. And as Hansie Cronje, South Africa's captain, pointed out: 'It is winning away from home that really boosts your reputation.'

But it took 28 minutes yesterday to make a start. South Africa, entering the final day at 185 for eight, were dismissed for 195, leaving England victors by 23 runs. Angus Fraser had Allan Donald caught at the wicket from the merest sliver of an outside edge, and Darren Gough completed his best Test figures, six for 42, by having Makhaya Ntini lbw. Ntini, who had faced only one ball all summer, and that against Ireland, was a perfect No. 11 when there was a Test to be won.

In all, 10 batsmen fell lbw, nine of them given by the Pakistani umpire Javed Akhtar. If eight lbws were against South Africa, such an imbalance can readily be explained by the different methods of the English seam attack, who pitched the ball up further and cut it back far more regularly than their South African counterparts.

There is no magic formula for England's victory in this series. It is the reward for several years' striving by up to a dozen key individuals. But Alec Stewart, whose appointment to the captaincy in the spring was deemed to be a stopgap, will deserve the recognition he receives.

Stewart brushes aside excuses and soft thinking as he brushes dust from his shoes. His conviction that English cricket must toughen up is hardly a unique

A cracking few days

insight. It is shared by the collection of senior players – Mike Atherton, Nasser Hussain, Graham Thorpe, Fraser and Gough – who have committed themselves so intensively to breaking the mould. What Stewart has done is draw the 'bottom line' in a forceful fashion.

To emphasise, however, that England's advancement has been a team effort, one only has to consider the turning point in the series. In the third Test at Old Trafford, South Africa led by 369 runs on first innings and with nearly two days remaining looked certain to go 2–0 up in the series. Then, with World Cup football monopolising attentions, Test cricket seemed almost inconsequential.

The recovery was begun by Atherton and Stewart, captains past and present, both aware that another England crisis loomed. Had either fallen cheaply then, this summer would have ended with the usual bout of recriminations. Instead they remained in a stand of 226, and the following day Robert Croft's unbeaten 37 in three hours scraped a draw.

Croft was left out of the Headingley squad, but he received a mobile phone call from the England dressing-room yesterday only minutes after their victory. 'We sang him a little song,' said Stewart. 'We didn't want to forget him.' It was a small but important touch, which spoke volumes for England's present morale.

Consistency will take a little longer. English cricket remains as mercurial as ever – this fluctuating Test was in many ways a microcosm of the ups and downs of the past 12 years – but at least it is learning how to take a punch on the chin and stay on its feet.

If Stewart was assisted by a past captain, Atherton, at Old Trafford, Headingley provided another symbolic moment in the shape of Hussain, who had been the only other serious candidate for the captaincy.

This is an impatient age, weaned on instant entertainment, but England won a Test series because a man toiled for more than seven hours for 94; a batsman, more to the point, who was once dismissed as chancy but who has worked tirelessly for the past five years to prove otherwise.

When Hussain was dismissed on Sunday he trailed from the field, head bowed, and punched the boundary rail in distress not at a lost Test hundred but that he might not have carried the job through. Thanks to the dependability of Fraser and yes, these days, the dependability of Gough, too, he had done enough.

Atherton, England's Man of the Series, had visited hospital before play, because of stomach trouble, and arrived at the ground by taxi, rushing across the football ground to arrive just as the first bottle of champagne was being uncorked.

Later he was repeatedly asked if he was frustrated that England had not won a major series under his captaincy. He invariably looked as if he did not quite grasp the question. A good thing too. Team England, yesterday, did not seem just a glib phrase. •

A cracking few days

1 December 1997

Chris Hawkins
Bradley hits the heights on Suny Bay

Sir Peter O'Sullevan's final hour, Graham Bradley's finest; the 1997 Hennessy Cognac Gold Cup at Newbury on Saturday will linger long in the memory as one of the special races. It will be remembered for the consummate caller and the reluctant faller; for O'Sullevan's gasp and Bradley's miraculous recovery.

Rarely can a horse have hit a fence as hard as Suny Bay when he rooted the fourth and got away with it. That he survived was down to the jockey, whose balancing act would have done justice to Blondin. 'It's the only mistake he's ever made,' said Bradley. 'He put in an extra stride and guessed. I was lucky. There would have been no way back if the reins had gone over his head instead of catching his right ear.'

It was a monster blunder, but incredibly seemed to take nothing out of the grey chaser, who had soon moved back into the lead and proceeded to jump with a faultless fluency matched only by Barton Bank.

The 11-year-old Barton Bank, who, swinging for home was going just as well as Suny Bay, ran the race of his life, carrying 11st 13lb and trying to give the winner 5lb. He was beaten by 13 lengths in the end, but it was a gallant effort in cloying ground which one would normally expect to anchor the top weights. For a stride or two as they came into the home straight those nearer the bottom of the handicap, Time for a Run and Trying Again, threatened, but neither was able to mount a serious challenge. Trying Again patently failed to stay the trip.

Bradley and Suny Bay, accompanied by his dazzlingly yellow-coated trainer, Charlie Brooks, returned to a rapturous reception. For Brooks, who had watched the race from the middle of the track, it had been an intensely nerve-racking experience. 'I went into the middle so that people wouldn't talk to me, but that didn't really work,' he said. 'When I saw him hit the fourth my heart stopped and from then on I couldn't watch another jump. This is a very good horse and we'll take on One Man in the King George at Kempton. We'll know after three days how he's come out of the race. One Man might be faster, but sometimes a battler can win. Brad has got to take most of the credit — and to think I was saying he should retire last summer! I think he's been one of those unlucky jockeys — last year he would have fallen off. But the luck's changed. He's a loyal, really nice man and deserves it.'

Bradley, 37, mused that when he last won the Hennessy, on Bregawn 15

A cracking few days

years ago, Tony McCoy, the champion jockey, was still in short trousers. 'The reason that I've been able to keep going is because of advice I had from Michael Dickinson when I was starting,' he explained. 'He told me never to ride bad horses if I could help it. They do in your confidence and do in your bottle. Generally speaking, I've done that and I've been quite happy riding about 300 horses a season instead of the 800 or so that you need to win the championship.'

O'Sullevan, of course, has had an even longer innings: his journalistic and broadcasting career has spanned 50 years. This refined, dignified man with the perfectly timbred voice has done so much to promote racing's popularity with the public. It was highly appropriate at the end of it all that Bradley should present him with a magnum of champagne from the jockeys. One supreme pro honouring another. •